edited by
Sandro Castaldo

CUSTOMER LOYALTY

Theory, Measurement, and Management

contributions
Emanuele Acconciamessa · Generoso Branca · Bruno Busacca
Andrea Ciacci · Alice Mantovani · Lara Penco · Ginevra Testa

This book was made possible thanks to the support of

Cover: Cristina Bernasconi, Milan
Typesetting: Corpo4 Team, Milan

EGEA S.p.A.
Via Salasco, 5 – 20136 Milan
Tel. 02/5836.5751 – Fax 02/5836.5753
egea.edizioni@unibocconi.it – www.egeaeditore.it

First Edition: November 2024

Domestic Edition 979-12-806-2355-3
Digital Domestic Edition 978-88-238-8914-9
International Edition 979-12-816-2737-6

TCC Edition 978-88-238-4787-3

TABLE OF CONTENTS

CHAPTER 3
LOYALTY PROMOTION MONITOR: THE PERSPECTIVE
OF RETAIL MANAGERS
[Emanuele Acconciamessa]

CHAPTER 4
AN ANALYSIS OF PREVIOUS REVIEWS ON LOYALTY:
CONCEPTUALIZATIONS, MEASUREMENTS, AND IMPLICATIONS
[Generoso Branca, Andrea Ciacci]

CHAPTER 5
CONCEPTUALIZATIONS, DIMENSIONS, AND MEASUREMENTS
OF LOYALTY: A SYSTEMATIC LITERATURE REVIEW
[Andrea Ciacci, Alice Mantovani, Generoso Branca]

CHAPTER 6
RESEARCH ON MEASURING LOYALTY
[Lara Penco, Ginevra Testa]

CHAPTER 7
CONCLUDING CONSIDERATIONS AND MANAGERIAL
IMPLICATIONS
*[Emanuele Acconciamessa, Bruno Busacca, Generoso Branca, Sandro Castaldo,
Andrea Ciacci, Alice Mantovani, Lara Penco and Ginevra Testa]*

Part Two
CORPORATE EXPERIENCE

CHAPTER 8
LOYALTY MANAGEMENT AND MEASUREMENT ACCORDING
TO TCC: A DATA-DRIVEN APPROACH
[Generoso Branca, Andrea Ciacci, Damien Katris and Yana Rubashkina]

BIBLIOGRAPHY

AUTHORS

APPENDICES

The appendices are available on the book's webpage. To access them, you can scan the QR Code or manually enter the following address.

PREFACE

1992 saw the publication of an essay entitled *Supermarket Customer Loyalty Promotions. An Empirical Study*, authored by Sandro Castaldo and Chiara Mauri. This work was published by Egea and promoted by the then newly formed The Continuity Company (or TCC as it is known today), along with the collaboration of several Italian retail companies.

The objective was to analyze how retailers manage their sales promotions, particularly "loyalty promotions." This is what they called marketing actions aimed at achieving immediate results (typically short-term increases in turnover), but which also served to secure the stability of sales volumes and enhance the company image by creating a base of loyal customers (hence the name "loyalty promotion").

Over the next ten years, fueled by growing interest in this specific marketing solution, the partnership between SDA Bocconi and TCC consolidated. This resulted in two more rounds of research, with accompanying publications. Meanwhile, TCC has carried out more than 9,000 loyalty programs in large-scale retail, petroleum and FMCG sectors, involving more than one billion consumers. Today, more than 30 years after that first study, we are faced with a highly competitive, mature market, where it's more essential than ever before to consider customer loyalty as the main driver of business performance. For this reason, TCC wanted to put its experience into the hands of researchers. To do so, they forged relations with the *SDA Bocconi Channel & Retail Lab*, which studies the development of distribution channels and retail. This led to the creation of the *Loyalty Promotion Monitor*, which draws comparisons between companies to define the main levers that determine growth in retail.

TCC has always had a privileged, international perspective on the dynamics of customer loyalty. Zeroing in on Italy, there is no doubt that companies are experiencing a historical period of great change, in particular large retailers. Several factors are impacting this transformation:

1. We are in a period of socioeconomic instability. Its effects can be felt both on purchasing processes and on shoppers, changing the criteria consumers apply to make their choices and the reasons behind their decision to concentrate their spending at one retailer rather than another.
2. The competitive scenario is rapidly transforming. On the one hand, interest is turning to the international scene, and on the other, we're seeing dramatic growth in convenience-oriented distribution formulas and the development of private labels.
3. Opportunities are multiplying thanks to new technologies, which offer multiple digital shopping experiences, and the development of e-commerce, which is increasingly integrated with physical distribution.

These are just some of the phenomena that contribute to a highly complex competitive scenario. At the same time, it's becoming more and more difficult for companies to pursue effective differentiation strategies. In this context, clear priorities include sustainability, digitization, and communication and loyalty strategies that are more customer oriented; this is true for all the retailers TCC has the pleasure of collaborating with. The goal is to win consumer trust, an ambitious objective that is the foundation of any valuable, solid, long-lasting relationship. Trust determines loyalty, and loyalty produces positive economic results and market share that is consistent, stable, and may even grow over time.

For years, TCC has been working closely with retailers and companies to develop programs that are designed to incentivize desired buying behaviors and strengthen the emotional connection between consumers and brands. These efforts are based on three key pillars:

• Tailored design and integrated marketing solutions
• Performance monitoring and optimization
• Post-campaign analysis

The ability to measure and optimize loyalty programs is an important strategic resource for retailers. But how is loyalty measured? What are the right KPIs to act on to maximize return on investment (ROI) and return on emotion (ROE) for retailers? The answers to these and other related questions can be found in this book, which is the result of the in-depth study carried out by professors and researchers from the Channel & Retail Lab at SDA Bocconi. We would like to thank them for having us by their side during this year of intensive work.

TCC collaborated by pooling its own experience and providing advice from the Data & Analytics team, which over the years has developed a diverse set of trust measurement methodologies that go beyond simple sales KPIs, embracing a more complex, multifaceted analysis of loyalty program performance. We would also like to thank the management teams from the companies for their participation, present and future, in insights from this observatory. Their willingness to share their data to enable timely and effective research is essential to continue our work on optimizing loyalty strategies.

For TCC, this is one more step towards increasing trust in our partnerships with retailers. A path of continuous evolution, guided by the common goal of designing truly customer-oriented loyalty solutions. Importantly, the customer in "customer-oriented" isn't just the purchasing decision-maker, but their entire family and the community in which they live.

Fabrizio Losa and Chiara Landini, TCC

Part One

CUSTOMER LOYALTY: CONCEPTUAL ASPECTS AND EMPIRICAL EVIDENCE

CHAPTER 1
CUSTOMER LOYALTY: AN INTRODUCTION

[Bruno Busacca, Sandro Castaldo]

1.1 The competitive environment

We are experiencing a complex period both economically and socially. Consumption is stagnant. Inflation is slowing down. But it has triggered an upsurge in the price of consumer goods in all European countries, negatively affecting the purchasing power of families. This has been further depleted by rising energy and financing costs, due to interest rates that persist at high levels and weigh significantly on the budgets of indebted households.

As a result, the customer has limited resources, and more price-oriented distribution formulas are developing rapidly in Italy, as they are throughout Europe. Discounters continue to grow (in our country they have surpassed hypermarkets in share) along with drugstores and e-commerce. This last format, although proliferating, remains a residual channel in the grocery world, unlike the consumer electronics and household appliances sector.

As we will see in more detail in the next chapter (Chapter 2), retail companies are dealing with a challenging competitive scenario. In fact, major players are trying to find new ways to face competition more effectively, often turning to digital transformation.

Competition is increasingly articulated and aggressive, which makes it ever more critical to be able to anticipate the evolving dynamics of demand expectations by continuously reinforcing the value proposition. In volatile, complex contexts, this is the most appropriate strategy to avoid missing the *"strategic window"* – the distance between the value a company offers to customers and the value they desire – a window which could close at any moment. In summary, in today's competitive environment, customers have truly become a scarce resource for companies. What's more, acquiring new customers is more difficult than ever because competing value propositions have proliferated, and technology has expanded the spectrum of substitutability between products and stores. Maintaining relationships with paying customers is also problematic, as the diversity of available alternatives diminishes their loyalty to a given brand or store.

In the past few years, particularly during COVID-19, many companies had solid performances in the grocery retail industry, which (in part due to the health crisis) had substantially reduced investments in undifferentiated price promotions (e.g. flyers and price cuts). For some time, the hope was that retailers would realize the importance of investing in customers to win over and build up their loyalty. In reality, the scenario has rapidly transformed, almost returning to the pre-COVID-19 situation: price promotions are on the rise again, favored in part by the recent reduction in inflation. Also noteworthy in this context is a significant upsurge in the market share of private labels (PLs), a trend which partly offsets the strong competitive tension on price and brings Italian retailers closer to average European levels.

1.2 The concept of loyalty

In the complicated environment briefly described above, companies have no choice but to invest in enhancing customer loyalty, which is coming to be seen as an increasingly critical resource in retail management. As we will see later, customer loyalty also allows for stabilizing relationships with customers, boosting economic value, and in turn maximizing the current and potential income streams.

Loyalty can be defined as a particular type of shopper behavior in which systematic repurchase is motivated by the existence, in the customer's cognitive system, of a significant stock of trust in the brand/store in question. This definition highlights the fact that different forms of loyalty emerge throughout the life cycle of the relationship with the company.

For this reason, in the next two sections of this chapter (1.3, 1.4) we'll explore the various forms of loyalty that come to fruition respectively from a *cross-sectional perspective* (different kinds of relationships existing simultaneously) and a *longitudinal perspective* (different evolutionary stages within the same relationship) (Busacca and Castaldo, 2002). Only through the in-depth study of these two analytical perspectives can we gain a full understanding of the different types of customer loyalty.

Following the definition of the construct and its morphology, we'll investigate two additional aspects that are particularly vital to store loyalty management. The first is the issue of measurement (1.5). Indeed, only through precise quantification of the level of loyalty can we identify its real effect on promotional initiatives. Without adequate measurement systems, we can neither understand the results of such initiatives, nor finetune future loyalty management actions. With this in mind, then, the fifth section of the chapter is devoted to measuring the various analytical dimensions of loyalty. Finally, Section 1.6 investigates the economic value of customer loyalty for the company. Indeed, as mentioned above, the attention given to the construct and the amount of cognitive and financial resources devoted to understanding, measuring, and developing customer loyalty are justifiable only if loyalty management programs actually increase the economic value generated by the company. The last section of this chapter aims to demonstrate the link between customer loyalty, the consistency and duration of income streams, and the magnitude of discount rates. What emerges is that as customer loyalty grows, so does the value of the firm's economic capital.

1.3 Typologies of customer loyalty from a cross-sectional perspective

As anticipated, while there is a clear link between repetitive behavior and customer loyalty, the former is a necessary but insufficient condition for the concrete manifestation of the latter. In the *resource-based perspective*, customer loyalty is an intangible resource, endowed with value only if the repeated purchase from the same store derives from the trust that the consumer has developed toward it.

That said, to identify the different forms of loyalty, we need to specify the meaning attributed to the construct of *trust.* As an initial approximation, it can be interpreted as *a form of knowledge* (Vicari, 1991; 2024) built on a flow of perceptions that conform to expectations about the counterpart's behavior, which acts as an *information structuring model.* This makes it possible to minimize the amount of data needed to make the final choice.

Trust has a multidimensional nature, arising from:

- beliefs about the *competencies/skills* of the company and the motivations that guide its market behaviors, with particular reference to integrity, customer orientation, and absence of opportunism (*cognitive dimension*);
- a set of *affective* valences, derived from feelings of self-connection, passion, tolerance, and emotions arising from repeated confirmation of the firm's behavior expectations (*affective dimension*);
- *orientations to action,* consistent with the above cognitive and affective components, resulting in a growing interdependence with the enterprise and a commitment to adopt collaborative behaviors designed to ensure the longevity of the relationship with it (*conative dimension*).

Analyzing these dimensions is crucial for classifying the forms of loyalty. For example, considering the elements that define the cognitive dimension of trust (beliefs about the firm's motivations and capabilities), we can distinguish three types of trust (Andaleeb, 1992):

- *Hopeful trust* arises when consumers believe that the firm's behaviors are aimed at achieving common benefits, but they aren't fully convinced the firm has the competencies/skills necessary to achieve that goal.
- *Unstable trust* arises from positive judgments of the firm's competencies/skills, but this is associated with the belief that the firm is driven by opportunistic motivations.
- *Full trust* is characterized by positive perceptions regarding the firm's motivations and competencies/skills.

The proposed classification, providing a scale for trust, is useful from two perspectives.

First, it facilitates the construction of an interpretive framework of customer loyalty intersecting the cognitive and behavioral dimensions of trust (Figure 1.1). Next to loyalty relationships, which are characterized by full trust and a high repurchase rate of the product offered by the company (upper right quadrant), we see three other forms of loyalty, which can be easily traced back to the types of trust discussed above:

Figure 1.1   A classification of possible forms of loyalty

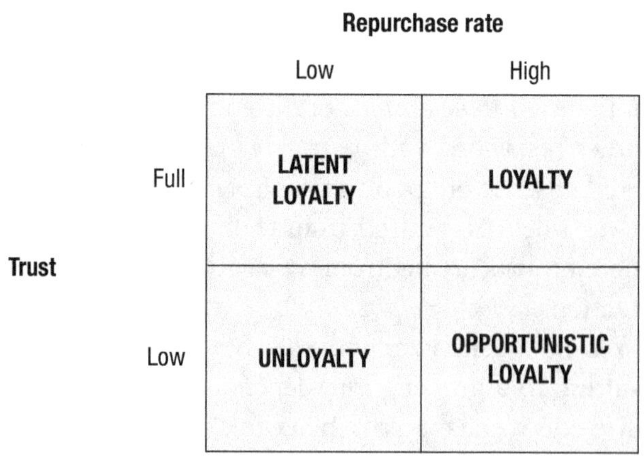

		Repurchase rate	
		Low	High
Trust	Full	LATENT LOYALTY	LOYALTY
	Low	UNLOYALTY	OPPORTUNISTIC LOYALTY

- *Opportunistic loyalty* is when repurchase is solely motivated by the high competencies attributed to the firm, whose opportunistic motives are taken for granted. In this case, the relationship is dominated by the consumer's attempt to repurchase all or part of the payoffs obtained from the firm.
- *Tolerant loyalty* emerges when repurchase is justified primarily by beliefs about the firm's willingness to pursue common benefits, beliefs that induce the consumer to accept its skills deficit (albeit not indefinitely).
- *Latent loyalty* happens when cognitive or affective barriers are still preventing full trust in the enterprise to translate into consistent behavioral orientations.

As we can easily deduce from the classification above, it isn't enough to survey the number of consumers who make repeat purchases from a certain retailer to determine the strength of that company's relational network, let alone its ability to build up customer-based intangible resources. In fact, only the relationships in the upper right quadrant can be considered true loyalty; the preferences of other consumer clusters are clearly transitory. In particular with regard to buyers linked to the firm by loyalty that is *unstable* or *hopeful*, these segments are high-risk. Moreover, their repetitive behavior can be explained by a lack of alternatives, or the substantial undifferentiation among alternatives, the existence of affective bonds (in the case of hopeful trust), or barriers to exit. The relationship may also be informed by conversion costs or other lock-in mechanisms.

Second, by identifying different types of trust, we highlight the need to complement the cross-sectional analysis of loyalty with a longitudinal analysis, aimed at capturing the transformative pattern typical of customer relationships characterized by greater longevity. For example, Mayer et al. (1995, p. 722) put forward the idea that perceptions about the company's competencies/skills prove decisive in the early stages of the relationship, when the limited number of interactions does not allow customers to glean sufficient information to ascertain whether opportunism is coming into play. This would support the hypothesis that customer loyalty represents the final state of an evolutionary process, which justifies the transition of the same customer through multiple forms of loyalty.

1.4 Forms of loyalty in a dynamic perspective

Several explanatory models of the customer relationship lifecycle can be found in the marketing literature (e.g. Ford, 1980; Dwyer et al., 1987; Gronroos, 1990; Wilson, 1995; Deighton & Grayson, 1995; Iacobucci & Zerillo, 1997; Fontenot & Wilson, 1997; Costabile, 2000; Castaldo 2002). All are grounded on the hypothesis that the nature and influence of the determinants of these relationships are subject to relevant changes over time.

In an extreme synthesis of the results of this line of research (beyond the differences regarding the number of stages and the variables of influence included in the different models), two aspects are particularly noteworthy:

1. Customer relationships follow a typical evolutionary process, in which the interaction between the determinants and consequences of trust leads to more intense forms of loyalty over time (in the best-case scenario).
2. Among the main marketing drivers, perceptions of value of the partners involved in the relationship assume a prominent role.

With reference to the first aspect, from the consumer's point of view, the longest-lasting market relationships spring from the recognition of significant differentiating elements in the company's offerings, which result in clear cut expectations of value. Repeated confirmation of these expectations generates a stream of customer satisfaction perceptions, which consolidates positive beliefs about the enterprise. So as the relationship progresses, the areas of brand/consumer interaction expand, and the interdependence between the partners enriches the stock of trust accumulated in previous stages with affective valences. These further strengthen the cognitive dimension of trust and bolster the consumer's determination to overcome any critical moments that would likely threaten the continuation of the relationship.

In relation to the second aspect, adopting the perspective of the firm in this case, there are various determinants of the evolutionary cycle underlying the transition of relationships to more intense forms of loyalty over time. Assuming central importance is the value generated for the customer in terms of the usefulness (*utility value*) and fairness (*equity value*) of the exchange process. Indeed, the creation of utility value acts on the consumers' cognitive system, reinforcing their motivations, beliefs and attitudes; equity value instead nurtures relational involvement and commitment. The latter, in particular, translates into greater effort from the parties involved and manifests any time the relationship is considered so meaningful as to justify the maximum exertion to maintain it. This entails the desire to establish a stable relationship, and the willingness to endure short-term sacrifices to consolidate that relationship while relying on its stability.

At this point, with regard to consumers' expectations and perceptions of value, we must consider the impact of the economies associated with replicating purchasing choices. First of all, the relationship with the company is activated by a comparative process that highlights the superiority of a given product it offers, measured up against the alternatives included in the evoked set, with an eye to utility value. The latter is deduced by weighing expectations concerning the benefits and costs of acquiring the product in question. After the consumption experience, the positive confirmation (or disconfirmation) of these expectations fuels trust in the firm and in turn the probability of repurchase. At this point, economies of various kinds come into play, the most significant of which reduce the costs associated with information gathering and processing, psychological costs, learning costs, conversion costs and any costs related to the purchase of complementary goods or services.

This means that, assuming the customer makes a compensatory valuation, the utility value could remain unchanged, or possibly increase, even with a decrease in expected benefits, *if* this decrease is compensated, or more than compensated, by a savings in cognitive and monetary resources that would otherwise be invested in the purchase and consumption process. The hypothesis advanced here is that, in such a case, the intermediary's behavior is judged negatively, even if the utility value is higher than available alternatives. In other words, we assume when consumers note that the firm offers fewer benefits, even if this is offset by trust economies, they develop the perception of opportunistic behavior. Specifically, they believe that the company is seeking to exploit the advantageous position it has gained from investing in the relationship.

In sum, by adopting a dynamic perspective to analyze customer loyalty, we can distinguish different forms of loyalty which are shaped decisively by the value produced for the customer, both in terms of utility and equity.

While it is not unreasonable to assume that the evolution of different forms of loyalty depends on the progressive development of perceptions of value (functional, symbolic and affective, equity), extant research cannot yet corroborate the existence of a strict sequence. In fact, the evolutionary cycle of customer relationships depends on the influence of multiple intervening variables (Costabile, 2001, pp. 133-138). Worth mentioning are information asymmetries and power imbalances among the parties to the relationship, the level of psychological involvement of the customer, the degree of perceived differentiation among alternatives offered by competitors, and the nature of the benefits sought in the good or service in question.

1.5 Measuring customer loyalty

In a nutshell, customer loyalty represents a construct that can be articulated into two dimensions: cognitive and behavioral. (See Chapter 4 for a more detailed review.) Therefore, it only materializes when the systematic choice of the same brand (repeated purchase behavior) results from a specific act of will of the buyer, who manifests a particular preference and clear trust in the firm offering that brand (cognitive dimension). What this means is if no cognitive component is involved, it's simply a matter of repetitive buying behavior. But since this behavior does not spring from ingrained beliefs or preferences, it is susceptible to sudden alterations when even minor changes in the competitive scenario happen. As a result, the firm gets no lasting competitive advantage.

Among the works devoted to the study of customer loyalty, several have addressed the problem of measuring this construct. As we see in Chapters 4 and 5, recommended indicators have often focused on measuring only one dimension of loyalty, simplifying the articulation of the construct. However, some authors, to overcome the problems associated with this methodological limitation, have proposed parameters capable of capturing both aspects.

In the following sections, we first introduce indicators aimed at evaluating the behavioral dimension of customer loyalty, and then those centering on the cognitive dimension. We end with synthetic indicators which attempt to assess both dimensions, sourcing to key scientific contributions. Later, in Chapter 5, we provide a detailed analysis of the international academic literature, including the most recent content and developments.

Before proceeding, however, it is worth noting as far as reductionist approaches to measuring customer loyalty that the scope is considerably limited, considering the increasing integration between channels, platforms, and devices. In a single customer journey, the same individual repeatedly passes through several different touchpoints. Hence the need to collect and process data on customer orientations and behaviors in an integrated way at every point of contact with the company: at the physical store, on the website, on social networks, on the phone, and on the different contact platforms (e.g., chats, e-mails, chatbots and virtual assistants).

In-store technologies undoubtedly facilitate data collection to build loyalty indicators consistent with the omnichannel logic that drives purchasing and consumption behavior. Here we're referring to the digital technologies available to retailers today: QR codes, sensors (e.g., beacons, NFS-near, RFID), interactive storefronts, smart mirrors, kiosks, mobile POS, and so on. Thanks to all these tools, more than ever before companies can integrate online and offline customer behavior data to have a comprehensive view of the level of loyalty throughout the entire customer journey.

1.5.1 *Behavioral indicators*

Behavioral indicators have been aggregated by Jacoby & Chestnut (1978) into four main categories, broken down as follows.

The first set is *purchase share indices*, which serve to measure loyalty by quantifying the share of the total spending budget allocated by a consumer to a particular store. Several threshold values have been proposed which mark the level above which buying behavior is considered loyal.

The second category is *purchase sequence indices*. These are compiled by tracking a series of purchases by an individual consumer. Some postulate, for example, that a sequence of three or more consecutive purchases of the same brand is indicative of loyal behavior. Others, also leveraging the sequence of purchases in a given period, propose more nuanced measures which can capture purchasing behaviors that are less easily coded, such as shared loyalty between two or more brands or unstable loyalty.

Purchase probability indices, the third category of behavioral indicators, compute inferential statistics derived the sequence of purchases detected during a series of past observations revealing the likelihood that consumers will select a particular brand for subsequent purchases. Among the indicators that fall into this category, some evaluate the probability that shoppers, who have recently changed the store where they normally make their purchases, will return to the original store the next time they go shopping.

Finally, *synthetic behavioral indices* are obtained by combining the methodologies in the previous categories.

As we discussed above, behavioral indicators are not sufficient to fully assess customer loyalty. If we state that consumers who allocate 60% of their spending budget to a particular store are considered loyal, while individuals who only spend 50% percent are not, or if we affirm that customers are loyal if they visit the same store more than three times in a row: these are claims that cannot be made without reservation. To fully appreciate the phenomenon of loyalty, we mustn't neglect to measure its cognitive dimension and, as we'll see later, additional dimensions which have yet to be investigated in depth. We need to explore consumer attitudes and how marketing actions affect them in the context of determining the level of loyalty. More specifically, the effectiveness of a marketing initiative, such as an ongoing promotion, should be read not only in terms of its impact on behavior, but also – and more importantly – on consumer attitudes, which constitute the cognitive basis of loyalty.

1.5.2 *Cognitive indicators*

Cognitive indices, which measure the type of trust attitude toward a certain brand, are mainly based on consumer preferences or purchase intentions. Unlike behavioral indices, these are more suitable for understanding the underlying causes of a change in loyalty, since by measuring the level of preference accorded to a given brand, they serve to assess the *determinants* of behavior.

This category of indicators considers the level of customer loyalty to be inversely proportional to the "cognitive distance" existing between the image of the store and the configuration of the ideal profile expressed by the consumer, in other words, the store that most customers would prefer. Therefore, to gauge the cognitive dimension of loyalty, we can measure the space that divides the perceptions of different brands and ideal store profiles as expressed by consumers.

Jacoby & Chestnut (1978, p. 48) propose a measurement methodology that aims to rank stores on a preference scale. From consumer evaluations, three ranking areas emerge: acceptance, neutral behavior, and rejection. The greater the cognitive distance between the acceptance and rejection areas (or the neutral area) with reference to an individual consumer or market segment, the greater the degree of loyalty to the stores included in the acceptance area.

To fully understand how to measure the cognitive dimension of loyalty, we need to investigate some of the main quantitative methodologies adopted for detecting the brand image profile, which, as we shall see below, is the primary cognitive determinant of loyalty. For our purposes, we need to classify the above methodologies into two basic categories: (1) *attribute-based*, and (2) *non-attribute-based*, i.e. grounded in comprehensive evaluations.

Attribute-based methodologies center on consumer assessments concerning a set of pre-determined characteristics of the offer. To reveal these judgments, rating scales are mainly used. Sometimes, precisely to isolate the most relevant attributes of the offer, the importance of individual attributes in defining the image of the product or retail brand is measured. Underlying this methodology is the hypothesis that not all attributes of the offering contribute equally to determining the image. This methodology, called the Multi-Attribute Attitude Model (Fishbein and Ajzen, 1975), is used to build an attitude index related to each store, calculated as the sum of the products of the importance and ratings of each attribute.

For *non-attribute-based* methodologies, an overall evaluation is gleaned from consumers which presumably incorporates opinions on the single attributes that make up the offer. In the past, the most common technique, and the simplest in terms of data collection and processing methods, was to rank consumer preferences in well-defined purchasing situations, and then associate these preferences with socio-demographic data (e.g., Weale, 1961). However, the growing variety expressed by consumers makes it increasingly difficult to accept the hypothesis of a biunivocal correspondence between customers' socio-demographic profile and individual preferred brands. This is the reason why non-attribute-based methodologies have been gradually replaced by others, such as Multidimensional Scaling (MDS), which measures the degree of similarity between different stores or brands. MDS makes it possible to assess the image profile of a set of stimuli, and then map perceptions and preferences.

In addition to quantitative image assessment methodologies, there are other techniques that can be defined as qualitative. These are particularly useful for conducting exploratory surveys to subsequently set up quantitative research. A common qualitative methodology uses questionnaires with semi-open-ended questions. This technique is based on the concept of image as a set of attributes, adopting a de-structured approach to defining them, discounting predefined characteristics. Another set of de-structured methodologies is represented by psycholinguistic techniques. Here consumer interviews serve to directly determine the stimuli to consider and the attributes to evaluate. Then personalized positioning maps can be drawn up from the evaluations expressed by the interviewees (Cardozo, 1974, p. 85). A final type of de-structured technique for image assessment is laddering, which is aimed at reconstructing the means-end chain. The focus of the model is on the relationship that exists between attributes (of a product, a store, a retail brand, and so on), consequences (positive--that is, beneficial--or undesirable), and personal values. The framework, which links attributes, benefits and values, provides insight into the way mental associations are formed. As such it serves as a useful starting point for a deeper understanding of brand image formation.

1.5.3 Synthetic indicators

To complete this brief review on measuring loyalty, we now turn to the wide-ranging category of *synthetic indicators*, which represent as many combinations as possible of behavioral and cognitive indices. Among these, the composite index of store loyalty proposed by Bellenger et al. (1976) is particularly interesting, albeit for illustrative purposes only. This index is calculated as follows:

1. First, customers estimate the percentage of total spending they allocate to a certain store.
2. Then, a store ranking is compiled by incorporating the following criteria: product assortment, distance and time required for shopping, staff attitude,

store atmosphere, and availability of parking. Next, the score for a given store on each of the above factors is used to weigh the percentage estimated in the previous step.

3. Finally, consumers are asked to rate on a Likert scale from 5 (I completely agree) to 1 (I completely disagree) the following assessment, "I make my purchases at store X when I need a product that I believe is sold at that store." This score is used to weigh the values resulting from the previous step.

The first figure (share of the budget) represents the behavioral component of the indicator, while the other two refer to the cognitive dimension of loyalty, in terms of attitudes and purchase intentions, respectively. Synthetic indices such as the one described above, while offering the advantage of conciseness, are to be evaluated with extreme caution, bearing in mind that offsets may occur between the behavioral and cognitive dimensions which are not reported by the indicator. This limits its interpretive potential. When using summary measures, in any case, it is always advisable to analyze the components of loyalty separately, so as to reconstruct the cause-and-effect relationships between them and fully understand the reasons behind any changes in the level of loyalty.

In conclusion, as we will see in Chapters 4 and 5, conceptualizations and measurements of loyalty have evolved over time and have become more sophisticated, allowing for an enriched understanding and ability to analyze this multidimensional construct.

1.6 The value of customer loyalty

After discussing some indicators of loyalty, it becomes crucial for our purposes to analyze the economic value of customer loyalty. The impact of loyalty on the value creation process has long been the focus of interest of business scholars and practitioners alike. This attention has resulted in a proliferation of interpretive models and empirical evidence which have clarified the areas of influence of customer loyalty on the economic capital of the firm (and on shareholder value as well). The results achievable through the systematic accumulation of this asset have also come into sharper focus.

A useful concept for understanding the value that a customer creates over time for the firm is *Customer Lifetime Value* (CLV), which can factor in both the size of the purchase periodically made and the stability and duration of the series of purchases reserved for the trusted brand. In summary, CLV measures the value expressed in terms of margins which an individual customer is expected to generate for the company during the time horizon of the relationship. In symbols, we have (Gupta and Zeithaml, 2006, p. 724):

$$CLV = \sum_{t=0}^{T^*} \frac{(p_t - c_t)}{(1 + i)^t} - AC$$

where:

- p_t is the price paid by the customer at time t
- c_t denotes the direct cost incurred to serve the customer at time t
- $p_t - c_t$ represents the customer's contribution margin at time t
- i corresponds to the discount rate or cost of capital
- T^* equals the expected life of the customer relationship
- AC is the cost of acquiring the customer

We can also include in the above formula the probability (r_t) that the customer remains loyal for a certain time horizon, which would then become:

$$CLV = \sum_{t=0}^{T^*} \frac{(p_t - c_t) r^t}{(1 + i)^t} - AC$$

where, with respect to the variables already known, r^t represents the probability that the customer repeats the purchase or is still "alive" at time t.

Customer loyalty affects all components of the value of the customer relationship, multiplying contribution margins and their duration while reducing the capitalization rate (and often also the cost of acquiring new customers, thanks to positive word of mouth). In the following pages we aim to investigate these impacts more specifically.

1.6.1 *Customer loyalty and customer contribution margin*

Numerous studies have shown that customers characterized by high loyalty have certain distinctive characteristics which increase their contribution margin. These include:

- lower price sensitivity;
- a greater propensity to consume;
- the willingness to trade up, i.e., to purchase higher quality goods and services from the same company, and cross-buying, i.e., extending their demand to other goods and/or services offered by that company;
- the need for lower sales and service costs; and

- the propensity to "spread the word" about the company and to collaborate on its innovation projects.

The characteristics of customer loyalty, listed above, represent growth options that progressively expand the scope of the relationship. In essence, the options indicated arise from the high transferability that characterizes customer loyalty, like all invisible assets based on consumers' cognitive systems. This transferability can be traced back to the generalization of the positive values attributed by the customer to the purchase and usage experience. It takes the form of the so-called halo effect, inducing the customer to extend the loyalty developed towards a certain asset (tangible or intangible) to other products/services marketed under the same brand.

Added to this is the decrease in operating costs associated with customer management. Loyal customers are known entities for the company; they are accustomed to using its system/business, and integrated into the related processes of logistics, product development, communication and so on. These individuals often entail lower costs compared to newly acquired customers, who inevitably require adaptation investments and give rise to business and credit risks, which are instead lower and more predictable with loyal customers. Moreover, we can easily understand that being able to count on a congruent base of loyal customers facilitates sales forecasting and simplifies all business planning processes: from purchasing to production scheduling, from staffing to financial forecasting, and so on.

An additional factor to consider is the greater bargaining power for firms that enjoy high customer loyalty. For example, the creation of store loyalty translates into fewer constraints in building product assortments, as well as the possibility of increasing contribution margins by directing consumer choices toward own brands or toward the most profitable references (which are typically unbranded). Moreover, taking a non-confrontational approach, it's possible to consolidate interactions with industrial firms.

1.6.2 *Customer loyalty and customer relationship longevity*

As an initial approximation, the influence exerted by customer loyalty on the expected life of the customer relationship can be determined by clarifying the connection between the concepts of customer retention rate (CRR) and average prospective longevity (APL). In practice, the first indicator is used as an expressive measure of the loyalty coefficient of the customer base. CRR is constructed by taking the number of customers at the beginning and end of a given time interval (usually, but not necessarily, a year), and comparing that to the initial number of customers, net of newly acquired customers. The second indicator (again assuming year as the time interval) is defined by the following ratio: 1/ (1-CRR). The relationship between the indicators is expressed by an exponential curve: as the loyalty rate rises, the duration of relationships gradually increases as well, and in turn the income and profit generated by customers.

The indicators we briefly described here are built on certain simplifying assumptions (Busacca & Bertoli, 2024), which can be removed by focusing attention not on the total customer base at a given time interval, but on the various cohorts that make up the portfolio, i.e., the homogeneous sets of customers relative to the year the year the firm acquires them (Costabile & Marzocchi, 1995). Second, we should not think in terms of the average time customers remain in the corporate portfolio, but instead project the prospective duration of current relationships by estimating the interval at which each cohort resets.

1.6.3 *Customer loyalty and flow discount rate*

A final but no less significant area of influence on customer loyalty on Customer Lifetime Value (CLV) relates to the impact of this resource on the discount rate of economic flows produced by market relationships. As anticipated in part in our discussion of the customer contribution margin, as customer loyalty grows, the competitive position of the firm is strengthened, and consequently, the risk profile characterizing these economic flows is reduced. This results in lower discount rates and higher CLV.

On a conceptual level, the positive correlation between customer loyalty and the strength of a firm's competitive position is justified by the fact that loyal buyers are less sensitive to the actions of competitors and pay more attention to the firm's initiatives. These elements translate into lower competitive vulnerability. In essence, customer loyalty reinforces the mechanisms of enterprise isolation, (Rumelt, 1984, pp. 566-569) i.e., barriers to the imitability of resources, the foundation of competitive advantage.

1.7 Conclusions

In light of the impact exerted by loyalty on the value of the firm's relationship portfolio and, more generally, its economic capital, we need to have a thorough understanding of the construct, its determinants (primarily trust), and its antecedents (e.g., Castaldo, 2002). This understanding will provide companies with valuable analytical support to design behaviors aimed at implementing trust-enhancing strategies that can translate into higher levels of customer loyalty and, more generally, in the economic value of the firm. In particular, by first identifying the cognitive antecedents of trust and its enhancement mechanisms, it is possible to isolate those elements capable of eliciting a positive impact on customers' trust and, consequently, on their level of loyalty. This impact, as we have seen in the previous section, results in multiplying customer lifetime value, incrementing margins generated by customers, extending their duration, amplifying the potential growth rate, and reducing the capitalization rate. These effects, combining variously, result in an increase in the economic value of the firm.

The framework in Figure 1.2. summarizes the main analytical steps of the loyalty management process described in this chapter.

In the next chapter, we will first delve into the distribution scenario in Italy, providing the main market data and exploring recent evolutionary trends. We'll see that the retail grocery retail sector is an extremely competitive one, where convenience-oriented distribution formulas are emerging along with a sharp rise in private labels (PL).

In Chapter 3, the research team of SDA Bocconi's Loyalty Promotion Monitor conducts a scenario analysis, interviewing the main players in Italy's large-scale organized distribution (GDO) grocery sector, and drawing cognitive maps that project possible and probable future competitive scenarios. Specifically, these scenarios foresee the growing relevance of digital technologies, which are affecting loyalty more than ever, both on the big data analysis front and in terms of digital device usage. The issue of sustainability is also a pertinent vector which inevitably affects retail strategies and loyalty management initiatives.

Chapters 4 and 5 are devoted to a review of the literature on customer loyalty. As anticipated earlier in this chapter, the topic has been extensively analyzed in the marketing literature, which has offered numerous insights into the conceptualization of the construct, its constituent dimensions, and its measurement. Specifically, Chapter 4 builds on the main reviews conducted on the topic of

Figure 1.2   A summary view of the process governing trust enhancement policies

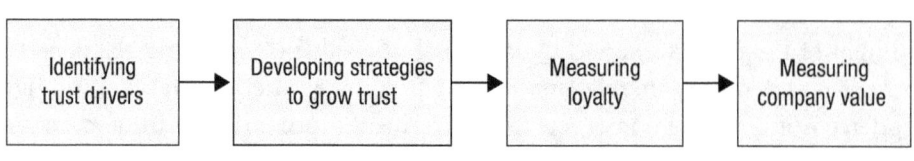

customer loyalty, while Chapter 5 analyzes all the major papers published in the leading journals, investigating the construct, its constituent dimensions, sectoral areas of analysis, and methods of measurement, and proposing a focus on retail and store loyalty. These analyses reveal the relevance of the topic, gradually focusing on the digital dimension of loyalty as well. In addition, what clearly emerges is the multidimensional nature of the construct and the relevance of managing and measuring all these dimensions: behavioral, cognitive, conative, and attitudinal.

Chapter 6 reports the results of a survey of a sample of managers on the specific topic of measuring loyalty at their companies, a critical issue both for practitioners and researchers. In light of the current situation at the companies in our sample, careful reflection is needed, first and foremost to focus on the analytical dimensions of the construct and the most effective ways to measure it. This also considering the new digital touchpoints, which require prompt adaptation of systems for gauging customer status and customer relationships.

The book closes with a chapter that sets down some managerial guidelines for developing more conscientious and effective loyalty management for companies, to boost their competitiveness by developing and optimizing trust relationships with customers over time.

CHAPTER 2
CHALLENGES AND TRENDS FOR RETAILERS: LOYALTY, UNCERTAINTY, AND RESPONSIBILITY

[Emanuele Acconciamessa, Sandro Castaldo]

2.1 The role of retail as an interface between industry and demand

The uncertainty that pervades the contemporary economy is significant and multifaceted. It affects all sectors of society and, inevitably, every level of the supply chain. In such rapidly changing environments, the end market transforms quickly, creating even greater uncertainty for both brands and retailers. Trust becomes a crucial resource for reassuring consumers, who are more sensitive when uncertainty in their world proliferates. External disruptions threaten to upend entrenched purchasing and consumption patterns, exposing both manufacturing and retail brands to the risk of customer churn. To mitigate this risk, customer loyalty is the key asset.

Customer loyalty is a crucial element in business strategies. Loyalty Programs (LPs), designed to build and maintain long-term relationships between shoppers and brands, are now an essential tool for retailers seeking to differentiate themselves in an increasingly competitive market. With the evolution of digital technologies and changes in purchasing and consumption habits, LPs must continuously adapt and renew to remain effective. In the current context, loyalty is no longer just about accumulating points or offering occasional discounts; it involves a deep understanding of customer needs and preferences. Retailers must leverage data and advanced analytics to create personalized experiences and distinctive advantages that strengthen their relationship with their customer base, maximizing acquisition and minimizing churn (Castaldo & Mauri, 1993; 2002).

Today's economic uncertainty is influenced by multiple factors, including fluctuations in global markets, changes in international trade policies, and technological innovations that are reshaping the boundaries of the traditional economy. This volatility affects all levels of the supply chain, from raw materials to final distribution. Brands must navigate this complex landscape, striving to keep their value creation processes stable while flexibly addressing new challenges and opportunities.

In the midst of growing uncertainty, trust becomes a valuable resource. Indeed, consumers seek security in the brands they trust, especially when the economic and social landscape becomes unstable. Trust not only reassures customers but also emotionally binds them to brands, reducing the risk of churn. LPs play a fundamental role in this context, helping to build and maintain trust through consistent and positive interactions. Technological advancements allow for the collection of detailed data on customer behaviors, enabling retailers to develop more targeted and personalized loyalty strategies.

Advanced data analysis is key to discovering emerging trends and preferences, allowing retailers to predict customer needs and adapt their value propositions accordingly. This proactive approach not only enhances the customer experience but also strengthens the emotional connection between the brand and its customer base. Digital technologies, such as Artificial Intelligence (AI) and machine learning, are transforming retail and offering new opportunities to improve customer engagement and satisfaction.

Retail is the interface between supply chains and the end customer, assimilating all the complexities coming from both: from inflation to supply shortages, everything passes through retail before reaching consumers. Grocery retailing, due to its high-frequency customer interaction, absorbs the drivers of change, often mitigating their effects on the final market. The role of retail as a critical interface between the supply chain and end consumers is of fundamental importance. Retailers not only distribute products but also filter and moderate the complexities of the global market for their customers. This buffering function is essential to preserving market stability and supporting consumer trust towards brands. Effective loyalty management requires a deep comprehension of the economic landscape and market dynamics, as well as an ability to adapt quickly to changing conditions.

Customer loyalty, in fact, is not just a marketing issue but is central to business management. Decisions on how to implement and manage LPs depend on understanding market dynamics and customer expectations. Retailers must be able to integrate customer data into their daily operations, using it to continuously improve their value proposition and respond nimbly to new challenges. This integrated approach is crucial for building lasting, valuable relationships with customers, while ensuring the long-term sustainability and competitiveness of the business.

The close relationship between retailers and customers requires companies to make careful assessments of their "loyalty asset." However, to understand the choices and expectations of players around this issue, we must first explore the environment in which they work.

2.2 The macro-scenario for retailers

Environmental and market changes require careful analysis to fully understand relative transformations and adjust business strategies accordingly. Macro-environment analysis is, in fact, the first step of any go-to-market process, followed by strategy development, implementation, and monitoring. In an increasingly complex and dynamic environment, there is a growing need to constantly and consistently track phenomena at all environmental levels, to assess the likelihood of occurrence and potential impacts (Castaldo, 2010). In recent years, various interconnected events have significantly influenced the balance of distribution channels and the performance of the commercial sector: the pandemic, the rise of e-commerce, geopolitical instability and conflicts, the energy crisis, shortages of certain raw materials, rising inflation, and high interest rates. Interpreting macroeconomic scenarios and translating them into micro-management decisions is the necessary path to follow for success in the market.

At the macro level, social transformations have triggered new purchasing behaviors and needs, prompting companies to innovate their offerings to satisfy new customer segments (e.g., seniors, singles, travelers, etc.). These changes have transformed both industrial and commercial supply and demand, making continuous innovation essential to addressing new target markets with proper products and services (Wang et al., 2024). These developments are unfolding in five main directions:

- Geography and demographics: Analyzing the territorial and demographic factors that influence consumption and purchasing behaviors is critical for any company. Italy is one of the most densely populated countries in the European Union, with a sizeable urban population and regional differences in population density, requiring flexible distribution organizations. Mountain regions, though sparsely inhabited, represent important market opportunities. Additionally, Italy has one of the oldest populations in Europe, with a high average life expectancy, albeit reduced due to the pandemic. This demographic trend offers opportunities for the silver economy, but low birth rates that continue to decline pose a challenge for the country's demographic future.

- Culture and society: Cultural and social variables influence purchasing and consumption decisions. Trends and imitative consumption, driven by opinion leaders and influencers, play a significant role. Companies use endorsers to promote products across various sectors. Additionally, internet access has grown appreciably, offering new communication and distribution opportunities from an omnichannel perspective.
- Economy and business: Economic variables influence customer and market behavior. The global economic crisis and the pandemic have had an enormous impact on consumption and employment. Unemployment has risen, particularly among women and young people. Remote work has altered the work-life balance, with an upsurge in psychological issues. Economic uncertainty has led consumers to postpone buying durable goods, causing a recession in various sectors.
- Science and technology: Technological innovations have reshaped business and consumer behavior in meaningful ways. The advent of information and communication technology has changed social habits, information processes, and purchasing behavior. Digital innovations have created new touchpoints, although they haven't been adopted across the board in all product categories or demographic segments.
- Politics and regulations: Political stances, the liberalization of economic activities, and regulatory constraints influence business strategies. In terms of regulations, environmental protection and health safeguards are opening up new markets. The liberalization of distribution has had limited effects but with positive outcomes on large modern retail spaces. The creation of an adequate regulatory framework is crucial for improving the competitiveness of the Italian distribution system at an international level.

In brief, looking beyond their own businesses, retailers must necessarily manage the following factors:

- Growing geopolitical instability is affecting the prices and supply of raw materials and energy.
- Demographic shifts will reveal new market segments and new value proposition opportunities associated with them (e.g., single-person households), especially considering immigration, which calls for profound rethinking of assortments and store design.
- Climate change is generating rising business-to-consumer (B2C) awareness driving the demand for sustainability from companies/brands.
- Uneven distribution of wealth is leading to a growing income-related social

divide (with a corresponding increase in families living in absolute or relative poverty), reflected in a polarization of retailers' positioning, ranging from discount stores to specialized shops.
- Inflation is shrinking household buying power, influencing pricing policies and the quantity of purchased products.
- Interest rates are a crucial variable in determining fluctuations in consumer purchasing power.

These factors create a sort of "perfect storm" (especially when they overlap). Retailers can only emerge by differentiating themselves in the eyes of customers, who are increasingly focused on the economic and value-driven benefits they receive.

2.3 A more demanding, more informed customer base

The trends in the macro-environment inevitably trigger a transformative process in customer demand, giving shape to a new profile of consumers, summarized as follows.

- The propensity to save is one of the clearest factors in this historical moment, in line with the period of crisis and economic pressure. Uncertainty about the future leads to decisions to reduce consumption, especially of durable goods. This creates savings pockets for families, who aim to minimize the erosion of accumulated savings over time. Families tend to reassess their spending priorities, focusing more on essential goods and reducing unnecessary purchases, seeking promotions and special offers that allow them to maximize the value of their limited budget.
- In parallel, the growing attention to health and personal well-being is a promising opportunity for both manufacturing and distribution companies. The end market is more and more interested in goods and services that support a healthy lifestyle, ranging from nutrition (e.g., free-from products) to fitness products, as well as food supplements and solutions that promote psychological balance. This trend is driven by a heightened awareness of the importance of self-care, both on a physical and mental level, stimulating demand for functional and organic food, and personalized fitness programs.
- Another fundamental aspect of the new consumer is their sensitivity toward sustainability. Today's consumers prefer – and buy - products and services that are environmentally friendly, and sustainable. Companies that can prove

they've made a concrete commitment to both environmental and social sustainability can gain a considerable competitive advantage. Sustainability certifications and green labels denoting transparency throughout the supply chain become decisive factors in purchasing decisions. For example, the 2024 Diversity Brand Index showed that brands that address inclusion in the end market and actively work to break down barriers grow faster than their competitors (+23.4% in revenue growth).

- The demand for customized products and services is continually on the rise. Consumers want to feel unique and valued, seeking offers that cater to their specific needs and preferences. This trend is particularly clear in the e-commerce sector, where technological solutions enable highly personalized shopping experiences. Even in physical stores, customization has become a key element in attracting and keeping customers. Retailers use technologies such as AI and machine learning to analyze customer data and create tailored offers, enhancing the shopping experience and escalating the likelihood of repeated purchases.

- In a complex economic environment, consumers are looking for a good value-for-money ratio. Value is not just about low prices but the overall benefit that a product or service offers. That means companies must find a balance between quality and price to meet customer expectations, offering solutions that justify monetary investments. Consumers carefully assess product features, functionality, and durability, aiming to make purchases that represent a good long-term investment. Online reviews and peer recommendations play a crucial role in purchasing decisions, influencing perceptions of product value.

- Co-creation is becoming an increasingly relevant aspect of the relationship between consumers and companies. Customers don't just want customized products; they also want to have a hand in creating them. This approach allows companies to obtain valuable feedback and develop products that better respond to market needs. Co-creation also strengthens the bond between the brand and consumers, promoting greater loyalty.

- Social interaction is a crucial element for the modern shopper, amplified by the widespread use of social networks. Sharing shopping and consumption experiences with one's social network has become a common practice, influencing purchasing decisions through so-called influencer marketing. Companies are capitalizing on this trend by crafting engaging content and encouraging interactions on social media. Collaborations with influencers, the creation of viral campaigns, and testimonials on social media can significantly boost brand visibility and consumer trust.

In summary, the new consumer is attentive, informed, and conscientious. Companies that can understand and respond to these new demands can gain a major competitive advantage, building customer loyalty and capturing new market share. Crucial for success in the modern market is the ability to quickly adapt to the changing preferences of customers and to offer products and services that meet their expectations. Investing in advanced technologies, sustainable practices, and personalization strategies is not just a strategic choice, but a necessity to thrive in an ever-evolving competitive environment.

2.4 Retailer strategies and tactics

The inflationary trend in recent months has eased (Figure 2.1), though it is still positive, considering price variations for equivalent products and quantities purchased. However, since May 2024, after months of continuous upticks, prices have declined, considering the average price changes in the shopping cart (including increases, decreases, product types, and quantities purchased). This trend reversal is significant as it marks a change from the constant inflationary trajectory that characterized previous periods. A central role in this reversal has been played by private labels (PL). Retailers (with their own brands) have adopted aggressive pricing strategies, significantly contributing to making the shopping cart more affordable. In contrast, branded goods have shown values

Figure 2.1   **Trend Inflation and Price Variation**

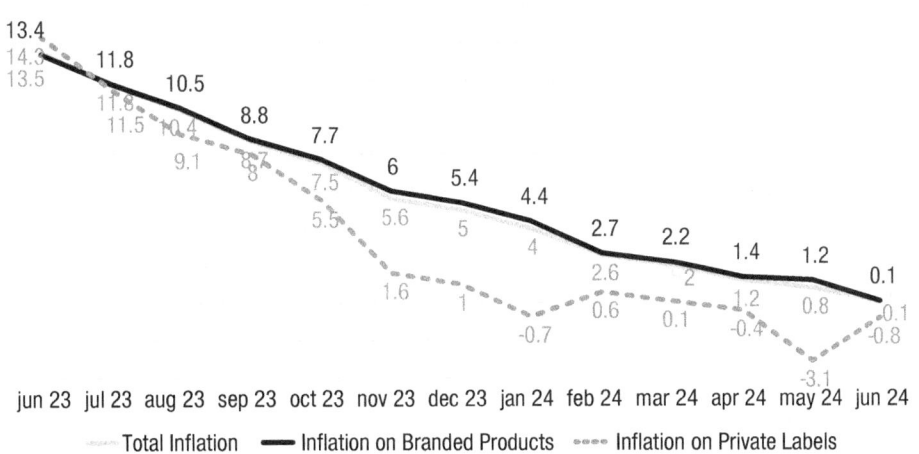

Source: Inflation Observatory NielsenIQ – Total Italy (2024)

that more closely align with overall inflation. Retailers have also ramped up promotions and improved supply chain efficiency to keep costs low, making private label products an attractive choice for consumers seeking value without compromising quality. This dynamic has not only bolstered consumer confidence but also allowed PLs to gain market share from traditional brands, highlighting their growing importance in the modern retail landscape.

In an inflationary scenario (Figure 2.1), as trends are absorbed and processed, four main areas of focus emerge for retailers:

- Assortment polarization
- Private labels (PLs)
- Discount stores
- Price promotions

The first point we should note is that as of June 2024, more than 50% of the market is represented by extreme price ranges: a price index above 150 (25.4%) or below/equal to 85 (27.7%), taking 100 as the average category price. The values adjust when focusing solely on hypermarkets, supermarkets, and self-service stores, confirming the mass market positioning of these formats, without radically changing the message of Figure 2.2. The market is, in fact, polarizing at the extremes, while thinning in the middle range.

As far as private labels (PLs), the trend is clear (Figure 2.3). From 2005 to 2023, the share of PLs has nearly doubled at the expense of manufacturer brands (both leaders and followers). This trend is confirmed by preliminary data for 2024. If we look at PL share (22.3% in hypermarkets, supermarkets, and self-service stores; 31.5% overall/omnichannel), this highlights major efforts by retailers in terms of both positioning and the value proposition (such as breadth and depth of assortment, price point, etc.). PLs have achieved impressive success thanks to pricing that is generally lower than the category average (Figure 2.4). In 2023, only 12.2% of private label products sold by retailers had a price index higher than 150 (hypermarkets, supermarkets, and self-service stores). On the other hand, more than 42% of PL SKUs were sold with a price index equal to or lower than 85. The differences between the omnichannel view and the hyper+super+self-service perspective stem from discount stores, which, being heavily focused on PL, reflect the performance of this product category overall.

Continuing with discount stores, Figure 2.5 shows the market shares of different distribution formats. Discount stores are represented by the line with the

Figure 2.2   **Sales Mix by Price Range**

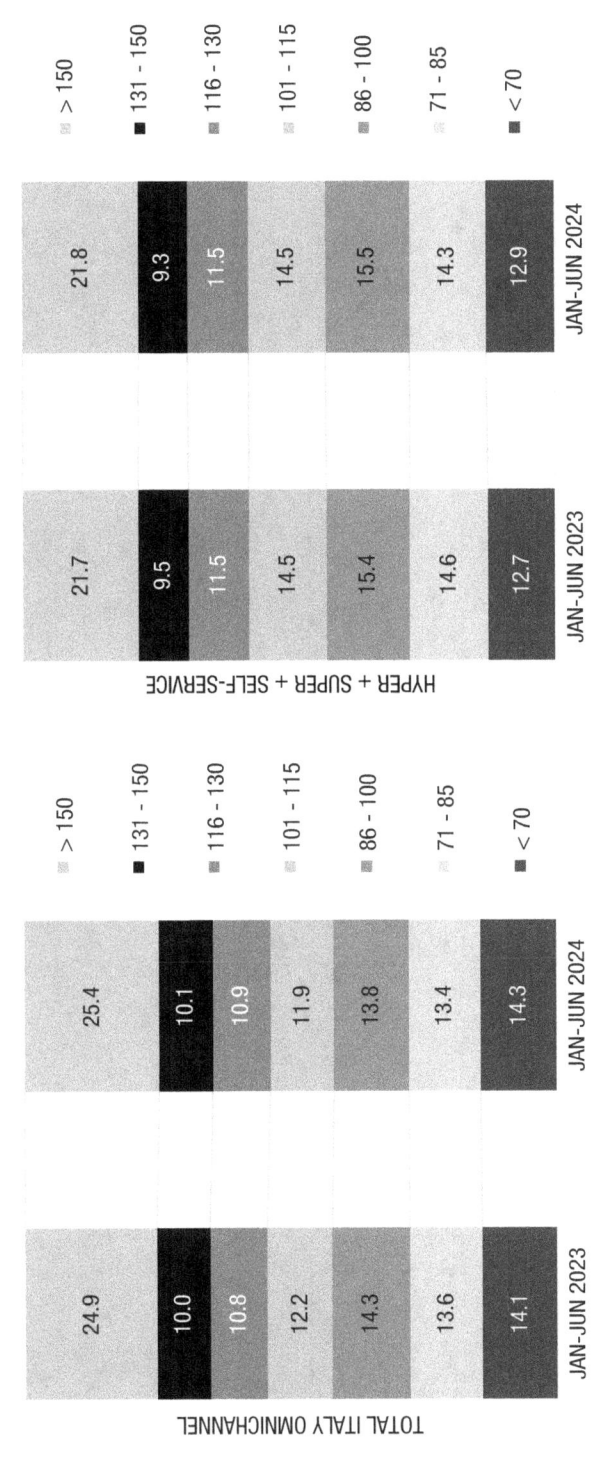

Source: NielsenIQ Discover – Grocery
Italy Omnichannel includes the following: Hypermaket+Supermarket+Self-Service+Discount+Drug Specialists + Ecommerce (2024)

Figure 2.3   Sales Mix by Brand Type (2005-2023)

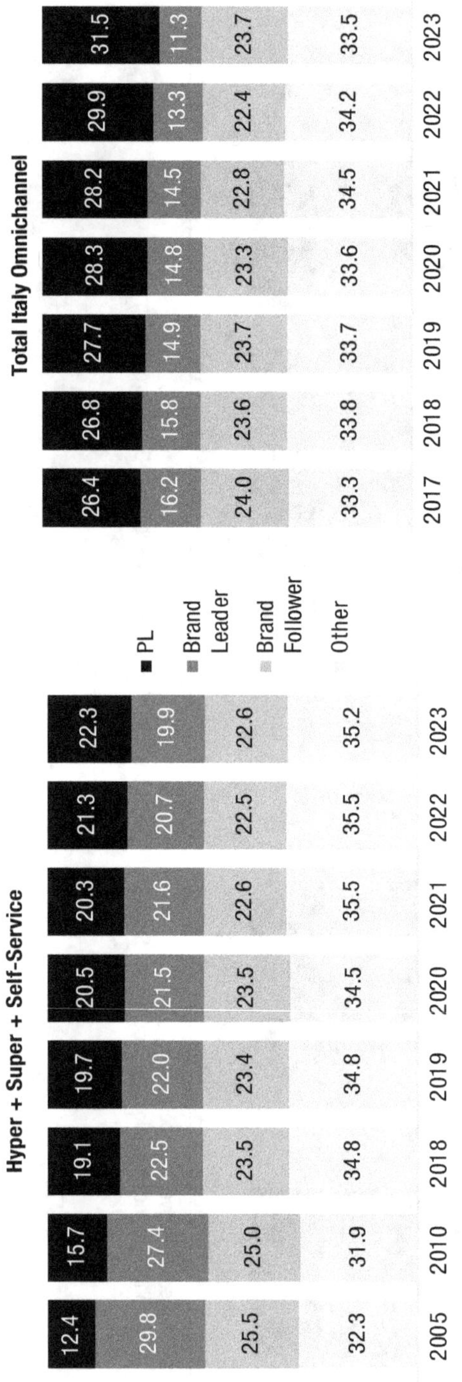

Total Italy Omnichannel

	2017	2018	2019	2020	2021	2022	2023
PL	26.4	26.8	27.7	28.3	28.2	29.9	31.5
Brand Leader	16.2	15.8	14.9	14.8	14.5	13.3	11.3
Brand Follower	24.0	23.6	23.7	23.3	22.8	22.4	23.7
Other	33.3	33.8	33.7	33.6	34.5	34.2	33.5

Hyper + Super + Self-Service

	2005	2010	2018	2019	2020	2021	2022	2023
PL	12.4	15.7	19.1	19.7	20.5	20.3	21.3	22.3
Brand Leader	29.8	27.4	22.5	22.0	21.5	21.6	20.7	19.9
Brand Follower	25.5	25.0	23.5	23.4	23.5	22.6	22.5	22.6
Other	32.3	31.9	34.8	34.8	34.5	35.5	35.5	35.2

Legend: ■ PL · Brand Leader · Brand Follower · Other

Source: NielsenIQ Trade*Mis – Hyper+Super+Self-Service (2023)

Figure 2.4   Private Label Sales Mix by Price Range (2005-2023)

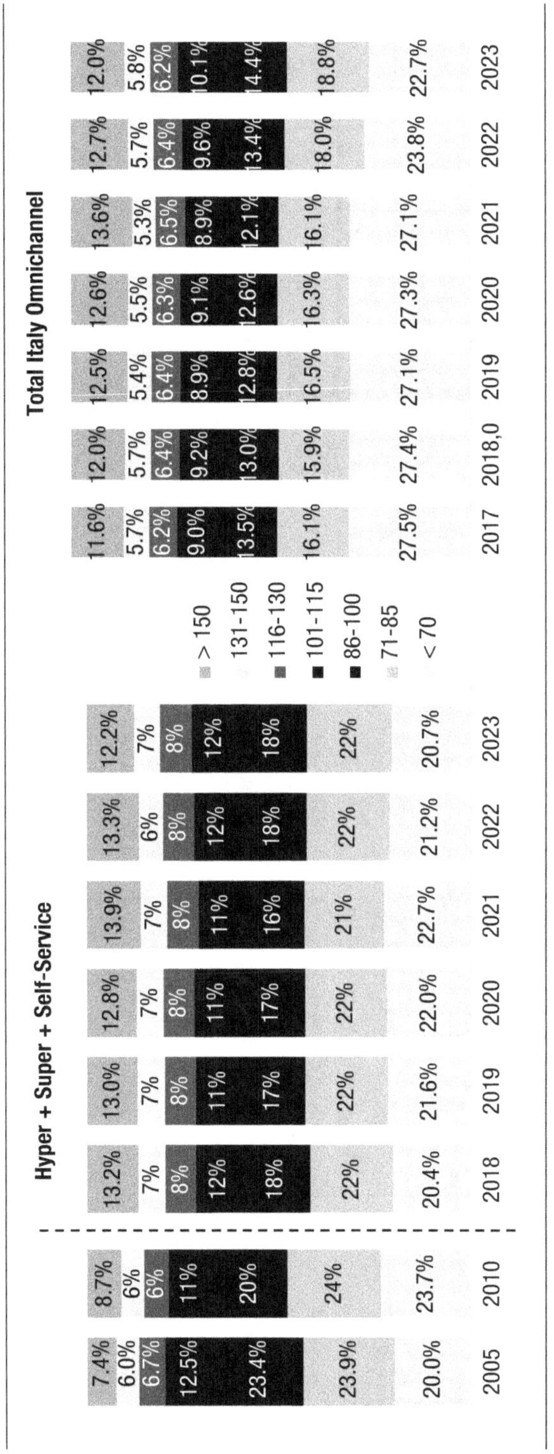

Hyper + Super + Self-Service

Price Range	2005	2010	2018	2019	2020	2021	2022	2023
>150	7.4%	8.7%	13.2%	13.0%	12.8%	13.9%	13.3%	12.2%
131-150	6.0%	6%	7%	7%	7%	7%	6%	7%
116-130	6.7%	6%	8%	8%	8%	8%	8%	8%
101-115	12.5%	11%	12%	11%	11%	11%	12%	12%
86-100	23.4%	20%	18%	17%	17%	16%	18%	18%
71-85	23.9%	24%	22%	22%	22%	21%	22%	22%
<70	20.0%	23.7%	20.4%	21.6%	22.0%	22.7%	21.2%	20.7%

Total Italy Omnichannel

Price Range	2017	2018,0	2019	2020	2021	2022	2023
>150	11.6%	12.0%	12.5%	12.6%	13.6%	12.7%	12.0%
131-150	5.7%	5.7%	5.4%	5.5%	5.3%	5.7%	5.8%
116-130	6.2%	6.4%	6.4%	6.3%	6.5%	6.4%	6.2%
101-115	9.0%	9.2%	8.9%	9.1%	8.9%	9.6%	10.1%
86-100	13.5%	13.0%	12.8%	12.6%	12.1%	13.4%	14.4%
71-85	16.1%	15.9%	16.5%	16.3%	16.1%	18.0%	18.8%
<70	27.5%	27.4%	27.1%	27.3%	27.1%	23.8%	22.7%

Source. NielsenIQ Trade*Mis – Hyper+Super+Self-Service (2023)

Figure 2.5   Market share by retail format (1998-2023)

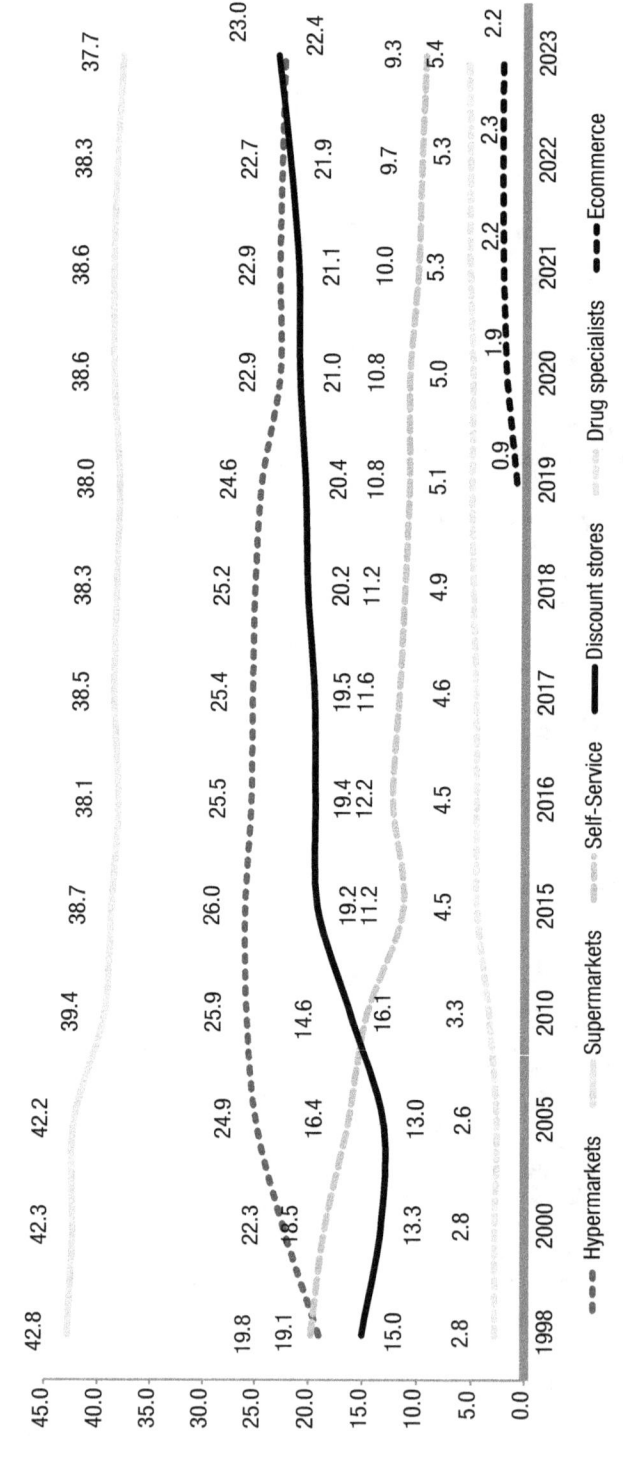

Source: Trade*Mis (2023)

Figure 2.6   Promotional pressure and SKUs affected by the promotions (1999-2023)

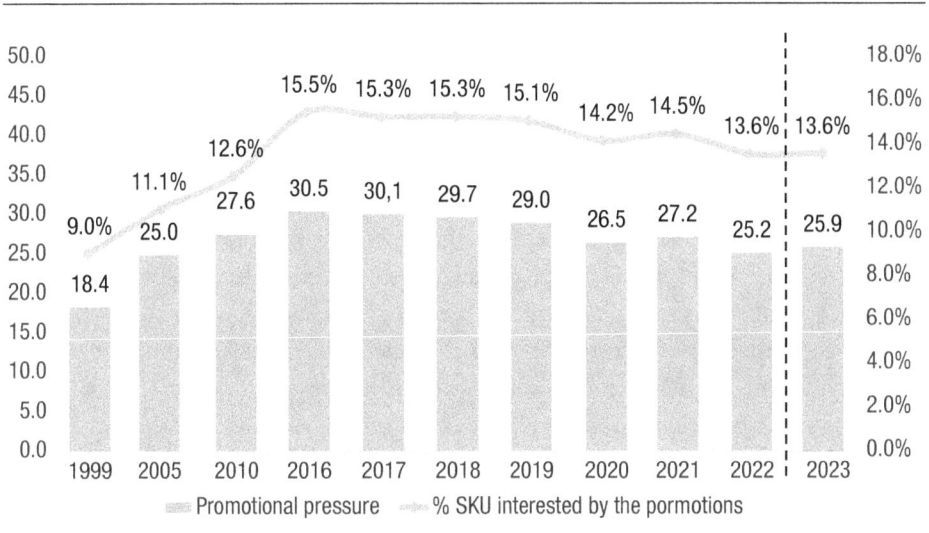

Source: NielsenIQ Trade*Mis - Hyper+Super+Self-Service (2023)

steepest upward trajectory, appearing as the fastest-growing format from 1998 to 2023, reaching 23% market share, eroding the shares of all other formats except for specialized stores and e-commerce. This trend highlights the ability of this format to respond to the changing needs of the target market, promoting the concept of "good value for money" and moving away from merely low prices and the basic shopping experience typical of hard discount stores.

In line with the spending sensitivity of the markets, promotions continue to play a significant role in retailers' strategies and performances. In 2023, the percentage of sales generated through promotions was 25.9% (Figure 2.6), which accounted for 13.6% of assortments (in terms of the number of products discounted in the promotions), with a slight uptick in promotional pressure compared to 2022. NielsenIQ data for 2023 and the first half of 2024 highlights hypermarkets as the format with the more intense promotional pressure, while discount stores, traditionally positioned at lower prices, generate proportionally lower volumes of "promoted" products.

2.5   The need for innovation

Combining affordability and added value is one of the traditional challenges in retail. Companies work along a spectrum, with maximum efficiency on one end, (as with discount stores), and maximum value on the other (typical of boutiques). For retailers, the traditional trade-off between these two dimensions is now evolving into a need for integration. In times of strong hybridization between formats and cross-industry convergence, stores are no longer defined solely by affordability or by the value they deliver. Consumers now expect a mix of both. Retailers must quickly boost their efficiency while effectively delivering new value. The value-for-money ratio takes center stage, where price is clearly not the only determinant. Customer experience is becoming a fundamental driver of a more attractive value proposition, achievable only through trust-based innovation, with loyalty serving as a key pillar.

The combination of affordability and value delivery is particularly crucial in a highly competitive market where consumers have access to a wide range of options and can easily compare products and prices online. Companies recognize the need to balance operational efficiency with the ability to offer a better customer experience, integrating advanced technologies to improve supply chain efficiency and optimize operations. This approach not only reduces costs but also allows companies to reinvest their savings into initiatives that increase perceived customer value, such as loyalty programs, improvements in customer service, and innovations in product assortment, among others.

In this context, the role of the value-for-money ratio becomes even more complex and multifaceted. It's not just about offering the lowest price but ensuring that every euro spent by the customer is perceived as a good investment. This requires a deep understanding of customer expectations and the ability to consistently meet them through a more and more personalized value proposition.

Customer experience emerges as a crucial element for long-term success. Contemporary consumers are not just looking for quality products at reasonable prices, but also for a rewarding and seamless shopping experience. This includes excellent customer service, ease of navigation both online and in-store, and clear, transparent communication. Therefore, consumers prioritize uninterrupted experiences. Innovating to improve customer experience also means adopting technologies like AI and big data analytics to offer an unprecedented level of personalization, enhancing customer engagement and satisfaction. The integration of online and offline channels must be managed in a way that offers a smooth, consistent customer experience (phygital). Consumers expect to start a shopping experience online and finish it in-store, or vice versa, without encountering any issues or disruptions. This requires robust technological infrastructure and agile operational management.

The ultimate goal of retailers is to enhance customer satisfaction and trust, creating a competitive "moat" to defend against the competition. Innovating also means responding promptly to market needs, continuously improving the product offering, and maintaining a high level of customer satisfaction. The ability to innovate effectively depends on the company's willingness to invest in research and development, actively listen to customer feedback, and be flexible in adapting its strategies in light of changing market conditions.

Innovating to set up a trust-based brand positioning allows for maximizing customer satisfaction, Net Promoter Score (NPS), and the company's financial results, stabilizing future revenue streams. Trust is built on a company's ability to fulfill its commitments, meet expectations, and keep its promises. A loyal customer base ensures stable and positive results over time. By focusing on competence, credibility, transparent communication, and the ability to deliver on promises, a retailer can build a trust capital that helps develop and solidify long-term customer relationships. Loyalty should be a constant goal at all levels of the company, measured and monitored in real time, to understand the impact of individual marketing actions.

Retailers must also always consider the importance of human contact in building customer trust and loyalty. Even in the digital age, face-to-face interaction with knowledgeable and helpful staff can make an appreciable difference in the perception of value and customer satisfaction. This means that continuous staff training and investment in quality human resources are crucial to maintaining an elevated level of service. Personalizing offers and experiences should go beyond simple product recommendations. Retailers must be able to offer tailor-made solutions that meet customers' specific needs, such as personalized consulting services (for example, in supermarket wine departments) and customized loyalty programs. All this requires a deep understanding of customer data and the use of advanced technologies to analyze and effectively leverage it.

Innovation in retail is not only about products and services, but also involves internal processes and operational methods. Companies must be willing to continually review and improve their processes to boost efficiency and cut costs. This can include automating repetitive processes, adopting new inventory management technologies, and optimizing logistics. Another crucial factor in combining convenience and added value is supply chain management. An efficient supply chain not only reduces operating costs but also ensures that products are available when and where consumers want them. Companies can adopt advanced tracking technologies and predictive analytics to optimize inventory management, reduce delivery times, and improve the accuracy of demand forecasting. This approach helps cut down on waste and improve sustainability while also meeting customer needs.

Furthermore, the market rewards companies that are capable of developing integrated marketing strategies that clearly communicate the added value they offer. This includes campaigns that not only highlight competitive prices but also superior quality, sustainability, and product innovation. Another essential element is the ability to tell a compelling story that aligns with consumer values to build a strong brand identity and foster customer loyalty. Physical stores must be designed to offer a pleasant, stress-free shopping experience, with intuitive layouts, clear signage, and helpful, knowledgeable staff. At the same time, the store environment should reflect the brand's values, conveying a sense of authenticity and trust that encourages customers to return.

In conclusion, combining convenience and added value is not just a challenge but an opportunity for retailers to stand out in a crowded market. Through an integrated approach that embraces operational efficiency, customer experience, technological innovation, and ethical values, companies can create a unique offering that meets the needs of modern consumers. This not only improves customer satisfaction and loyalty but also helps build a strong, sustainable brand in the long term.

The numbers referring to loyalty management prove that companies' vision and focus on this topic are clear. At a global level, this market will grow at an average annual rate of 17.3% over the next five years, more than doubling from an estimated $11.4 billion in 2024 to $25.4 billion by 2029 (Figure 2.7).

When considering the crucial role of the retailer and the new challenges char-

Figure 2.7   Loyalty management market trend (in billions of dollars)

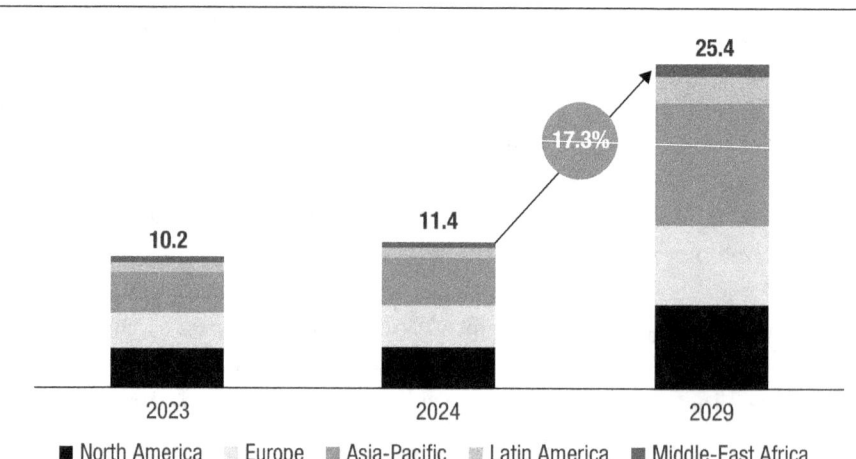

Source: Markets & Markets (2023)

acterizing the current competitive landscape, there are a series of opportunities to seize and challenges to tackle, as discussed in this chapter. These aspects will serve as the foundation for Chapter 3, which focuses on the managerial perspective and insights from key opinion leaders in the industry, highlighting, among other things, successful experiences that can overcome the challenges of today's competitive market.

CHAPTER 3
LOYALTY PROMOTION MONITOR:
THE PERSPECTIVE OF RETAIL MANAGERS

[Emanuele Acconciamessa]

To understand the role that modern grocery retail managers attribute to loyalty in their business strategies, orientations, current challenges, and successful experiences, the Channel & Retail Lab research team conducted a qualitative study of industry opinion leaders at the beginning of 2024.

In today's market context, both customers and retailers are evolving, and with them, the concept and role of Loyalty Programs (LPs). Our research aims to explore these dynamics, focusing on the Italian market. To this end, 19 in-depth interviews were carried out with senior managers in the grocery retail sector. The main findings highlight macroenvironment trends as well as the transformations loyalty management is undergoing. Big data and digital technologies can play a powerful part, although they still present challenges and issues. Nevertheless, physical spaces are still the most valuable assets. Additionally, our research emphasizes the importance of sustainability in LPs, reflecting the evolving values and expectations of the end market. Finally, our study focuses on the effectiveness of various Key Performance Indicators (KPIs) in measuring the success of LPs, suggesting the need for innovative metrics that capture the multifaceted nature of customer engagement and link it to broader organizational strategies.

3.1 Research background and methodology

LPs have become iconic elements in the retail industry, helping to establish lasting connections between shoppers and brands. They allow customers to accumulate points by purchasing directly from a retailer or an affiliated partner, and when they reach a preset threshold, they can redeem their points for rewards. An LP serves as a promotional tool (without focusing on price) that effectively promotes long-term relationships, increasing revenue streams and the retailer's share of the wallet. As the retail landscape changes, LPs have evolved in response to the latest trends, particularly in terms of the digitalization of the sector and a sharper focus on customer-centric strategies.

The digital revolution has redefined the nature of LPs, enabling new ways to interact with customers and collect big data, and facilitating the delivery of highly personalized incentives, rewards, products, and services. AI-based applications have further stimulated the evolution of these programs, allowing managers to predict individual preferences and estimate price sensitivity. These open up unprecedented opportunities for personalized communication and stronger customer-company relationships, though not without ethical concerns related to data security and privacy. The shift toward an omnichannel perspective in retail, driven by the integration of LPs online and offline across various touchpoints, highlights the evolving nature of modern loyalty programs. Retailers can leverage apps and personalized in-store offers to create a seamless shopping experience, promoting engagement and loyalty across multiple channels.

Recognizing the need for innovative and proactive initiatives in the retail arena, as proved by the numbers and trends highlighted earlier in Chapter, the qualitative research of the Loyalty Promotion Monitor aimed to focus on significant gaps in the current literature on LPs.

Given the recent spread of digitalization incorporated into retailer LPs, we find a gap in the literature as far as examining the opportunities and challenges posed by this transformative process. Specifically, there is limited focus on LPs from an omnichannel perspective. This key observation requires empirical evidence to evaluate the impact of retailers' digital strategies.

Many studies underscore the limitations of existing metrics for measuring customer engagement in LPs. Our research aims to understand the effectiveness of current Key Performance Indicators (KPIs) in measuring customer engagement and LP success, as well as the progress made in terms of innovative metrics and methods of calculation, based on big data and advanced technologies.

Despite the digital transformation in retail, physical stores continue to play a strategic role, serving not only as commercial and transactional spaces but also as venues for communicating the brand and creating emotional connections with consumers. Given the relevance of physical stores and the disruption generated by digital technologies and ever-changing needs in a more demanding market, the research delves into how retailers are reshaping the role of physical stores to enhance shopping experiences and service encounters.

In summary, the research conducted by the Channel & Retail Lab aims to enrich current knowledge about LPs in the digital era, investigating critical strategic areas for retailers such as omnichannel approaches, AI applications, KPIs, and sustainability. Through an exploratory qualitative study, we analyze the grocery retail sector with the aim of highlighting the convergence between scenarios and business behaviors.

In line with Yin (2017), this exploratory approach can support the understanding of specific phenomena and the discovery of new topics and perspectives. Nineteen in-depth interviews were conducted online between February and March 2024 with various senior managers (e.g., Marketing Directors, Sales Managers, Sales Directors) from leading grocery retailers operating in Italy. Each interview lasted an average of 45 minutes and was carried out by the same research team, following a semi-structured framework. With explicit consent, the interviews were recorded and transcribed for analysis using the content analysis method. After an introductory section, the interview focused on the changes and trends in the macroenvironment in which our informants' organizations operate, then moved on to the topic of loyalty and customer relationships.

In analyzing the scenario elements with the interviewees, we applied the cognitive mapping methodology, which is useful for graphically representing the thought process of the respondents, along with their underlying behavior and action. Concepts are represented hierarchically and linked by a cause/effect relationship indicated by an arrow. This technique is particularly useful for understanding a sector's orientation toward challenges, providing a clear view of the scenario, the main trends, and weak signals (Vicari & Troilo, 1997).

The research team then created a cognitive map for each individual and, through a process of overlap, identified the possible and probable scenarios on which there was the greatest convergence among the interviewees (Figure 3.1).

Figure 3.1   **Cognitive maps**

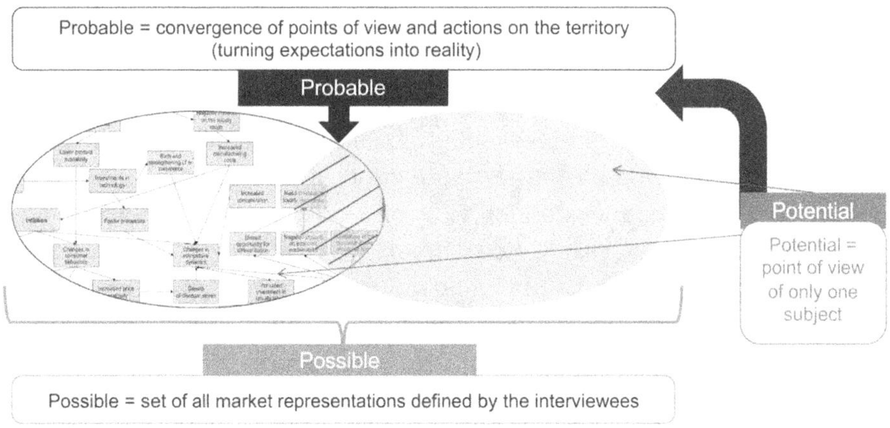

Source: Authors' elaboration

This methodology is a valuable tool for exploring and understanding the expectations of opinion leaders about specific topics, particularly those relevant to the development and future of a sector.

3.2 The main insights

The following sections present the main findings from the interviews with managers of leading Italian grocery retailers (informants), along with the corresponding summarized cognitive maps, focusing on the elements with the greatest convergence (Figures 3.2, 3.3, and 3.4).

3.2.1 *The retail perspective on the macro-environment*

International crises are a serious concern for retailers, both in geopolitical and business terms, creating relevant pressure on the supply chain. Added to this is inflation: a major factor of change that directly influences operating costs and companies' pricing strategies. This issue has been identified as a critical challenge, with potential impacts on customers' purchasing power and business strategies. Fluctuations in the prices of goods and services can squeeze retailers' profit margins, forcing them to continuously review their cost and pricing models to stay competitive in the market. Moreover, rising prices can influence consumer behavior, leading them to seek cheaper alternatives or cut the overall volume of their purchases. This forces companies to strike a delicate balance between maintaining competitive prices and protecting their profit margins (Figure 3.2).

The COVID-19 pandemic, along with subsequent global crises, has led to substantial changes in the macro-environment, influencing business models and consumer behaviors while accelerating the transition to digital. The pandemic exposed the vulnerability of global supply chains, pushing many companies to reconsider their sourcing and distribution strategies. The need for social distancing also accelerated the adoption of e-commerce solutions, leading to a significant increase in online sales. Retailers that were already primed for digital transitions capitalized on this shift, while those less prepared faced greater challenges in adapting quickly to this new context.

Digitalization emerged as a central theme, presenting both challenges and opportunities. Informants emphasized the importance of embracing advanced technologies to improve operational efficiency and customer experience. Technologies like AI, machine learning, and big data analytics allow retailers to bet-

Figure 3.2   **Cognitive map on the macro-environment**

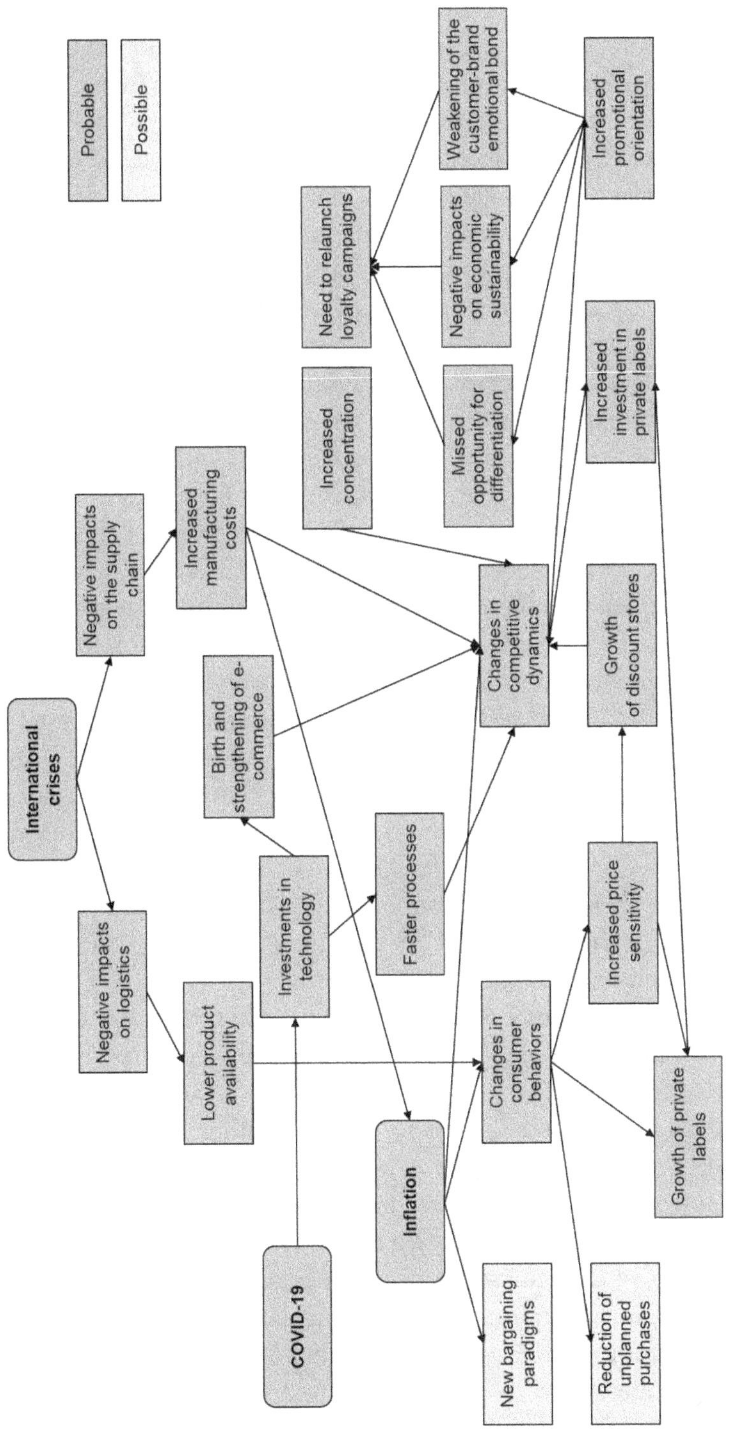

Source: Authors' elaboration

ter understand customer needs and preferences, personalize offers, and improve inventory management. Some predict further acceleration in digitalization, which not only involves adopting advanced technologies for business operations but also digitalizing the customer experience. This includes developing more sophisticated e-commerce platforms, integrating digital payment solutions, and implementing advanced customer relationship management (CRM) tools. The main challenge will be keeping pace with rapid technological changes while ensuring data security and accessibility for customers. Protecting customers' personal data is crucial for keeping public trust, and businesses must invest in robust security systems that follow privacy regulations.

Consumer behavior is undergoing noteworthy changes, with higher sensitivity to prices and promotions. The pandemic has made consumers more value-conscious, prompting them to seek deals and discounts more often. Interviewees expect to focus more intently on sustainability and personalized shopping experiences. Consumers are becoming more and more aware of the environmental impact of their purchases and prefer products and brands that demonstrate a commitment to sustainable practices. Personalization is another key factor, with consumers expecting tailored shopping experiences that reflect their individual preferences. Retailers must use data and analytics to create personalized shopping journeys and targeted offers that meet customer expectations. Several informants emphasized the rising importance of sustainability and corporate social responsibility (CSR) in business strategies. This is relevant not only in meeting consumer expectations but also in contributing positively to society and the environment. Companies that integrate sustainability into their operations not only improve their reputation but can also achieve operational efficiencies and reduce costs in the long term. CSR initiatives can include carbon emissions reduction programs, the use of recycled materials, the promotion of fair trade, and support for local communities. Addressing consumers' growing concerns about sustainability is crucial for building a loyal customer base and attracting new market segments.

Competition has intensified, and in line with other market changes, organizations need continuous innovation and greater adaptability. Retailers must be ready to introduce cutting-edge technologies, experiment with new business models, and quickly adapt to changing market conditions. Particular attention is given to the rise of discount stores and innovations in this distribution format. Discount stores are gaining market share due to their ability to offer quality products at competitive prices; they are also innovating in terms of assortment, services, and technologies.

These factors and trends outline a complex and ever-evolving landscape for retailers, who must navigate the challenges of inflation, digitalization, and sustainability while adapting their strategies to maintain competitiveness and build lasting relationships with customers.

3.2.2 *Loyalty management as a relational asset*

Loyalty Programs (LPs) play a fundamental role in building customer relationships, acting as a bridge that connects consumer needs to retailer value propositions. When implemented effectively, these programs can transform occasional customers into loyal brand advocates, fostering a relationship that goes beyond a mere economic transaction. Many informants in our study emphasized the importance of Customer Relationship Management (CRM) and personalization within these programs. Through accurate customer segmentation, based on demographic, behavioral, and psychographic data, retailers can offer more targeted experiences and rewards, which are extremely effective in creating lasting bonds (Figure 3.3).

The effectiveness of LPs is based on the ability to offer unique added value that differentiates a retailer from the competition. This value can take various forms, such as exclusive experiences, personalized services, or specific products that meet individual customer preferences. For example, a retailer might offer early access to special sales, exclusive events, or personalized consultations as part of its LP. Such offers not only incentivize loyalty but also strengthen the trust between the customer and the brand, creating a sense of belonging and recognition that is difficult to replicate through simple discounts or promotions.

Another crucial aspect is actively collecting and using customer feedback. These actions allow retailers to further finetune and personalize their LPs, continuously molding them to the needs and expectations of consumers. Actively involving customers in the feedback process not only offers valuable insights for improving the programs but also helps create a sense of belonging and engagement, improving loyalty and engagement. Customers who feel heard and valued are more likely to be loyal and promote the brand through positive word of mouth.

The use of digital technologies is indispensable in strengthening LPs. Online platforms and mobile apps are essential tools for making LPs more accessible and engaging. These technologies allow customers to easily interact with the program, track their rewards, and take part in real-time promotional activities. The integration of advanced technologies, such as AI and big data analytics, also enables an unprecedented level of personalization and relevance. For example, AI can analyze customer purchase and behavior data to predict future needs and

Figure 3.3 **Cognitive map on loyalty management**

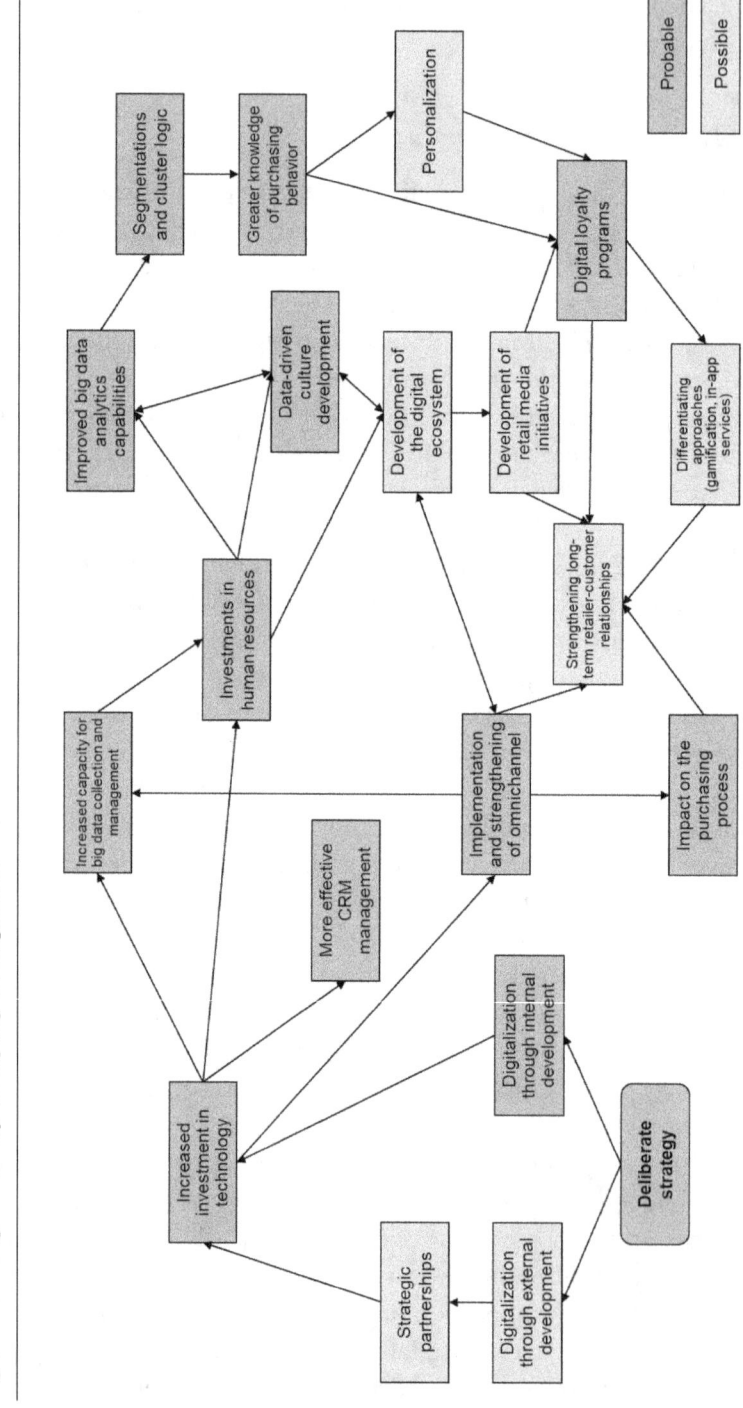

Source. Authors' elaboration

suggest tailored products or promotions, enhancing the overall customer experience. Digital platforms also allow retailers to collect detailed data on customer behavior, which can be used to further refine loyalty strategies. This can include information on which products are most popular, which promotions are most successful, and which communication channels are most effective. With this input, retailers can adjust their offerings more precisely and in a timely fashion, ensuring that their LPs remain relevant and attractive to customers.

However, some informants expressed concerns about traditional tools used in LPs, suggesting the need to identify and implement innovative solutions. This indicates that, despite the progress, there is still room to improve and evolve loyalty strategies to better respond to the ever-changing market dynamics and multiplying consumer expectations. Innovative solutions could include integrating emerging technologies like blockchain (to ensure the security and transparency of loyalty transactions) or using augmented reality to create unique, immersive shopping experiences. Blockchain, in particular, could revolutionize the way LPs are managed by offering a secure and transparent platform to track customer points and transactions. This technology could reduce the risk of fraud and augment customer trust in the program. Additionally, augmented reality could provide immersive shopping experiences that engage customers in new and innovative ways, creating deeper interaction with the brand.

In summary, LPs should be seen as a dynamic ecosystem where personalization, digital technologies, and continuous customer feedback are fundamental elements in building strong, lasting relationships. Companies need to adopt innovative solutions and constantly adapt to new market trends to maintain the effectiveness and relevance of these programs over time. Retailers who can fully leverage the potential of digital technologies and proactively respond to customer needs will be able to create LPs that not only retain but also transform customers into true brand ambassadors.

A concrete example of success can be seen in some of the leading retailers who have implemented these advanced strategies. For instance, some integrate LPs with their mobile apps, offering real-time rewards and personalized promotions based on customer purchasing behavior. Others use social media platforms to engage customers through exclusive content and direct interactions, strengthening the sense of community and belonging. Moreover, retailers that have invested in big data analytics technologies can gain deeper insights into their customers' behavior, which in turn allows them to anticipate trends and respond more quickly to changes in consumer preferences. This ability to be proactive and reactive is a critical success factor in an increasingly competitive market.

In conclusion, LPs are no longer just marketing tools but integral components of business strategy that can determine a retailer's long-term success. The key is to keep a constant focus on innovation, personalization, and customer interaction, using the most advanced technologies to create memorable experiences that foster loyalty and build lasting, profitable relationships.

3.2.3 *The challenge of digitalization*

Most of our informants emphasized the importance of digitalization in loyalty strategies, recognizing it as a key factor for improving efficiency, personalization, and customer engagement. Digitalization allows for the collection and analysis of large amounts of data, known as big data, which is essential for better understanding customers and personalizing offers. Data analysis helps companies make more informed decisions and optimize loyalty strategies, enabling them to create tailored experiences that meet the specific needs of consumers.

The ability to analyze and utilize big data provides retailers with a more detailed view of customer behaviors, preferences, and purchasing trends. This data-driven approach is fundamental for developing personalized offers that not only meet but exceed customer expectations, creating a stronger emotional connection with the brand. For example, data can reveal which products are most appreciated by specific customer segments, allowing retailers to propose targeted promotions and optimize inventory based on real consumer preferences.

Similarly, several respondents highlighted the adoption of advanced technologies, such as AI, to improve data analysis and process automation. These technologies allow deeper insights to be extracted from the data collected, identifying patterns and trends that would otherwise go unnoticed. AI can also automate various aspects of loyalty strategies, from customer segmentation to personalized communications, making loyalty strategies more effective and scalable. Massive volumes of data can be analyzed in real-time, providing retailers with the ability to react quickly to market changes and customer needs. Additionally, AI can enhance the customer experience through chatbots and virtual assistants, offering personalized support and immediate responses to customer inquiries. These digital interactions not only improve customer satisfaction but also free up human resources for more strategic and creative tasks.

However, managing big data presents big challenges. The need for advanced technical skills to analyze and interpret data is one of the main difficulties companies face. Training or hiring people skilled in data science, machine learning, and data analytics can be expensive and time-consuming. Moreover, issues related to data privacy and security are increasingly critical, as customers become more aware of and concerned about how their personal information is used and protected. Ensuring compliance with privacy regulations and implementing robust security measures are crucial steps for maintaining customer trust and fully leveraging the benefits of digitalization. Companies must develop data security policies that not only comply with existing laws (e.g., GDPR in Europe) but also go above and beyond to establish a trust-based relationship with customers. Transparency in data collection and usage, along with providing control options for customers, can help build this trust. Additionally, businesses must be prepared to respond quickly to potential security breaches, with well-defined contingency plans to mitigate damage and communicate effectively with affected customers.

Lastly, some informants expressed concerns about the delay in digitalizing their organizations, stressing the need to accelerate this process to remain competitive. Companies that fail to adapt quickly to new technologies risk falling behind more innovative competitors. Therefore, it is vital for organizations to invest in digital infrastructure and develop the necessary skills to support digital transformation, ensuring they can seize the opportunities offered by big data and advanced technologies to improve their loyalty strategies.

Digitalization is an ongoing process that requires constant commitment and strategic vision. Organizations must be willing to invest not only in technologies but also in continuous staff training and in revising business processes to better integrate them with new technologies. The ability to innovate and quickly adapt to new technological trends becomes a crucial competitive advantage in an increasingly dynamic and digital market.

3.2.4 *The culture of measurement*

A wide range of KPIs has emerged for measuring the success of loyalty initiatives. These include metrics related to customer value, purchase frequency, retention, penetration, and customer satisfaction. Such measures allow companies to evaluate how effectively their LPs are contributing to keeping and growing their base of loyal customers. For example, customer value measures how much a customer spends on average over a given period, while purchase frequency provides insights into how often customers return to make purchases. Measuring these aspects helps identify the most valuable customers and develop targeted strategies to boost their loyalty and long-term value (Figure 3.4).

Customer retention is another crucial KPI, as keeping an existing customer is generally more cost-effective than acquiring a new one. Companies must closely

Figure 3.4   Cognitive map on KPIs and sustainability

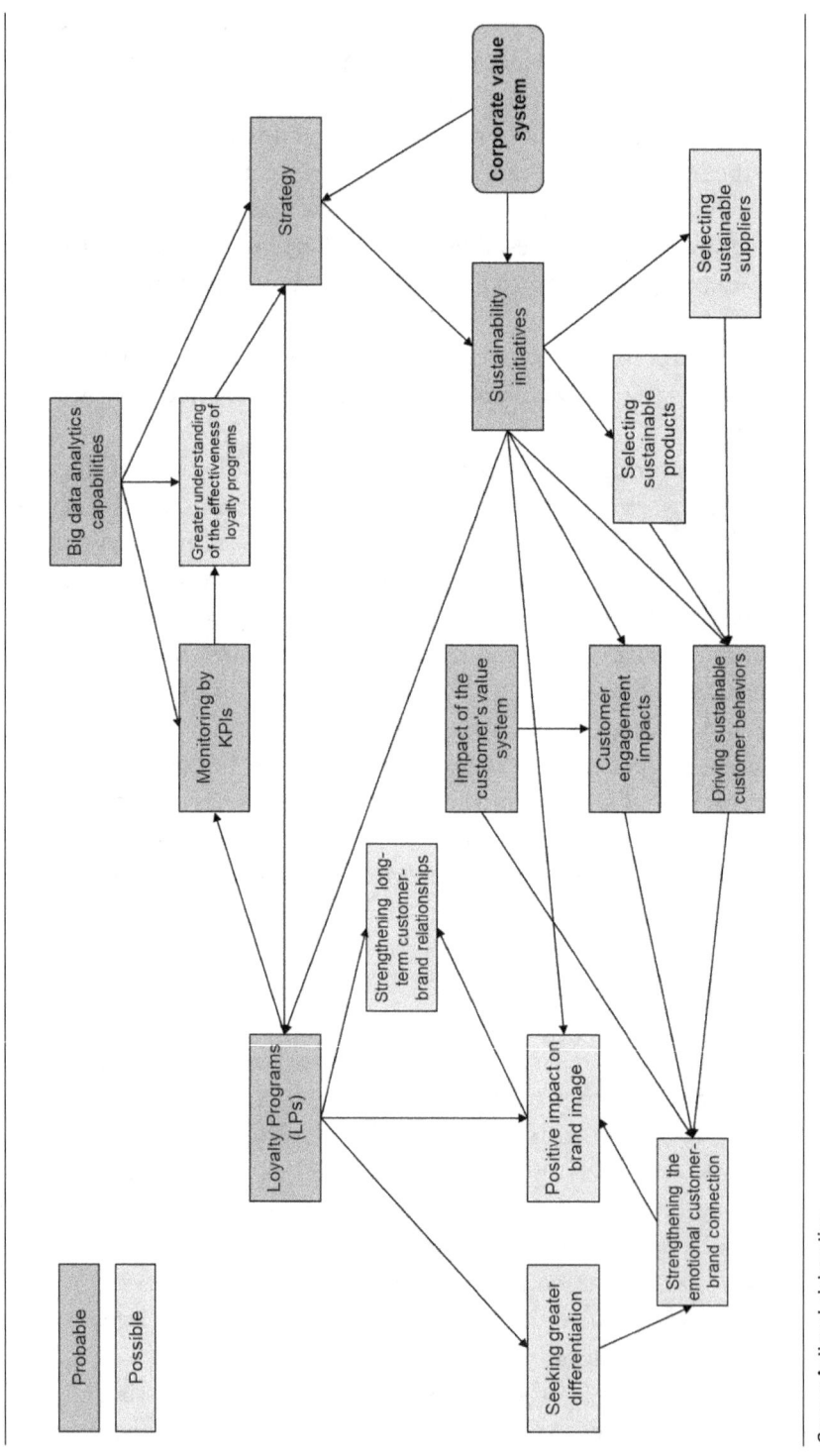

Source: Authors' elaboration

monitor retention rates to identify any signs of decline in customer loyalty and act promptly with corrective measures. Penetration gauges the market share that an LP is able to cover, indicating how widespread and accepted it is among the customer base. High penetration means that the program is effective in reaching a large market segment, while low penetration may signal the need to revise and improve the value proposition to attract more customers.

Finally, customer satisfaction is essential for understanding how customers perceive the value offered by the LP and their propensity to remain loyal over time. Using surveys, reviews, and other forms of direct feedback provides a clear view of the program's strengths and areas for improvement. Customer satisfaction not only reflects the effectiveness of loyalty initiatives but also influences word of mouth and the overall reputation of the brand.

Despite the importance of these KPIs, they are often not fully integrated into broader business strategies. Instead, to maximize the impact of LPs, companies should use KPIs to support marketing, sales, and customer service decisions and to create a direct link between these programs and the overall objectives. Without this integration, loyalty initiatives risk being viewed as separate entities, not fully aligned with other business activities. For example, an increase in purchase frequency might indicate greater promotional effectiveness or improved customer experience, but without a direct connection to the company's overall objectives, this data may not be fully utilized.

Challenges in measuring and interpreting KPIs include the difficulty of directly linking them to customer behavior and the importance of analyzing indicators in the appropriate context. For instance, an uptick in purchase frequency might not necessarily reflect greater loyalty but could be influenced by external factors like seasonal promotions or changes in economic conditions. Therefore, KPIs must be analyzed in the context of market conditions and specific promotional initiatives to gain a complete picture of their effectiveness. Moreover, superficial analysis of KPIs can lead to erroneous conclusions; it is necessary to dig deeper and understand the underlying factors that influence these metrics to derive truly useful insights.

Another formidable challenge relates to the quality and accuracy of the data used to calculate KPIs. Companies must ensure that their data collection systems are robust and reliable; data should be regularly updated to accurately reflect customer interactions. Managing big data requires advanced technical skills to analyze and interpret information effectively. This may involve hiring data scientists and investing in advanced data analytics technologies. Only with accurate and up-to-date data companies gain a clear view of their LPs' performance and make informed decisions.

Additionally, we note that loyalty KPIs can evolve over time in response to business needs and changing market dynamics. This calls for continually updating and adapting these indicators to maintain their relevance and effectiveness. Companies must be prepared to periodically review their KPIs to ensure they accurately reflect LP performance and contribute to achieving the company's strategic goals. For example, with new technologies and digital platforms coming online, new KPIs might be introduced to measure customer engagement through digital channels or social media.

Companies must adopt a flexible, dynamic approach to managing KPIs, updating and adapting them based on market and business needs, to ensure that LPs continue to deliver value both to customers and to the company itself. This involves not only monitoring existing KPIs but also being proactive in identifying new metrics that can provide further insights into LP performance. For example, integrating qualitative customer feedback, collected through surveys and reviews, can enrich the analysis of quantitative KPIs, offering a more complete and nuanced view of the effectiveness of loyalty initiatives.

The adoption of emerging technologies, such as AI and machine learning, can significantly improve KPI analysis, enabling the identification of hidden trends and patterns that may not be evident through traditional analysis techniques. These technologies can automate data collection and analysis, making the process more efficient and less prone to human error. Additionally, they can provide accurate forecasts of future customer behavior trends, allowing retailers to proactively adjust their loyalty strategies.

In summary, KPIs are essential tools for measuring the success of loyalty initiatives, and it is crucial to integrate these metrics into broader business strategies and interpret them accurately to achieve meaningful results. Only through careful and contextual analysis of KPIs can the full impact of LPs be understood, and corrective measures or improvements implemented in real time. The adoption of new technologies, investment in analytical skills, and strategic alignment between LPs and the company's overall aims are key factors for success in an increasingly competitive and customer-driven market.

The continuous evolution of the technological landscape and consumer expectations requires an agile and responsive approach to managing KPIs. Companies that successfully integrate these indicators into their broader strategies not only gain a clear view of current performance but are also better prepared to respond quickly to market changes, ensuring that their LPs remain effective and relevant over time.

3.2.5 *The link between loyalty and sustainability*

Some informants discussed the specific objectives of their sustainability and CSR initiatives, such as achieving environmental or social standards, and how they measure their progress, for example through social impact reports. Sustainability and CSR initiatives can positively influence customer perception and loyalty. What's more, consumers are becoming more and more attentive to the environmental and social impact of brands and tend to be more loyal to the ones they perceive as responsible and committed to the environment and society. This has led many organizations to integrate sustainability and CSR into their customer interaction strategies, emphasizing the need for ethical and responsible practices. These practices can include offering sustainable products, adopting green policies, and promoting eco-conscious behavior among customers.

Sustainability initiatives not only enhance a brand's image in the eyes of customers but can also have a positive impact on customer engagement and loyalty. For instance, companies that offer products made from recycled materials or promote energy-saving measures can attract customers who share these values and enhance their commitment and loyalty. Additionally, green policies, such as reducing plastic use or adopting biodegradable packaging, not only address consumers' environmental concerns but also strengthen the company's reputation as a leader in sustainability.

The link between sustainability-CSR initiatives and LPs could be expressed by incorporating sustainability into reward programs, such as offering extra points for purchasing eco-friendly products or taking part in recycling programs. Furthermore, the use of CSR initiatives can enhance brand image and customer relationships, creating a sense of community and belonging that goes beyond mere commercial transactions. In other words, companies that effectively integrate sustainability into their LPs not only improve brand perception but also grow customer loyalty, as customers feel part of a larger, more meaningful mission.

For example, an LP could incentivize customers to take part in tree-planting initiatives or donate to environmental causes by offering points or discounts if they participate. This type of active engagement not only rewards customers for their sustainable behaviors but also strengthens the emotional connection between the customer and the brand, fostering a sense of participation and contribution to a common cause. Campaigns that combine sustainability and loyalty have the potential to create a lasting positive impact for both the brand and the environment.

Additionally, companies can use their digital platforms to educate and raise awareness among customers about sustainable best practices. For instance, through loyalty apps, retailers can provide them with information about the environmental benefits of sustainable products or tips on how to reduce environmental impact in their daily lives. This type of communication not only reinforces the perception of the brand as responsible and committed but can also positively influence customer behavior outside the commercial context.

In some cases, sustainability and CSR initiatives can be used to differentiate the brand in a competitive market. For example, companies can communicate their sustainability achievements through marketing campaigns that emphasize their ethical and responsible practices. These communications can include success stories, statistics on emissions reductions or energy savings, and testimonials from satisfied customers. Clearly and regularly communicating these successes can augment transparency and customer trust, further strengthening brand loyalty.

However, we also noted that in some organizations, there is no direct connection between sustainability/CSR initiatives and LPs, showing a lack of strategic integration between these two areas. This disconnection can limit the positive impact that such initiatives could have on customer loyalty and brand perception. Companies that fail to link their sustainability initiatives to LPs may miss meaningful opportunities to engage customers and differentiate themselves from the competition.

To maximize the benefits of sustainability and CSR initiatives, it is crucial that companies develop an integrated strategy that clearly connects these efforts to their LPs. This way, businesses can fully leverage the potential of relevant initiatives to build a more loyal and engaged customer base and promote a brand image that is responsible and committed to the well-being of society and the environment. Effective strategic integration requires careful planning and collaboration between different business functions, including marketing, CSR, and customer relationship management, to ensure that efforts are aligned and that messages are consistent.

Furthermore, companies must be willing to invest in the necessary resources to implement and sustain these initiatives. This can include training staff on sustainable practices, adopting green technologies, and committing to long-term environmental and social goals. By creating a corporate environment that values sustainability and social responsibility as fundamental pillars, companies not only improve their brand's perception but also foster a sense of pride and belonging among employees, both essential elements for long-term success.

In conclusion, sustainability and CSR initiatives represent a powerful lever for improving brand perception and customer loyalty. However, to fully realize this potential, companies must closely integrate these efforts with their LPs, creating synergies that enhance customer engagement and foster a sense of participation in important causes. Investing in sustainability is not only an ethical choice, but also a winning strategy for building lasting, lucrative relationships with customers.

3.3 Conclusions: relevant topics for the future of loyalty management

The informants in our sample shared their thoughts on areas that need further exploration. Their feedback will guide the future research work of the Loyalty Promotion Monitor and help identify the main directions for loyalty management in Italian grocery retailing.

One key topic that emerged is the importance of sustainability and environmental impact. The interviewees suggested research projects that explore how sustainability practices can be more effectively integrated into business strategies and loyalty programs (LPs). This integration could include adopting green policies, promoting sustainable products, and implementing initiatives that reduce the ecological footprint of business operations. Sustainability not only addresses the growing consumer expectations around environmental responsibility, but it can also positively differentiate a brand in a competitive market. Moreover, the integration of sustainable practices can lead to cost reductions through energy efficiency and waste reduction, thereby improving business profitability.

Another salient area of attention is the need for projects investigating strategies to improve customer experience, with particular attention to personalizing customer interactions and optimizing the shopping experience. Personalization can occur through the use of advanced technologies like AI, which enables the analysis of customer data to offer tailored product recommendations, personalized promotions, and more responsive customer service. Optimizing the shopping experience also means enhancing the user interface, reducing wait times, and making the purchasing process as smooth and enjoyable as possible. Creating a frictionless, personalized shopping experience can lead to higher customer satisfaction and loyalty, ultimately increasing sales and long-term retention.

Some informants also proposed further exploration of specific innovations in the retail industry, particularly around new approaches to LPs and their evolution in response to changing consumer behavior. With the growing use of digital platforms and the adoption of new technologies, LPs must continually be updated to remain relevant and engaging. This could include integrating interactive games, using augmented reality to create immersive shopping experiences, and gamifying LPs to bolster customer engagement. The ability to innovate and adapt quickly to new market trends is critical to the long-term success of LPs. Technological innovations might also include using blockchain to ensure transparency and security in loyalty transactions, creating a more reliable and attractive system for customers.

Regarding KPIs, while there was general interest from the interviewees, several challenges were mentioned, indicating a need for support in identifying and using relevant indicators. Defining clear and measurable KPIs is essential to evaluate the effectiveness of loyalty strategies and to make data-driven adjustments. Some participants in our study expressed interest in projects focusing on data use, particularly predictive analysis and big data processing, to improve the understanding of customer behavior and forecast trends. Predictive analysis can help companies identify behavior patterns, anticipate future preferences, and proactively personalize offers. KPIs, when used effectively, allow companies to monitor performance and make informed decisions to optimize LP results. Data collection and analysis must be integrated into a broader business strategy to ensure that all business functions can benefit from the insights obtained.

Moreover, there was interest in research projects examining the impact of new technologies, such as AI, on the retail sector and consumer shopping experiences. AI, with its advanced analytics and automation capabilities, can revolutionize how companies understand and interact with customers, offering highly personalized and optimized shopping experiences. Exploring these topics through targeted research projects can help companies remain competitive in a rapidly evolving market, providing them with the tools and knowledge necessary to implement innovative solutions that enhance both sustainability and customer experience. What's more, the introduction of AI-powered virtual assistants and chatbots can significantly improve customer service by offering immediate, personalized support 24/7.

Investing in these areas of research not only offers the opportunity to innovate LPs but also helps build a more robust knowledge base around how to continuously improve business strategies. This is essential to help companies navigate an increasingly complex and competitive market. By integrating these elements into their strategies, companies can create long-lasting value for both customers and the environment, while strengthening their market position at the same time. These projects offer a roadmap for innovation and sustainable growth, promoting a holistic approach that combines operational efficiency with social and environmental responsibility. The ability to quickly adapt to market changes, continually innovate, and meet customer needs through personalized and sustainable solutions is what distinguishes successful companies in an ever-evolving competitive landscape. Investing in research and development in these areas not only prepares companies to respond to current challenges but also positions them to seize future opportunities and drive change in the retail sector. Through a continued commitment to innovation and sustainability, companies can build trust and loyalty with their customers, creating a competitive advantage that will endure over time.

Chapter 3 reveals the importance of loyalty as a relational asset and addresses the need to adapt to new market dynamics, such as digitalization and sustainability. This chapter also underscores the necessity of identifying new, more effective ways to measure and analyze loyalty. Moving on, Chapter 4 examines academic literature reviews on the topic of loyalty to gain a deeper understanding of this multidimensional concept.

CHAPTER 4
AN ANALYSIS OF PREVIOUS REVIEWS ON LOYALTY: CONCEPTUALIZATIONS, MEASUREMENTS, AND IMPLICATIONS

[Generoso Branca, Andrea Ciacci]

4.1 Introduction

Loyalty is a central theme in marketing and management disciplines, and it can represent a crucial element for the success and sustainability of a business. The concept of customer loyalty has become pervasive in several industries, driven by an increasingly competitive environment, with companies in the same sector vying for the same group of customers (Kumar & Shah, 2004; Toufaily et al., 2013). It is worth noting that, lacking a clear differentiation strategy or a relevant value proposition, companies risk wasting valuable marketing resources in an attempt to build loyalty that might not lead to profitable results (Kumar & Shah, 2004).

Although there is no commonly accepted definition of customer loyalty, the consensus in the literature is that this multidimensional construct encompasses a set of attitudes, intentions, and behaviors that benefit one player over its competitors, resulting in improved performance (Belli et al., 2022; Watson et al., 2015). However, the approach to measuring loyalty is often fuzzy (Watson et al., 2015). As highlighted by Grace et al. (2018), findings in the literature show significant challenges in conceptualizing and measuring key consumer-related constructs such as brand loyalty.

A deeper understanding of loyalty can benefit the entire business activity. As McManus & Guilding (2008) point out, by integrating marketing constructs such as customer satisfaction and loyalty into accounting systems, companies can get a more comprehensive view of business performance.

This chapter aims to examine previous reviews and relevant conceptual articles on loyalty, to synthesize the main findings that have emerged over the years. The intent is to gain an overview of the available evidence, identifying the most significant contributions on the topic, with particular attention to the conceptualization and measurement of loyalty. The insights from this review also provide a solid foundation for the systematic literature review presented in Chapter 5.

4.2 Methodology

This research was conducted using Scopus, a bibliographic database of scientific literature by Elsevier. Scopus is widely utilized for academic research as it represents one of the largest databases of its kind and covers a broad range of scientific disciplines.

We selected a series of keywords to identify potentially relevant articles, analyzing titles, abstracts, and keywords. The query was characterized by three main semantic groups:

- loyalty and related constructs, such as *fidelity, retention,* and *attachment*
- measurements and related constructs, such as *key performance indicator (KPI), measurement, metric, scale, index,* and *performance*
- *review*

We then refined our search to include only articles published in peer-reviewed academic journals. These journals conduct critical assessments by experts with competencies similar to those of the article's authors. This approach ensures that contributions meet the highest standards of rigor and transparency in scientific research. Only scientific publications (articles and reviews) written in English were included, while other types of publications, such as conference proceedings and book chapters, were not. Additionally, we applied a filter for the subject area *business, management, and accounting* to focus our analysis only on articles related to management and marketing. Finally, considering all articles published in any country up until April 2024, we obtained 758 items in total.

We conducted our initial screening based on this dataset. First, considering the Chartered Association of Business Schools - Academic Journal Guide (CABS AJG) 2021, we filtered the journals ranked 2, 3, 4, or 4* to ensure the relevance and quality of our results (in line with Campbell et al., 2023). This process resulted in a total of 290 documents, as 468 articles were published in journals ranked 1 (which is the lowest) or were not included in the CABS AJG list.

The next step was reading the titles, abstracts, introductions, and conclusions of each record. An article was considered potentially relevant if: a) it is a review or a conceptual article; b) it focuses on loyalty or related constructs; or c) it centers on the measurement of loyalty or related constructs.

Based on this procedure, the final number of articles selected was four. However, to enrich the analysis, we chose two additional articles manually ex-post due to their relevance to the analysis, bringing the total to six.

4.3 Results and Discussion

4.3.1 Descriptive analysis

Table 4.1 provides an overview of the reviews we selected. For each one, the objectives, methodology, keywords (if present), and context of analysis are reported. These articles represent an advancement in the topic of conceptualizing or measuring loyalty at various levels of analysis, including consumer, brand, digital, and service.

4.3.2 The nature and dimensions of loyalty

Although there is not a generally accepted definition, recent research agrees that loyalty represents a set of attitudes and behaviors that benefit a company over its competitors (Belli et al., 2022; Watson et al., 2015).

Starting from an early conceptualization, Jacoby & Kyner (1973) define brand loyalty based on six necessary, collectively sufficient conditions. According to these authors, brand loyalty is (Toufaily et al., 2013, p. 1436):

1. *a biased (i.e., nonrandom) response;*
2. *a behavioral response (i.e., purchase);*
3. *expressed over time;*
4. *by one or more decision-making units;*
5. *where several alternatives are possible;*
6. *a function of a psychological process (evaluating alternatives, decision-making, etc.).*

Research has often examined loyalty as an attitude, purchasing behavior, or a multidimensional construct (for example, attitudes, purchase behaviors, and word-of-mouth (WOM) (Watson et al., 2015). However, there is considerable variation in how loyalty is conceptualized and measured, which may account for the differences in loyalty-related outcomes.

Table 4.1 Summary of selected literature reviews and relevant conceptual articles

Article	Objectives	Methodology	Keywords (*)	Context
Belli et al. (2022)	Analyze effectiveness, and underlying processes of loyalty programs, by program type and industry.	Meta-analysis	*Loyalty, loyalty program, loyalty scheme, effectiveness, loyalty card, rewards program, points program, relationship program, fidelity card*	Loyalty program
Jai et al. (2022)	Study the evolution of brand loyalty through social media platforms.	Systematic literature review	*Loyalty, social media, social network, consumer relationship, customer relationship, brand*	Brand loyalty on social media
Grace et al. (2018)	Analyze the evolution of brand and consumer research, highlighting challenges in conceptualizing and measuring constructs such as brand loyalty, brand commitment and brand love. Define brand loyalty as a new approach.	Literature review	-	Relation between consumers and brand
Watson et al. (2015)	Analyze and synthesize different approaches in measuring and understanding loyalty	Meta-analysis	*Loyalty, attitudes, repurchase*	Customer loyalty measurement
Toufaily et al. (2013)	Analyze the academic literature dealing with loyalty relative to commercial websites, focusing on the conceptualizations, measurements, antecedents and consequences of e-loyalty	Descriptive meta-analysis	*Online loyalty, electronic loyalty, Internet loyalty, website loyalty, online retention*	Customer loyalty toward commercial websites
Kumar & Shah (2004)	Develop an integrative conceptual framework for simultaneously building and sustaining customer loyalty and profitability	Literature review	-	Customer loyalty and profitability

(*) Please refer to the original articles for the exact combination of search queries.
Source: authors' elaboration.

According to Grace et al. (2018, p. 579), *"the nature and measurement of brand loyalty have long been debated."* Conceptualizations of the loyalty construct have traditionally been based on the behavioral traits of "loyal customers," measured through repeated purchasing, purchase intentions, and switching intentions. However, loyalty also includes cognitive dimensions, which are reflected in the decision-making process through evaluation, brand preference, and customer attitudes. According to Grace et al. (2018, p. 579), the generally accepted definition of brand loyalty as a non-random behavioral response expressed over time by a specific decision-making unit toward one or more brand alternatives, based on psychological evaluation processes, does not fully capture the relational perspective between brand and consumer. McManus & Guilding (2008, p. 779) define customer loyalty in two ways:

1. an attitude whereby the customer develops an attachment to a product, service, brand, or organization; and
2. a behavior, such as continuing to purchase from the same provider, recommending a particular seller, or increasing the scope of a relationship with a supplier.

Several studies on customer loyalty have focused on measuring behaviors, such as repeated purchases, which have clear advantages for a company's financial performance. This perspective has led to the development of stochastic models of loyalty, including recency, frequency, churn/retention, and purchase sequence models (Watson et al., 2015). However, purely behavioral approaches often disregard the psychological factors driving customer actions. They fail to account for the possibility that repeated purchasing may result from situational constraints (e.g., limited alternatives) or ingrained habits rather than true loyalty.

As noted by Kumar & Shah (2004), loyalty has traditionally been measured in terms of customer behavior, with metrics including purchase percentage, likelihood of purchase, repurchase probability, purchase frequency, repeated buying patterns, purchase sequences, and various other aspects of purchasing behavior. In retail, commonly used measures include share of purchase (SOP), share of visit (SOV), share of wallet (SOW), past customer value (PCV), recency, frequency, and monetary value (RFM), which help in assessing behavioral loyalty. Following this logic, the more a customer spends with a company, the more rewards they earn, leading to the risk that the customer associates loyalty (in terms of purchasing behavior) with a specific rewards program rather than with the brand or retailer. Therefore, purely behavioral loyalty cannot be considered a foolproof predictor of profitability and, by itself, cannot be considered a measure of *true* customer loyalty (Kumar & Shah, 2004). Building and sustaining loyalty is challenging without including the attitudinal factors influencing customer behavior. As highlighted by Jai et al. (2022), customer loyalty should extend beyond repeated purchasing behavior to include dimensions like belief, affection, and intentionality.

From the discussion above, the understanding of loyalty transitions from a behavioral perspective (where loyalty is defined and assessed through purchasing) to a cognitive perspective, which emphasizes the attitudinal aspects of loyalty. Finally, this comprehension culminates in a composite perspective that illustrates how both attitudinal preferences and repeated purchasing behaviors are essential components of the concept of loyalty (Toufaily et al., 2013). Moreover, loyalty develops sequentially through a process consisting of several phases (cognition, affection, conation, action), and this occurs despite the influence of situational factors and marketing actions (Toufaily et al., 2013).

According to Watson et al. (2015), attitudes are a fundamental component of customer loyalty. Attitudinal loyalty can be described as a form of cognition or a sense of satisfaction that supports a specific entity. When customers have strong positive attitudes, they tend to engage in "defensive processes" against competition, making them resistant to competitive offers, even if those offers are appreciably better. As such, attitudinal loyalty signifies a deeper, long-term commitment from customers to a company, which cannot be solely inferred from observing their purchasing habits (Kumar & Shah, 2004). Attitudinal loyalty is pertinent because it indicates the propensity to exhibit certain behaviors, such as the likelihood of future use or WOM. As noted by Jai et al. (2022), attitudinal loyalty follows the schema of cognition (preference for the brand based on information or past experiences), affection (emotional attachment, liking, or satisfaction with the brand), and conation (the conversion of behavioral intentions into actions).

Purchasing behavior is the second element of loyalty (Watson et al., 2015). Behavioral loyalty involves repeated purchases that result from a conation or action orientation that implies a "readiness to act" to the benefit of a specific entity. As highlighted by Belli et al. (2022), behavioral loyalty includes metrics driven by observable behaviors, such as purchase volume, purchase frequency, customer retention, and company performance. For any company, customer loyalty holds greater importance when it leads to purchasing behavior, as this produces direct and measurable returns. In contrast, attitudinal loyalty, while it may indicate commitment or trust, does not always result in actual purchases (Kumar & Shah, 2004).

According to Watson et al. (2015), loyalty can be viewed as a set of attitudes aligned with a series of purchasing behaviors that systematically favor one company over its competitors. The authors also suggest considering the temporal aspect (backward-looking vs. forward-looking) due to its influence on how loyalty is psychologically processed and its effect on performance outcomes. On one hand, viewing loyalty from a backward-looking perspective can lead to more accurate measurements based on the psychological mechanisms that determine past behaviors. Doing so allows companies to identify the most relevant behavioral drivers. On the other hand, if companies adopt forward-looking approaches, with a predictive orientation, they can avoid being constrained by an analysis based only on the past, which may not predict future purchasing behaviors in changing conditions (e.g., the launch of innovative competitor products). By understanding the true nature of consumers, for example, through the study of their value system and behaviors outside the customer journey, forecasting future behaviors is possible. Therefore, the literature suggests considering both attitudinal and behavioral aspects from the two different temporal orientations to achieve *true* loyalty, proposing indices based on both approaches (Kumar & Shah, 2004; Watson et al., 2015).

Belli et al. (2022) contribute to the discussion by exploring conative loyalty, which closely resembles motivation, reflecting a customer's intention to engage with the company. This type of loyalty is often measured by indicators such as repurchase intentions or a commitment to stay with the company and maintain the relationship in the future. Conative loyalty is marked by a strong commitment to the brand that surpasses mere liking or satisfaction, representing a deeper level of loyalty than attitudinal loyalty (Belli et al., 2022).

The difference between customer retention and customer loyalty lies in customers' emotional commitment, beyond repeat visits or purchases, indicating their preference for one provider over others. Loyalty and retention measures are often combined in a single study. Unlike retention, however, loyalty outcomes include the willingness to pay more, positive WOM, commitment, trust, and first-choice preference. Retention or frequency does not always imply loyalty; however, loyal customers will visit or purchase repeatedly from a preferred company.

In line with the above, Belli et al. (2022) show that although the literature agrees on the multidimensionality of loyalty, studies on loyalty programs have generally focused on one dimension of loyalty at a time. Indeed, LPs are institutionalized incentive systems aimed at improving people's consumption behavior over time to create or strengthen customer loyalty, which means such programs are primarily designed to influence behavioral loyalty (Belli et al., 2022). Instead, customer loyalty includes both attitudinal and behavioral elements.

Finally, Kumar & Shah (2004) highlighted several key challenges in managing customer loyalty. One issue is the broad, generalized approach that lacks differentiation across the customer base, which can lead to overlooking individual-level differences such as psychographic, demographic, behavioral, and attitudinal factors. Additionally, the link between loyalty and profitability is often weak. Furthermore, many loyalty programs lack scalability and become less profitable as more customers participate, since they are typically based on spending or usage frequency rather than profitability.

4.3.3 *Contributions and insights of the loyalty research*

In their article published in the Journal of Retailing, Kumar & Shah (2004) studied customer behavior and attitude in the context of loyalty, reviewing research that linked loyalty to profitability and forecasting metrics. The authors proposed a conceptual framework with the objectives to (1) strengthen behavioral loyalty, (2) foster attitudinal loyalty, and (3) connect loyalty to profitability.

Kumar & Shah (2004) addressed behavioral loyalty and attitudinal loyalty. For the former, the authors emphasize the importance of tangible returns through customers' purchasing behavior; the latter focuses instead on the psychological commitment of customers to a brand, potentially leading to long-term loyalty beyond mere purchasing behavior.

To operationalize the framework, Kumar & Shah (2004) propose a two-tier reward structure.

1. Tier 1 provides a simple, transparent way to reward all customers for past and current purchases, regardless of their attitudes or behaviors. It ensures that all customers, including new ones, are aware of the program and encourages them to register their transactions. Rewards are based on spending, making the program scalable.
2. Tier 2 rewards focus on influencing future customer behavior and attitudes based on past performance. These selective rewards are given to promote attitudinal and behavioral loyalty, targeting customers whose loyalty the company aims to nurture.

While all customers are eligible for Tier 1 rewards, companies can select specific people from this group for Tier 2 rewards. The latter are not publicly disclosed but instead are personalized and distributed by the company, keeping them hidden from competitors. This approach allows for flexible resource allocation and reward customization, ensuring loyalty programs stay both profitable and effective.

The authors also stress the importance of tying loyalty programs to profitability, recommending customer lifetime value (CLV) as a more effective metric than traditional measures like RFM, SOW, and PCV (Kumar & Shah, 2004).

More recently, Watson et al. (2015) examined customer loyalty, providing insights into measuring and effectively managing loyalty to improve business performance. According to the authors, there are variations in how loyalty is conceptualized and measured. Their findings highlight how different antecedents contribute differently to attitudinal and behavioral loyalty, and how these dimensions affect business outcomes differently as well, in terms of WOM and performance (such as sales, SOW, and profits). Relying on loyalty measures based solely on attitude or behavior can give conflicting results about the impact on performance. Watson et al. (2015) noted that most studies view loyalty only as an outcome, which may be misleading as a performance indicator. They also explored measurement composition (e.g., the ratio of attitudinal to behavioral items and the inclusion of WOM) and research characteristics (e.g., temporal focus), and how they affect loyalty outcomes. The authors found that combining attitudinal and behavioral items yields better results than using just one type. Finally, they recommend strategies that integrate both kinds of loyalty, prioritize predictive performance measures, and include contextual factors.

Watson et al. (2015) provide key recommendations for research.

- To understand how factors drive loyalty, measure attitudinal and behavioral loyalty separately, as they are influenced differently (e.g., satisfaction impacts attitudinal loyalty more than behavioral).
- When analyzing loyalty's effect on performance (e.g., revenue), combine attitudinal and behavioral measures for the most accurate results.
- For predicting WOM, attitudinal loyalty is more reliable, as behavioral factors like budget and location don't affect WOM as much.
- Retrospective measures can help avoid overestimating the connection between loyalty and WOM.

In terms of business practices:

- Loyalty measurements should combine attitudes and behaviors, as this mix has a stronger impact on performance than using just one. When customers exhibit high attitudinal loyalty (e.g., a high NPS) but low behavioral loyalty, performance outcomes may be less effective, leading to potential misallocation of marketing efforts.

- Customer loyalty is not gained through incentives but by building relationships based on commitment, trust, and satisfaction.
- Strategies for leveraging WOM should differ from those aimed at boosting loyalty. In B2B markets, loyalty impacts WOM more than performance, so investing in attitudinal loyalty should focus on maximizing customer portfolio value.

As summarized by Kumar & Shah (2004), a shift in LP paradigms has emerged from a program-centric to a customer-centric approach. This is reflected in the following dimensions.

- At the operational level, the most significant change is the move in LP management from an aggregate level to an individual customer level.
- LP has transitioned from being standardized, i.e., based on usage or spending, to being customized, that is, based on the *type* of usage or spending.
- The reward scheme, which was once identical across the board and aimed at repeat purchases, has evolved into a personalized, customer-relevant system, designed to influence specific behavioral changes or attitudinal gratification.
- Reward options are now structured as multiple choices, usually in partnership or alliance with other players.
- The reward mechanism has changed from reactive, based on past/current spending and service usage, to proactive, offering high-value rewards to influence future behavior and purchase motivation.
- Companies are becoming more and more creative, promoting intangible and experiential rewards for their customers, in addition to traditional tangible rewards.
- The objectives of LP are moving toward linking loyalty to profitability, aiming to influence behavioral loyalty and cultivate attitudinal loyalty, as opposed to previous loyalty programs that focused on increasing market share, boosting revenue, and building behavioral loyalty through repeat purchases and frequency of use.
- CLV is positioned as a preferable metric to RFM, PCV, and SOW.
- The use of technology and analytical techniques is becoming more intensive.

Despite the widespread use of LPs by companies and the numerous studies on their effectiveness, the effects of LPs on customer loyalty remain highly debated (Belli et al., 2022). LPs are developed based on the premise that it is more cost-effective to retain existing customers than to acquire new ones. In their research, Belli et al. (2022) provided useful insights for designing effective LPs, highlighting the importance of cognitive and affective elements in driving loyalty. According to the authors, several relevant theoretical and managerial implications emerge from the literature.

- LPs may boost favorable consumption behaviors more than fostering genuine loyalty, so monitoring all loyalty dimensions is essential.
- Closed LPs outperform open ones by enhancing group prestige and loyalty, though overly strict conditions may limit participation. Fees and tiers have minimal impact, while coalition LPs are as effective as single-company LPs.
- Savings and exclusive rewards increase loyalty, but discounts and personalized attention rewards (e.g., event invites) can reduce it by promoting cross-price sensitivity or feelings of unfairness.
- Direct rewards shore up loyalty, while indirect or deferred rewards are less effective.
- LPs work best in low-frequency, high-value purchase sectors, helping reduce risk and build trust.
- Cognitive benefits should be prioritized, as they play a key role in fostering affective benefits and enhancing loyalty.

Two previous literature reviews have focused on loyalty in digital contexts. Jai et al. (2022) analyzed the development of brand loyalty through social media platforms, identifying five main theoretical clusters related to:

a. customer self-identity
b. brand community
c. consumer decision-making
d. platforms as communication channels
e. relationships

The authors organized the concepts and constructs using the ADO framework (Antecedents, Decisions, and Outcomes) (Paul & Benito, 2018). Jai et al. (2022) identified the following measures of loyalty:

- increased interaction with the brand
- intention to repurchase
- purchase intention
- attachment, namely emotional attachment to or liking the brand
- positive WOM

- satisfaction
- willingness to pay more for the brand
- favoring the brand over others
- trust toward the brand
- commitment
- unwillingness to switch brands

According to the authors, there are eight main antecedents of brand loyalty related to consumers, brands, and social media:

- brand characteristics
- consumer-brand relationship and engagement
- social media marketing activities
- consumer characteristics
- social media characteristics
- social media engagement
- online brand community
- perceived value and risk

Moreover, based on the framework of the four stages of loyalty proposed by Oliver (1999), the study categorized brand loyalty measurements into:

- cognitive
- affective
- conative
- action

Finally, among loyalty outcomes, Jai et al. (2022) identified constructs such as:

- WOM and e-WOM
- repurchase or repeat-purchase intention
- purchase intention
- branding co-creation
- brand equity

Toufaily et al. (2013) conducted a meta-analysis of the empirical literature on customer loyalty toward commercial websites. The study revealed significant diversity in how online loyalty is conceptualized and measured across different studies. Some scales are based on behavioral measures, others assess loyalty using an attitudinal psychological approach, and still others use a composite approach that views online loyalty as a multifaceted construct, accounting for both attitudinal and behavioral components. The antecedents of online loyalty are varied and were classified by the authors into five main categories:

- product/service attributes
- customer/consumer characteristics
- company/seller/retailer characteristics
- website characteristics
- environmental characteristics such as culture

Online loyalty can lead to various outcomes, such as customer profitability, SOW, purchase frequency, visit count, price sensitivity, alternative searches, WOM, willingness to pay more, the likelihood of purchasing from the website, overall satisfaction, cross-selling opportunities, and customer retention (Toufaily et al., 2013). The authors categorize several measures of online loyalty, including behavioral loyalty, behavioral loyalty with a positive attitude, intentional (attitudinal) loyalty, cognitive loyalty, affective loyalty, conative loyalty, and action loyalty.

Finally, Grace et al. (2018) introduced the concept of brand fidelity as an innovative approach to understanding consumer-brand relationships. This construct includes cognitive and behavioral mechanisms that maintain the stability and longevity of the relationship, drawing inspiration from theories on maintaining romantic relationships. Behaviors such as accommodation/forgiveness, willingness to sacrifice, and cognitive manifestations like derogation of alternatives, cognitive interdependence, and positive illusions are crucial for understanding brand fidelity. The relationship is based on product-related elements (price, performance, category involvement) and market factors (type of exchange, B2B vs. B2C, accessibility); the relationship develops through brand commitment (the desire to develop a long-term relationship) and brand love (a strong emotional bond).

4.4 Conclusions

This chapter offers an analysis of previous marketing literature reviews on loyalty, highlighting the various conceptualizations, measurement methodologies, and practical implications that have emerged over time. Research has revealed that the nature of loyalty is complex and multidimensional, requiring an integrated approach that considers all its different aspects. Furthermore, we have seen that various theoretical perspectives contribute to a more articulated understanding of the phenomenon, but there are still open challenges, particularly regarding the practical application of models and knowledge.

Considering the previous contributions reviewed here, we might ask how the conceptualization and measurement of loyalty have evolved, and what progress has been made in the scientific literature. This critical analysis has allowed us to establish the knowledge base for Chapter 5, which will present a systematic literature review of empirical research, aimed at consolidating current knowledge and exploring new research directions and applications in the field of loyalty, with a specific focus on the retail context.

CHAPTER 5
CONCEPTUALIZATIONS, DIMENSIONS, AND MEASUREMENTS OF LOYALTY: A SYSTEMATIC LITERATURE REVIEW

[Andrea Ciacci, Alice Mantovani, Generoso Branca]

5.1 Introduction

Loyalty is a key concept in management and marketing literature. Investing in loyalty implies embarking on a journey aimed at strengthening long-term relationships between customers and the firm (Homburg & Tischer, 2023; Lewis, 2004), with the ultimate goal of increasing sales, raising profits, gaining market share, and guiding consumers in their purchasing choices (Baehre et al., 2022; Chaudhuri & Holbrook, 2001; Guadagni & Little, 2008; Petersen et al., 2018; Rossi, 2021; van Doorn et al., 2013). For these reasons, embracing loyalty means acting at the core of the corporate strategy to leverage a true differentiator.

Despite the efforts undertaken by many companies to secure the benefits of loyalty and the related rise in loyalty management expenditures globally (Watson et al., 2015), some estimates suggest that overall, loyalty programs (LPs) do not always ensure high returns or certain outcomes (Chen et al., 2021).

The mixed results in achieving loyalty stem, to a large extent, from divergent theoretical and operational approaches, such as analyzing only one category of loyalty while leaving out all others, or using metrics that don't align with the specific stage of the customer loyalty journey that we want to assess (Watson et al., 2015). Moreover, given the complexity and heterogeneity underlying the concept of loyalty, the variability of the empirical evidence is a direct result of the multiple conceptualizations and operationalizations proposed in the literature (Hill et al., 2022; Shaalan et al., 2023), as well as a variety of theoretical scenarios (Demoulin & Zidda, 2009; Homburg et al., 2009; Sipilä et al., 2021).

The systematic literature review (SLR) in this chapter aims to take stock of how far research has advanced and reconcile the abovementioned divergences. Considering the findings that have emerged from the different approaches and industries, in this chapter, we aim to provide empirical generalizations about the loyalty literature and the processes underpinning it.

Specifically, we'll answer the following research questions:

1. *What conceptions of loyalty emerge over time?*
2. *What are the key theories, contexts, characteristics (antecedents, outcomes, moderators), and methodologies of loyalty research?*
3. *What measurement approaches are applied to loyalty?*
4. *Where are the gaps in current research on loyalty and what are the possible future directions?*

In this context, our SLR differs from previous ones in that it provides a comprehensive review of the many theoretical and empirical aspects of loyalty research, including the most recent contributions to the scientific literature. We intend to capture the latest advancements in a field that is constantly evolving and map out future research directions as well. To this end, our SLR applies the review protocol known as Theory-Context-Characteristics-Methodology (TCCM) (Paul & Rosado-Serrano, 2019), which sheds light on various dimensions of a specific field of research.

Following the systematic selection of a set of articles, our review included 192 papers published in business, management, and marketing journals from 1974 to 2024. This literature review not only aims to fill existing gaps in our understanding of loyalty but also provides an integrated, up-to-date overview of the wide range of conceptions, theories, and methods of measuring loyalty. By applying the TCCM protocol, we provide a structured framework of the empirical evidence and theoretical implications that have emerged over the decades. In doing so, we help strengthen the knowledge base needed to guide future research and support business strategies in a changing marketplace.

5.2 Approach and structure of the systematic literature review

A systematic literature review requires admissible and reproducible criteria, from journal selection to article identification (Paul & Criado, 2020). We adopted a process that would ensure the representativeness, completeness, and high quality of the studies we included in our review. This SLR (Fink, 2009; Tranfield et al., 2003) follows the Preferred Reporting Items for Systematic Literature Reviews and Meta-Analyses (PRISMA) guidelines (Page et al., 2021).

Consistent with our objectives and the PRISMA process, we produced an algorithm to accurately identify relevant search items. To this end, because loyalty is often labeled differently depending on the specific domain and conceptualization provided by the authors of any given paper, we took special care to pinpoint all proximate (e.g., *"retention"*) or related (e.g., *"patronage"*) terms. Accordingly, the search query was stratified to encompass a wide range of keywords, categorized by various semantic groups, including:

- loyalty and related constructs, such as *fidelity, retention, patronage,* and *attachment*
- additional information to better contextualize and recognize various interpretations of loyalty, such as *store, retail, shop, channel, customer, consumer, buy, brand, distributor, dealer, private label,* and *commerce*
- references to measurements, in response to the search query, such as *key performance indicator (KPI), measure, metric, scale, score, index, performance,* and *margin*

Therefore, the search query was structured as follows:

TITLE-ABS-KEY (stor* OR retail* OR shop* OR channel* OR customer* OR consumer* OR buy* OR brand* OR distribut* OR dealer* OR "private label*" OR *commerce*) AND TITLE-ABS-KEY (loyal* OR fidel* OR retention* OR patronag* OR attach*) AND TITLE-ABS-KEY (kpi* OR "key performance indicator*" OR measur* OR metric* OR scale* OR scor* OR index* OR perform* OR margin*)

The asterisk (*) allows us to search for keywords with different suffixes, while quotation marks (" ") detect exact phrases. When a combination of words is enclosed in quotation marks, Scopus locates only papers in which the words appear in the order specified, as in the case of *"key performance indicator*"*. This tool is useful for refining search results and tagging publications that contain certain exact phrases or combinations of terms.

We identified papers by filtering keywords from the titles, abstracts, and keywords of English-language scientific articles in the Scopus database, and then refined our search to comprise only articles published in peer-reviewed academic journals. Our review included only scientific publications (articles) written in English and excluded other types of publications, such as reviews, conference proceedings, or book chapters. In addition, as in Chapter 4, we applied the subject area filter "business, management and accounting" to focus the analysis only on articles related to management and marketing. Finally, we considered all articles published in any country until May 22, 2024, applying no time limitation to the analysis to capture how the loyalty concept has evolved over time. In total, we obtained 5377 items.

After screening this initial result, we later decided to focus attention only on the most influential journals according to CABS AJG 2021, i.e., with a score of 4* and 4. This included: the Journal of Marketing, Journal of Retailing, Journal of the Academy of Marketing Science, Marketing Science, Journal of Management Information Systems, and Journal of Service Research, among others. A total of 401 articles fell into this classification.

To make a careful selection that considers the relevance to the topic under investigation and the research questions, two researchers read the abstracts and, where necessary, the text of each paper to decide whether to consider the article for our review. Exclusion criteria included:

1. conceptual articles or previous literature reviews
2. commentaries or editorials
3. articles not focused on customer-related loyalty, such as articles dealing with employee loyalty, which align more with organizational studies
4. the articles that are outside the scope of this literature review, that is, unrelated to the research objectives of this study, such as destination loyalty
5. articles not related to management or marketing (e.g., organizational behavior, finance, accounting, etc.)

In conclusion, this step-by-step approach resulted in the identification of 192 articles, published in 28 journals classified as 2021 ABS 4* or 4. The complete list can be found in Appendix A1.

The analysis phase involved reading the entire textual corpus of the selected papers to identify the following elements of interest: the loyalty construct used (e.g., customer loyalty, brand loyalty, etc.); theory, context, characteristics, and method applied according to the TCCM framework; the loyalty categories analyzed (e.g., affective, behavioral, etc.) and their measurements and operationalizations; antecedents, outcomes, and moderators of loyalty.

5.3   General overview

The loyalty literature investigates factors that determine customer loyalty, including customer attitudes and behaviors, key variables that impact on or arise from loyalty, and aspects concerning measurement. To better understand the characteristics of the object of study, this section (5.3) includes a review of the most studied loyalty constructs and an outline of the temporal evolution of the loyalty literature. In the following sections, we present the results of the systematic application of the TCCM analytical framework to assess the theoretical orientations in the literature (5.4), the contexts studied (5.5), the salient features of the contributions we analyzed (5.6) and the methods adopted to conduct the analyses (5.7). Added to these are considerations concerning the measurement of loyalty (5.8). We end the SLR with a description of loyalty in the retail sector (5.9) before presenting some brief conclusions (5.10).

5.3.1 *The concept of loyalty and its temporal evolution*

Concerning the loyalty constructs investigated in the scientific literature, customer loyalty appears to be the most studied (56 articles, 26% of the total loyalty concepts identified). This is a relatively broad concept, including both behavioral aspects (e.g., repeated purchases) and attitudinal aspects (e.g., preference, affection) (Demoulin & Zidda, 2009; Homburg et al., 2009; Kim et al., 2004). In other words, customer loyalty can indicate people's commitment to a brand, retail store, product, or service over time (Homburg et al., 2023; Morgeson et al., 2024; Srinivasan et al., 2002).

Customer retention, on the other hand, is more focused on behavioral considerations, that is, a company's ability to keep its current customers while minimizing the churn rate (Ascarza et al., 2016; Burnham et al., 2003; Tamaddoni et al., 2016). While loyalty is an attitude translated into behaviors, retention directly measures results in behavioral terms, indicating the continuity of the customer relationship (Cooil et al., 2007). Among the articles we analyzed, 37 focused on customer retention (17%).

As far as brand loyalty, this is not contingent on where the brand's products are purchased (Koll & Plank, 2022; Sprott et al., 2009; Tankersley, 1977). This construct emphasizes the importance of the brand in consumer decision-making (Papatla & Krishnamurthi, 1996; Villas-Boas, 2004). Overall, the brand loyalty concept appears central in 30 articles (14%).

Store loyalty (10 items, 5%) specifically indicates a connection to a particular retail outlet and not necessarily to a product or brand (Ailawadi et al., 2008; Bell et al., 1998; Koschate-Fischer et al., 2014; Seenivasan et al., 2016; Sirohi et al., 1998). Indeed, customers can be loyal to a specific store even though they purchase a variety of brands there.

The concept of loyalty intention, found in 10 articles (5%), measures a customer's willingness to continue buying from a company or to recommend it to others (Arens & Rust, 2012; Briggs & Grisaffe, 2010; Shaalan et al., 2023; Sipilä et al., 2021). It represents an earlier stage than actual behavior and reflects future intentions. In these terms, loyalty intention can be a predictive indicator of customer loyalty and customer retention (Petersen et al., 2018).

Table 5.1 summarizes the results regarding loyalty concepts that emerged during the literature review.

Based on the year of publication, the loyalty studies included in this SLR are distributed as in Figure 5.1.

The period from the 1970s to the 1990s saw the rise of the theoretical foundations of the loyalty concept. Newman & Werbel (1974) and Tankersley (1977) produce the first studies on brand attachment and behavioral loyalty. These works were centered on understanding why consumers repeatedly choose the same brands. At that time, brand loyalty was primarily viewed as repetitive behavior related to customer satisfaction and habit.

Subsequently, Bell et al. (1998) and Sirohi et al. (1998) begin to explore store loyalty, considering factors such as perceived quality and shopping experiences that are central to driving customer decision-making. At the same time, custom-

Table 5.1   Constructs employed in the studies on loyalty

Constructs	Frequencies	Examples of relevant contributions
Customer loyalty	56	Brady et al. (2012); Chitturi et al. (2008); Demoulin & Zidda (2009); Harris & Goode (2004); Haumann et al. (2014); Hill et al. (2022); Homburg et al. (2009); Hult et al. (2019); Liao & Chuang (2004); Mithas et al. (2006); Morgan & Rego (2008); Otim & Grover (2006); Rahman et al. (2022); Sirdeshmukh et al. (2002); Wolfinbarger & Gilly (2003)
Customer retention	37	Ascarza et al. (2016); Borle et al. (2005); Burnham et al. (2003); Gao et al. (2023); Lander et al. (2017); Lewis (2004); Lynch Jr. & Ariely (2000); Kamakura et al. (2002); Narayandas (1998); Tamaddoni et al. (2016); Vlachos et al. (2009)
Brand loyalty	30	Agrawal (1996); Batra et al. (2012); Burton et al. (1998); Kim & Kim (2005); Koll & Plank (2022); Miller et al. (2019); Newman & Werbel (1974); Ortmeyer et al. (1991); Papatla & Krishnamurthi (1996); Tankersley (1977)
Store loyalty	10	Ailawadi et al. (2008); Bell et al. (1998); Bleck & Gao (2023); Hansen & Singh (2008); Koschate-Fischer et al. (2014); Liaukonytė et al. (2023); Maxham III et al. (2008); Seenivasan et al. (2016); Sirohi et al. (1998)
Loyalty intention	10	Arens & Rust (2012); Briggs & Grisaffe (2010); Johnson et al. (2006); Larivière et al. (2016); Ou et al. (2017); Petersen et al. (2018); Shaalan et al. (2023); Sipilä et al. (2021); van Doorn et al. (2013)
Other forms of loyalty	75	Becker et al. (2009); Guo et al. (2023); Hillebrand et al. (2011); Lemmink & Mattsson (1998); Ngobo (2017); Petrick (2004)

Note. The total number of constructs exceeds the total number of items in the sample because some items conceptualize loyalty in more than one way.

Source: authors' elaboration.

Figure 5.1   **Article distribution per year**

Source: authors' elaboration.

er retention takes on the contours of a strategic concept for maintaining a stable and profitable customer base (Narayandas, 1998). It was around the 2000s that the concept of loyalty expanded, and customer loyalty became the most studied topic (Kim et al., 2004; Morgan & Rego, 2009; Vickery et al., 2004). That period was marked by an expansion of knowledge on loyalty to previously little-explored fields, such as the importance of relationships in determining attachment to a brand or store and the contextual development of the satisfaction-loyalty theoretical axis (Brakus et al., 2009; Homburg et al., 2009; Jones & Reynolds, 2006). The concept of perceived customer value becomes another cornerstone for delineating loyalty strategies (Chitturi et al., 2008; Petrick & Backman, 2002; Sirdeshmukh et al., 2002).

During this decade, customer retention hinged on more complex strategies and advanced behavioral models (Burnham et al., 2003; Lewis, 2004). These models consider switching costs, promotions, long-term customer value, and the impact of targeted marketing campaigns (Fullerton, 2003; Guadagni & Little, 2008; Shaffer & Zhang, 2002).

Other contributions further explored the notion of brand trust and brand equity (Ailawadi et al., 2001; Chaudhuri & Holbrook, 2001), highlighting how emotions and perceptions influence loyalty. These two variables are also factors in the differentiation and strategic positioning of the firm (Harris & Goode, 2004; Kim & Kim, 2005).

It was during this period that the concept of online customer loyalty began to take up an increasingly relevant space (Borle et al., 2005; Koça' & Bohlmann, 2008; Srinivasan et al., 2002). This development is rooted in the emergence of the e-commerce paradigm, which compounds the need to develop an empirical corpus to improve our understanding of the phenomenon. Research in this field centers attention on the impact of loyalty on LPs and promotions, service quality in the online customer journey, customer perceived value, and website characteristics (Harris & Goode, 2004; Lewis, 2004; Otim & Grover, 2006; Wolfinbarger & Gilly, 2003).

During the 2010s, studies on customer engagement and experience proliferate (Arnold et al., 2011; Batra et al., 2012; Grissemann & Stokburger-Sauer, 2012). This reinforces the notion that loyalty is not just repetitive behavior, but an emotional connection and long-term proactive customer engagement with the brand (Batra et al., 2012; Beltagui & Candi, 2018). Experiential loyalty emerges as a key theme, where the focus is on customer interaction across various touchpoints, both physical and digital (Ascarza et al., 2018; Herhausen et al., 2019; Kuehnl et al., 2019; Rapp et al., 2013). These contributions reflect the shift toward digital integration and omnichannel marketing to build and maintain loyalty (Herhausen et al., 2019).

With the propagation of website use, the potential for businesses to collect data is expanding. These data hold the key to gaining greater insight into customers' habits and preferences (Hu et al., 2019). This reinforces retention strategies based on data analysis and subsequent optimization of experiences (Iyengar et al., 2011; Ascarza et al., 2016). Organizations are beginning to implement advanced customer relationship management (CRM) systems and technologies to predict and influence repurchase behavior (Dong et al., 2011b; Hillebrand et al., 2011). At the same time, corporate social responsibility (CSR), sustainability, and ethical values are beginning to play an increasingly central role in determining brand loyalty (Ailawadi et al., 2014).

Recent contributions (2020-2024) point out how technology and digitization have become central to the effective management of loyalty, particularly through Artificial Intelligence (AI) and big data analysis (Hochstein et al., 2023; Kim & So, 2024; Yang et al., 2022). Employees must adapt their behaviors to this wave of change to improve customer perceptions and maintain long-lasting relationships (Herhausen et al., 2020; Kim & So, 2024). There is ever sharper focus on personalizing experiences and integrating digital platforms to manage and analyze customer loyalty (Rahman et al., 2022; Schmitz et al., 2020; Yang et al., 2022; Yoganarasimhan et al., 2023). Loyalty is now seen as a combination of shared values, personalized experiences, and continuous engagement, achieved by leveraging digital technologies and social media more and more (Gu et al., 2022; Hill et al., 2022; Shin & Perdue, 2023). In particular, retention strategies in the 2020s center on dynamic adaptation to customer needs and predictive use of data to prevent abandonment (Gao et al., 2023; Hochstein et al., 2023; McCarthy & Oblander, 2021).

While tracking this trajectory, it appears that the field has not yet garnered sufficient substantiation from empirical evidence to draw broad generalizations about the effect of new technologies on loyalty. Relatively recent technological evolution is met with low adoption rates. Due to the lack of relevant use cases and the time required for research to catch up with such a rapidly evolving market, there is a knowledge gap at the intersection between customer loyalty and digital technologies. At the same time, sustainability and ethical values continue to play a relevant role in determining customer loyalty (Sipilä et al., 2021). However, once again the empirical evidence that has emerged over the past decade cannot offer exhaustive knowledge on a topic that is multidimensional, complex, and rich in potential implications. The reason for this gap may be associated with the difficulties in implementing measurements of sustainability and ethics where the customer and the company meet. Another possible obstacle is the challenge of incorporating CSR and sustainability into LPs.

Figure 5.2 outlines the main developments in the loyalty literature over time.

5.4 Theories

Loyalty research employs several theories to explain relationships among relevant variables (Table 5.2). In general, the term "theory" refers to a set of systematically related and empirically verifiable statements (Sutton & Staw, 1995). In an applied context, theories can be understood as reasoned propositions about how a set of relevant constructs (e.g., customer loyalty and profitability) relate to each other with the goal of explaining and/or predicting empirical phenomena.

In loyalty studies, the most frequently applied theories are psychological and behavioral (17 articles), investigating the mental processes and behaviors that drive consumer decisions. Construal level theory is employed to ascertain how a customer journey should be structured to maximize loyalty in the customer experience (Kuehnl et al., 2019) and integrate experiential components across touchpoints (Kim & So, 2024). Consumer behavior theory allows us to understand, for example, how consumers act as a result of attachment (Dwayne Ball & Tasaki, 1992) and the long-term effects of promotions on different consumer segments (Lim et al., 2005). With expectancy-disconfirmation theory, research-

Figure 5.2   **Temporal evolution of the literature on loyalty**

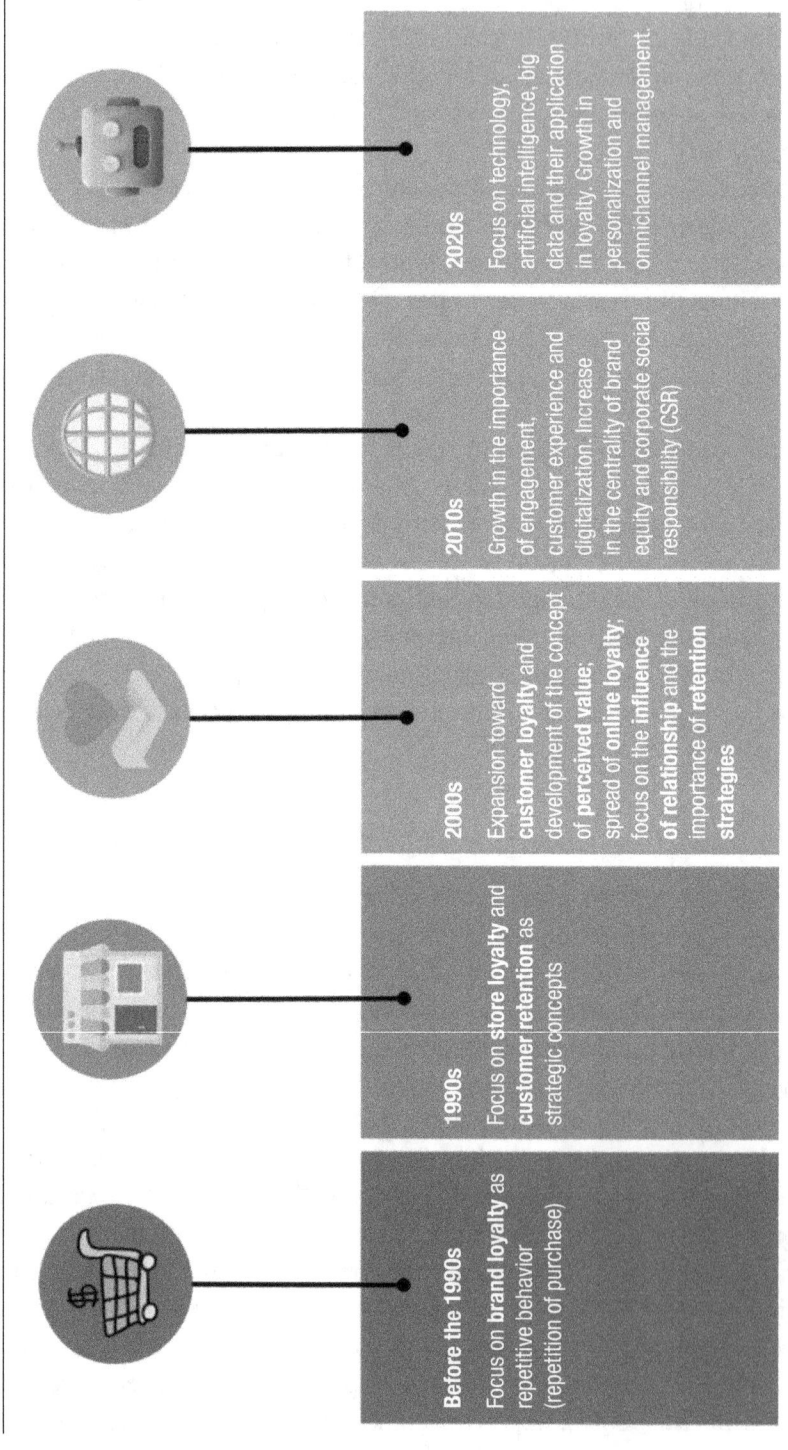

Before the 1990s

Focus on **brand loyalty** as repetitive behavior (repetition of purchase)

1990s

Focus on **store loyalty** and **customer retention** as strategic concepts

2000s

Expansion toward **customer loyalty** and development of the concept of **perceived value**; spread of **online loyalty**, focus on the **influence of relationship** and the importance of **retention strategies**

2010s

Growth in the importance of engagement, customer experience and digitalization. Increase in the centrality of brand equity and corporate social responsibility (CSR)

2020s

Focus on technology, artificial intelligence, big data and their application in loyalty. Growth in personalization and omnichannel management.

Note: In each of the periods there is a focus on a specific interpretation of loyalty. We should remember, however, that a particular construct is not analyzed in only one time slot. For example, although most of the contributions regarding store loyalty are attributable to the 1990s segment, we can identify others, to a lesser extent, in later periods as well.

Source: authors' elaboration.

Table 5.2   **Theories employed in loyalty studies**

Theoretical category	Examples of theories	Number of theories	Examples of relevant contributions
Psychological and behavioral theories	Attachment theory, attribution theory, construal level theory, consumer behavior theory, dual-process theories, equity theory, expectancy-disconfirmation theory, expectancy-value theory, grounded theory, metacognition theory, self-congruity theory, self-expansion theory, self-perception theory, theory of reasoned action	17	Arens & Rust (2012); Dwayne Ball & Tasaki (1992); Batra et al. (2012); Brady et al. (2012); Freling et al. (2011); Garnefeld et al. (2013); Kim & So (2024); Kuehnl et al. (2019); Lim et al. (2005); Mao et al. (2009); Mazodier & Merunka (2012); Pena-Marin & Wu (2019); del Rio Olivares et al. (2018); Otim & Grover (2006); Taplin (2013); Thomson et al. (2005)
Sociological and communication theories	Contagion theory, CSR theory, consumer empowerment theory, institutional theory, interactionist theory of place attachment, media richness theory, relationship lifecycle theory, social exchange theory, social identity theory, social presence theory, theory of interaction ritual chains, theory of attention trajectories	15	Briggs & Grisaffe (2010); Gao et al. (2023); Goel et al. (2011); Gu et al. (2022); Harrigan et al. (2017); Herhausen et al. (2020); Hill et al. (2022); Hillebrand et al. (2011); Homburg et al. (2009); Martinovici et al. (2023); Rapp et al. (2013); Schmitz et al. (2020); Vickery et al. (2004)
Economic and marketing theories	Adaptive expectations theory, anticipated utility theory, diffusion of innovations theory, information economics theory, price dispersion theory, prospect theory, random utility theory, sequential screening theory, theory of marketing mix response, transaction costs theory, sales theory, service climate theory	13	Aflaki & Popescu (2014); Ailawadi et al., (2001); Demoulin & Zidda (2009); Dixon & Verma (2013); Guo et al. (2023); Herhausen et al. (2019); Koçaş & Bohlmann (2008); Lynch Jr. & Ariely (2000); Temerak et al. (2024); Towler et al. (2011); Xue et al. (2011)
Management theories	Resource-based view, dynamic capabilities view, conservation of resources theory, micro-level behavioral theory, multi-level loyalty theory, organizational design theory, theory of information value	6	Arnold et al. (2011); Hays & Hill (2006); Homburg & Tisher (2023); Maria Stock et al. (2017); Padmanabhan et al. (2006); Schmitz et al. (2020)
Cognitive theories	Experiential learning theory, consumer learning theory, reconstructive memory theory	3	Gao et al. (2023); Herhausen et al. (2020); Villas-Boas (2004)

Note. Not all studies adopt a reference theory; therefore, the total number of theories is less than the number of articles analyzed.

Source: authors' elaboration.

ers analyze the extent to which the inaccuracy of a piece of information results in a decrease in the reliability of the source, affecting customer loyalty (Pena-Marin & Wu, 2019).

Sociological and communication theories (15 articles) examine social interactions, communication, and the relational and influence processes that take place between individuals and groups. For example, social exchange theory explains exchanges in dyadic relationships, suggesting that relationships form based on the interaction between two parties. Using this theory, Gao et al. (2023) study how the depth of the customer-firm relationship affects the link between customer experience and retention. In contrast, Harrigan et al. (2017) analyze the role of engagement with regard to loyalty. Another well-known concept is social identity theory, which argues that people define themselves by their membership in a relevant social group (Homburg et al., 2009). In addition, CSR theory inspires the study of how efforts in implementing responsible corporate behavior impact customer perceptions, affecting loyalty (Sipilä et al., 2021; Vlachos et al., 2009).

Economic and marketing theories (13 articles) examine the factors pertaining to these two areas, which influence consumer behavior. One of the most common in this domain is prospect theory, which explains individuals' asymmetric reactions to gains and losses and provides a conceptual framework for examining, for example, the effects of previous shopping experiences on customer retention dynamics (Aflaki & Popescu, 2014). Another is the random utility theory, which predicts that customers will choose the product that offers them the highest utility, given the relative costs and benefits and their personal tastes. This theory is being employed to explore the drivers of the adoption of Internet banking and health services, considering the loyalty dynamics that result (Dixon & Verma, 2013; Xue et al., 2011).

Management theories (6 articles) are concerned with the internal management of corporate resources and the organization of business activities to improve performance (Maria Stock et al., 2017). Homburg & Tisher (2023) apply the resource-based view to examine how resource engagement and dynamic capabilities are essential for ensuring customer journey effectiveness and maintaining loyalty orientation.

Cognitive theories (3 articles), on the other hand, examine how individuals learn new information and how they store and retrieve it from memory (Herhausen et al., 2020). Theories such as experiential learning and consumer learning help reveal how consumers' past experiences with a brand influence their future decisions and loyalty (Gao et al., 2023; Villas-Boas, 2004).

5.5 Contexts

Regarding context, this SLR analyzes the industries and countries found in the loyalty research. As some studies are set in multiple industries and countries

(Arnold et al., 2011; Lemmink & Mattsson, 1998), the frequency of industries and countries exceeds the number of articles in the sample.

5.5.1 *Industry*

Analysis of the context (Table 5.3) shows that the most represented industry is retail (i.e., 29% of all studies individually examined). This finding is not surprising considering that LPs were rapidly adopted by the retail industry after originally being launched by airlines. In addition, the retail industry has a wealth of data (e.g., from retailers' scanners, loyalty cards, and consumer panels), which makes it easier to develop and launch LPs.

In retail, most studies (75%) focus on offline retail stores and grocery stores (Ailawadi et al., 2014; Hansen & Singh, 2008; Seenivasan et al., 2016). Only a few (22%) examine online retail (Otim & Grover, 2006; Tamaddoni et al., 2016; Yang et al., 2022). The limited amount of research on this channel can be explained by the relatively recent emergence of e-commerce and the time it takes to investigate the phenomenon. The resulting knowledge gap needs to be filled with future research. Finally, two studies consider both offline and online contexts: the first is a comparative analysis of relative shopping experiences (Hult et al., 2019); the second explores omnichannel approaches (Rahman et al., 2022).

A substantial number of articles focus on hospitality (18%), divided between airline, hotel, restaurant, coffee shop, and other hospitality services (e.g., casinos, travel agencies, cruises) (Haumann et al., 2014; Li, 2010; Pritchard et al., 1999). The frequency of these studies can be attributed to the rapid rise of global tourism, as well as the high perishability of some services in the industry, such as hotel rooms and airplane seats. These characteristics lead to more intense competition among operators to secure customer loyalty.

In contrast, many researchers investigate information-oriented services (20%), goods-oriented services (9%), and people-oriented services (8%) (Gao et al., 2023; Temerak et al., 2024; Vickery et al., 2004). Information-oriented services include telecommunication, financial services, software and ICT, consulting, and marketing research (Guo et al., 2023; Raassens & Haans, 2017; Stock & Zacharias, 2013), while goods-oriented services refer to logistics, transportation rental, repairs, and home delivery (Hsu et al., 2010; Lemmink & Mattsson, 1998). Typical examples of people-oriented services are the healthcare sector, pharmacies, and insurance (Mangus et al., 2020; Maria Stock et al., 2017).

Finally, in brand loyalty research, several contributions consider consumer durables (12%) or nondurables (8%) (Ailawadi et al., 2007; Stahl et al., 2012). The most frequently investigated consumer durables are electronic products,

Table 5.3   **Industry investigated in loyalty studies**

Industry	Frequencies	Examples of relevant contributions
Retail	55	
Offline retail	41	Ailawadi et al. (2001); Arnold et al. (2011); Becker et al. (2009); Donthu & Cherian (1994); Keiningham et al. (2007); Koll & Plank (2022); Koschate-Fischer et al. (2014); Leenheer et al. (2007); Mangus et al. (2020); Ngobo (2017); Park et al. (2013); Sharp & Sharp (1997); Swaminathan & Bawa (2005)
Online retail	12	Borle et al. (2005); Herhausen et al. (2019); Koçaş & Bohlmann (2008); Otim & Grover (2006); Padmanabhan et al. (2006); Rapp et al. (2013); Tamaddoni et al. (2016); Yang et al. (2022)
Offline and online retail	2	Hult et al. (2019); Rahman et al. (2022)
Hospitality	35	
Airplanes	7	Harris & Goode (2004); Haumann et al. (2014); Liu & Ansari (2020); Sirdeshmukh et al. (2002); Steinhoff & Palmatier (2016)
Restaurants	7	Godes & Mayzlin (2009); Kim & Kim (2005); Liao & Chuang (2004); Stank et al. (1999); Thomson et al. (2005); Wang et al. (2022)
Hotels	5	Guo et al. (2023); Kirca (2011); Steinhoff & Palmatier (2016); Wang et al. (2016)
Coffee shops	3	Brakus et al. (2009); Guadagni & Little (2008); Ortmeyer et al. (1991)
Other services	13	Hu et al. (2019); Kim & So (2024); Maria Stock et al. (2017); Shin & Perdue (2023)
Other service industries	71	
Information-oriented services	38	Iyengar et al. (2011); Raassens & Haans (2017); Stock & Zacharias (2013); Tarasi et al. (2013); van Doorn et al. (2013); Vlachos et al. (2009)
Good-oriented services	17	Briggs & Grisaffe (2010); Hibbard et al. (2001); Hsu et al. (2010); Lemmink & Mattsson (1998); Rust et al. (2004)
Person-oriented services	16	Daryanto et al. (2010); Hays & Hill (2006); Lander et al. (2017); Musalem & Joshi (2009); Pena-Marin & Wu (2019)
Brand	38	
Consumer durables	23	Chitturi et al. (2008); Miller et al. (2019); Narayandas (1998); Sipilä et al. (2021); Towler et al. (2011)
Consumer non-durables	15	Ailawadi et al. (2007); Chaudhuri et al. (2019); Echambadi et al. (2013); Kuehnl et al. (2019); Liaukonytė et al (2023)
Other industries	19	Ascarza et al. (2018); Hill et al. (2022); Perkins-Munn et al. (2005); van Doorn et al. (2013)
Industry not explicitly stated	4	Morhart et al. (2015); Shaffer & Zhang (2002)

Note. The total frequency of industries exceeds the total number of articles because some articles investigate several different industries. Reference industries were identified following the scheme provided by Chen et al. (2021).

Source: authors' elaboration.

such as PCs and high-tech, and automobiles (Brakus et al., 2009; Narayandas, 1998; Petersen et al., 2018). In contrast, the most often recurring nondurable goods are food & beverage and gas/petrol (Chaudhuri et al., 2019; Echambadi et al., 2013).

Among the studies in our review, 54 (28%) include several industries in the same sample (cross-industry studies), that is, they analyze different sectors to compare results and identify common trends or significant divergence (Becker et al., 2009; Chaudhuri et al., 2019; Hochstein et al., 2023). Such studies allow for a broader, comparative view of market dynamics, providing useful insights to identify best practices and generalizations across sectors. Future research could develop additional cross-country studies to further explore these comparisons, delving into the influence of sector-specific variables and providing generalizable results on a broader scale.

The clear majority of the studies we analyzed belong to business-to-consumer (B2C) contexts (171, or 89%) (Otim & Grover, 2006; Srinivasan et al., 2002), while only 13 articles (7%) focus on the business-to-business (B2B) (Homburg & Tisher, 2023) and 9 articles (4%) consider both B2C and B2B (Petersen et al., 2018). Therefore, we can detect a research gap at the intersection of loyalty studies and B2B contexts.

5.5.2 *Countries*

Table 5.4 presents an overview of the countries studied in research where location was made explicit. As we can see, the United States is the most represented country. Europe figures in 74 studies run in 17 countries. The European countries analyzed most frequently are Germany, the United Kingdom, the Netherlands, and France. Asia is the context of reference in 12 studies, with China predominating over other countries in that area. Oceania is represented in 6 studies. Among the papers in our review, 19 are contextualized in multiple countries (cross-country studies), i.e., they count statistical units referable to distinct countries but included in the same sample (Daryanto et al., 2010; Shaalan et al., 2023). The remaining 174 are conducted in a single country. Developing cross-country studies allows for insights that include cultural, economic, and regulatory differences across national contexts, providing a more comprehensive and generalizable view of the dynamics under investigation. Therefore, one of the goals of future research could be to more often adopt approaches that span multiple countries.

Table 5.4 Countries investigated in the loyalty studies

Countries	Frequencies	Examples of relevant contributions
America	94	
United States	86	Baehre et al. (2022); Bell et al. (1998); Harrigan et al. (2017); Hochstein et al. (2023); Leclerc & Little (1997); McCarthy & Oblander (2021); Morgan & Rego (2009); Rahman et al. (2022); Seenivasan et al. (2016); Sprott et al. (2009); Thomson et al. (2005)
Canada	4	Fullerton (2003); Pritchard et al. (1999); Wolfinbarger & Gilly (2003)
Other countries	3	Morhart et al. (2014); Steenkamp (2024)
Europe	74	
Germany	16	Homburg et al. (2009); Koll & Plank (2022); Koschate-Fischer et al. (2014); Schmitt et al. (2011); Wallenburg (2009)
United Kingdom	9	Blocker et al. (2011); Bolton et al. (2006); Shaalan et al. (2023)
The Netherlands	8	De Haan et al. (2015); Hillebrand et al. (2011); van Doorn et al. (2013)
France	6	Aurier & N'goala (2010); Mazodier & Merunka (2012); Meyer-Waarden & Benavent (2009)
Belgium	3	Demoulin & Zidda (2009); Larivière (2008)
Italy	3	Rossi (2021); Steenkamp (2024)
Other countries	29	Barnes et al. (2014); Nitzan & Libai (2011); Temerak et al. (2024)
Asia	12	
China	3	Dong et al. (2011a); Dong et al. (2011b)
Other countries	9	Agyeiwaah et al. (2016); Kim et al. (2004); Liang et al. (2023)
Oceania	6	
Australia	4	Daryanto et al. (2010); Sharp & Sharp (1997); Taplin (2013)
New Zealand	2	Colgate & Danaher (2000); Yoganarasimhan et al. (2023)

Source: authors' elaboration.

5.6 Characteristics

5.6.1 *Antecedents*

The antecedents of loyalty refer to the factors that influence this phenomenon leading to changes in its intensity. An analysis of the literature reveals four macro-categories of antecedents, which can be detected at four distinct levels (Table 5.5). Starting from the microsphere, individual dynamics at the customer level can generate effects on loyalty. Customer satisfaction and experience along the customer journey, as well as customer characteristics, value systems, purchasing behaviors, and the quality they perceive: these are the main factors attributable to customer dynamics that can shape loyalty (Aflaki & Popescu, 2014; Homburg

Table 5.5   **Antecedents investigated in the loyalty studies**

Macro-categories	Categories	Examples of variables
Customer-level dynamics	Customer satisfaction and experience	Customer satisfaction, customer delight, journey satisfaction, product satisfaction, attitudinal commitment, involvement, omnichannel customer experience
	Customer behavior and characteristics	Consumer purchasing behavior, consumer browsing, past visit behavior, consumption value, dormancy length, ethnic identification, demographics (age, education, occupation), intrinsic customer preferences, cognitive absorption, moral identity, loyalty proneness, resistance to change
	Customer value and perceived quality	Perceived value, perceived quality, perceived differences in service quality, perceived value in CRM efforts, merchandise quality perceptions
	Employee performance and service levels	Employee service performance, satisfaction with the employee, employee motivation and vision, employee fairness, employee satisfaction, human capital, service quality, service quality perceptions, service experience, customer support, on-time delivery, customer journey management capability
Brand- and company-related drivers	Branding and loyalty programs	Brand authenticity, brand love, brand experience, brand personality, customer-based brand equity, brand quality, customer-company identification, loyalty program characteristics, loyalty program frequency, loyalty program structure, accumulation of reward points, redemption breadth, depth, and recency, brand engagement in self-concept, private labels
	Marketing and communication	Marketing communication, marketing investments, marketing actions, promotions, one-to-one promotions, frequency of promotions, price sensitivity, pricing structure, market orientation, online reviews, quality and content of e-mails, social media usage
	Technology and online factors	Website service quality, website features, customer insight, contact interactivity, transparency of billing, order tracking, adoption of internet banking, content co-creation, media richness
	Economic and strategic factors	Brand portfolio strategy, price strategy, store pricing strategy, switching costs, customer cost to serve, customer acquisition efforts and incentive mechanisms, proactive cost and performance improvement, CRM implementations
	CSR and ethics	CSR attributions, social and environmental responsibility, good employer practices, corporate citizenship
Relational influences	Interaction and relational dynamics	Perceived warmth during the service encounter, social atmosphere, interaction rituals, expectations of future relational benefits, relational switching costs, learning through service failure, moral hazard severity
	Trust and commitment	Customer trust, personal trust, brand trust, source trustworthiness, relationship commitment, customer commitment
Environmental forces	Environmental and contextual factors	Industry characteristics, contextual cues, market characteristics

Note. The categories were derived through manual (coding) and software-based analysis of the different variables. The macro-categories are the result of subsequent aggregation of the categories based on criteria of consistency and conceptual convergence.

Source: authors' elaboration.

et al., 2009; Gao et al., 2023; Koçaş & Bohlmann, 2008; Rahman et al., 2022; Villas-Boas, 2004; Wen et al., 2014). The performance and service provided by employees and the company can also affect the perceived quality and level of customer satisfaction, which reverberates into loyalty (Ailawadi et al., 2014; Liao & Chuang, 2004).

Significant elements for increasing loyalty emerge from the corporate sphere, related to brand enhancement and image, as well as LPs (e.g., structure, features, frequency), marketing and communication, and strategies (e.g., brand portfolio and pricing) (Batra et al., 2012; Brakus et al., 2009; Lewis, 2004; Liu & Ansari, 2020; Morgan & Rego, 2008; Morhart et al., 2015). In addition, e-commerce characteristics and the firm's online presence are relevant technological factors for the success of loyalty strategies (Herhausen et al., 2020; Wolfinbarger & Gilly, 2003). Finally, firms that adopt responsible behaviors toward their employees and the environment are more likely to foster customer loyalty (Sipilä et al., 2021; Walsh & Beatty, 2007).

Customer-business relationships are essential drivers for establishing loyalty. Constructing effective interaction systems from an omnichannel perspective, attending to the environment in which the interaction takes place, as well as investments in trust at various levels (e.g., personal, brand) and recommendations: these are key variables in building loyalty (Echambadi et al., 2013; Hill et al., 2022; Mangus et al., 2020; Mazodier & Merunka, 2012; Wang et al., 2022).

Finally, at a macro level, external factors such as competition, market trends, and socioeconomic changes can influence customer loyalty (Kirca, 2011; Ou et al., 2017; Vanier & Trippi, 1976). Such elements, despite being outside the control of the firm, if intercepted early, can become stimuli for the firm to affect change to embrace new trends.

5.6.2 Outcomes

Loyalty outcomes refer to the elements in which loyalty generates effects. The literature review shows four macro-categories of outcomes at three different levels (Table 5.6). Looking at the microsphere, it appears that loyalty can influence customer behavior, leading to repurchase, repeat visits, visit frequency, and an increase in share-of-wallet (SOW) (Kim et al., 2004; Larivière, 2008; Lee et al., 2014; Petrick, 2004; Raassens & Haans, 2017). In addition, loyalty affects consumers' choices by driving their spending, lessening their price sensitivity, and augmenting their propensity to redeem coupons (Guadagni & Little, 2008; Lynch Jr. & Ariely, 2000; Swaminathan & Bawa, 2005).

Loyalty also influences the firm's financial and operational performance. This

Table 5.6   **Outcomes investigated in the loyalty studies**

Macro-categories	Categories	Examples of variables
Customer behavior	Retention and repurchase	Behavioral loyalty, continued usage of service/product, usage levels, revisit intention, length of stay and visit frequency, enhanced share-of-wallet
	Consumer choices and preferences	Brand choice, brand utility, consumer spending, decrease in outshopping behavior, decline in attitudes toward private labels
	Sensitivity to price and promotions	Reduced price sensitivity, coupon efficiency, propensity to redeem coupons
Company financial and operational performance	Profits and margins	Higher revenue and profit, higher contribution margins, gross margins, financial returns, cash flow variability
	Growth and value creation	Sales growth, firm financial performance, market valuation, increase of CLV, market share acquisition
	Efficiency and decisions	Improved operational decisions, consumption efficiency, resource exploitation
Marketing and business strategies	Pricing and sales strategies	Retailer pricing strategies, retail sales performance, willingness to pay more
	Promotional strategies	More spent in advertising, promotional strategies
	Forecasting and targeting	Effective customer targeting, prediction of firm revenue growth, enhanced predictive accuracy
Engagement and relationships	Quality and strength of the relationship	Customer engagement levels, brand relationship motivational strength, relationship quality
	Long-term relationships	Long term relationship commitment
	Word-of-mouth	Increased Word-of-Mouth, online Word-of-Mouth

Note. The categories were derived through manual (coding) and software-based analysis of the different variables; the macro-categories are the result of subsequent aggregation of the categories based on criteria of consistency and conceptual convergence.

Source: authors' elaboration.

translates into bigger margins and profits and greater efficiency in resource consumption. Overall, loyalty contributes to higher firm value, sales, and customer lifetime value (CLV), and boosts market share (Aflaki & Popescu, 2014; Baehre et al., 2022; Chaudhuri & Holbrook, 2001; Dong & Chintagunta, 2016; Guo et al., 2023; Rapp et al., 2013; Rossi, 2018; Schmitt et al., 2011). Variations in loyalty levels also affect the design of pricing, sales, and promotional strategies, leading to more sizeable investments (van Doorn et al., 2013).

Finally, from the firm's perspective, stronger loyalty results in better, longer-lasting customer relationships, leading customers to recommend the brand or store through word-of-mouth (WOM) (Narayandas, 1998; Park et al., 2013; Srinivasan et al., 2002).

Figure 5.3 highlights the groups of antecedents and outcomes that emerged from the systematization of the literature. Loyalty is influenced by a combination of individual, business, relational, and environmental factors, and, in turn, affects a range of business behaviors and outcomes. All this has implications for customer engagement and relationships.

In practice, companies should monitor and manage these factors in an integrated way to build and maintain customer loyalty, which is crucial for sustaining competitive advantage and achieving long-term success.

5.6.3 *The mediating role of loyalty*

Among the articles considered for this literature review, 31 (16%) attribute a role to loyalty mediating between antecedent constructs and outcomes. From a conceptual point of view, this approach emphasizes the centrality of loyalty within the theoretical-analytic framework, making it a pivot element for certain cause-effect relationships to be meaningful and, therefore, to produce the expected effects. From a logical standpoint, the rationale behind mediation is that, in the absence of the mediator, the hypothesized relationship no longer has reason to exist or does not produce effects with the same intensity. Loyalty as a

Figure 5.3   Overview of the antecedents and outcomes of loyalty

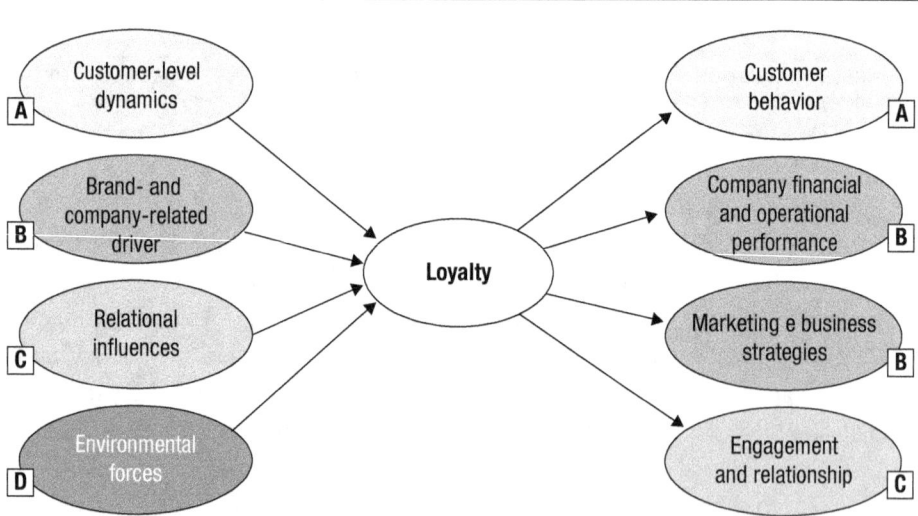

Note. *The letters corresponding to the ovals indicate the levels to which the macro-categories are attributable:* A for individual, B for corporate and organizational, C for relational, and D for macro-environmental.

Source: authors' elaboration.

mediator conveys the effect of the antecedent in such a way as to influence the outcome. An example of this perspective is provided by Homburg & Tischer (2023) who demonstrate the mediating role of loyalty in the B2B context in the relationship between customer journey management capability and return on sales (ROS). Further evidence is provided by Larivière et al. (2016) that loyalty intention serves as a mediator in the relationship between customer satisfaction and shareholder value metrics. Another contribution shows that loyalty toward retailers plays a significant role in conveying the effects of consumers' social media use on supplier brand sales performance and retailer sales performance (Rapp et al., 2013). The examples given here clearly show that loyalty is often seen as the link between intangible aspects and economic and financial performance indicators.

5.6.4 *Moderators*

Moderators are factors that can bolster or inhibit the effectiveness of certain relationships. In the presence of some moderators, the effect of a dependent variable on loyalty may be amplified, while when certain other factors are at play, the relationship may decline in intensity. In addition, depending on the conceptual framework of reference and the research hypotheses made, interchangeability between antecedents and moderators could occur. Therefore, as we explained in Section 5.6.1, some moderators might reflect the antecedents we previously discussed.

From the sample we analyzed, the most recurrent moderators can be traced to four macro-categories:

- consumer characteristics and behaviors
- products and markets
- firm or service characteristics
- contextual and environmental factors.

Among the most recurrent moderator variables, we note the socioeconomic and demographic characteristics of customers (e.g., salary, education level, customer status, cultural orientation, value system) (Cooil et al., 2007), item characteristics (e.g., perishability, category) (Becker et al., 2009; Dong et al, 2011a), industry characteristic dynamics (e.g., competitive intensity, territory-level market share) (Briggs & Grisaffe, 2010; Echambadi et al., 2013), firm type (e.g., products vs. services) (Homburg & Tisher, 2023), purchase channel (e.g., offline vs. online) (Hult et al., 2019), and country-level tax and government policy (Shaalan et al., 2023).

5.7 Methodology

To assess the methodology adopted in the literature, we reviewed the empirical articles according to the research approach (quantitative, qualitative, or mixed) and analytical methods used to investigate the relationships of interest. The results of our literature review indicate the prevalence of quantitative studies (180 articles, 94%). The most commonly used analytical methods include structural equation models (SEMs), regression analyses (including linear, logistic, and Bayesian regressions), experiments, multivariate analyses, and ANOVAs (Arens & Rust, 2012; Koschate-Fischer et al., 2014; Liang et al., 2023; Miller et al., 2019; Park et al., 2013). Methods such as SEMs and regression analyses allow us to understand causal relationships among complex variables, such as those that influence customer loyalty. For example, SEMs make it possible to explore not only correlations but also direct and indirect interactions between variables. Applying this method, Chaudhuri & Holbrook (2001) find that trust and fondness toward the brand are determinants of brand loyalty. Similarly, regression analyses help predict the impact of specific factors on purchasing behavior. For example, Garnefeld et al. (2013) apply logistic regression to evaluate the effect of attitudinal loyalty, indicating a strong, positive relationship with the brand based on trust, satisfaction, and affection, on behavioral by observing the positive effects exerted by attitudinal loyalty on customers' repeat purchase behavior. Multivariate experiments and analyses allow the effect of specific variables to be isolated and assessed, refining the accuracy of loyalty strategies (Godes & Mayzlin, 2009; Seenivasan et al., 2016).

The number of qualitative studies is significantly small (2 articles, 1%). This gap in the literature may indicate shortcomings in investigating the psychological mechanisms underlying consumers' behaviors, purchase intentions, or latent needs, preferences, and desires. The qualitative methods used in the two papers in our review include in-depth interviews, focus groups, and ethnographies (Hill et al., 2022; Hochstein et al., 2023).

Studies employing both quantitative and qualitative approaches number 10 (5%). These methods merge complementary analyses, such as in-depth interviews and SEM or regressions (Homburg & Tisher, 2023; Steinhoff & Palmatier, 2016; Wolter et al., 2022), to better comprehend the complex nature of loyalty. For example, Batra et al. (2012) propose an approach that combines two qualitative studies to identify variables relevant to brand love formation, and a quantitative study based on SEM to explore the structure of these variables and the effects of their relationships.

5.8 Loyalty measurements

The main loyalty measurements can be traced back to the loyalty journey categories previously described in Chapter 4. Specifically, to codify the loyalty measurements adopted in the articles in our review, we considered the definitions of cognitive, affective, conative, and behavioral loyalty provided by Oliver (1999). According to the conceptualization provided by the author, loyalty develops sequentially in different stages. By these definitions, cognitive loyalty indicates the initial stage of consumer loyalty, in which loyalty is based on evaluations of information about brand attributes (e.g., "*For me, this brand is the most functional for my needs*"). Affective loyalty occurs when the consumer has developed an affection or positive attitude toward the brand based on satisfactory user experiences (e.g., "*I like this brand*"). Conative loyalty is the intention to purchase the brand again (e.g., "*I intend to repurchase this brand*"). Behavioral loyalty is when customers transform their intentions into actions (e.g., "*I purchase this brand often*"). Behavioral loyalty refers to past actions, such as the actually making repeated purchases.

In our analysis, we find various types of indicators used to detect loyalty categories (Table 5.7). The one with the most empirical findings is behavioral loyalty, followed by affective loyalty, conative loyalty, and cognitive loyalty. The greatest variety of indicators emerges for the behavioral loyalty category, as measured by Likert scales (Lander et al., 2017; Wolter et al., 2022), share of spending and purchases (e.g., share of items, share of visit, SOW) (Ailawadi et al., 2008; Demoulin & Zidda, 2009), repeat purchases, and retention behavior (e.g., repeat purchase rates, time to churn) (Lewis, 2004; Yang et al., 2022). In addition, the literature proposes indicators related to customer participation and interaction, based on joining LPs, redeeming points, opening emails, unsubscribing to newsletters, and leaving online reviews (Ascarza et al., 2018; Li et al., 2024; Tarasi et al., 2013). Predictive indicators estimate the probability of future purchase or retention (e.g., switching probability, survival analysis) (Stahl et al., 2012; Xue et al., 2011). Other indicators focus on financial metrics related to customer spending behaviors (e.g., daily contribution margin) (Van Den Bulte et al., 2018).

Because they are not effectual/behavioral, but rather intentional and subjective in nature (i.e. based on the stated preferences and value judgments of respondents), Likert scales are the most common measurement approach to detect affective, conative, and cognitive loyalty (Harris & Goode, 2004; Kim & So, 2024; Pena-Marin & Wu, 2019; Steinhoff & Palmatier, 2016). Among the most widely used Likert scales are multi-item and reflexive scales, in particular, multi-categorical scales, whose items can be attributed to different loyalty

Table 5.7   **Measurements taken in loyalty studies**

Loyalty category	Examples of indicators	Number of measurements	Examples of relevant contributions
Behavioral	Likert scales, share of items, share of visits, share of wallet, repeat purchase rates, time to churn, average basket size, usage and customer tenure, daily contribution margin	114	Ailawadi et al. (2008); Demoulin & Zidda (2009); Iyengar et al. (2011); Kirca (2011); Lewis (2004); McCarthy & Oblander (2021); Ngobo (2017); Van Den Bulte et al., (2018); Meyer-Waarden & Benavent (2009); Wolter et al. (2022)
Affective	Likert scales, NPS	33	Dwayne Ball & Tasaki (1992); Gao et al. (2023); Liang et al. (2023); Maxham III et al. (2008); Rahman et al. (2022)
Conative	Likert scales	30	Barnes et al. (2014); Homburg & Tisher (2023); Kim & So (2024); Vlachos et al. (2009); Wolfinbarger & Gilly (2003)
Cognitive	Likert scales	1	Harris & Goode (2004)
Mixed measurements (multi-categorical)	Likert scales	44	Mao et al. (2009); MacCormick & Parker (2010); Sipilä et al. (2021); Srinivasan et al. (2002); Wen et al. (2014)

Note. The total number of measurements exceeds the total sample because some papers measure loyalty in more than one way.

Source: authors' elaboration.

categories. For example, a large number of Likert scales include affective and conative items (Shin & Perdue, 2023; Sipilä et al., 2021; Steenkamp, 2024), while others add in cognitive and behavioral items as well (Srinivasan et al., 2002; Wen et al., 2014). Adopting multi-categorical scales allows researchers to capture a wide range of dimensions of loyalty (e.g., purchase intention, emotional bonding, perception of product features), offering a more comprehensive and detailed view than a single-item scale. For example, Watson et al. (2015) point out that measurements that combine attitudinal and behavioral items prove more effective in accurately assessing customer loyalty than those based on only one type of item. However, because mixed scales include multiple dimensions of loyalty, interpreting the results may be difficult. In addition, approaches based on using multi-categorical scales prevent us from observing how different loyalty categories interact sequentially with each other.

Instead, there is a dearth of multidimensional scales that integrate the dimensions of loyalty into a single coherent and structured measurement. The reason may be that developing and validating multidimensional scales requires a complex and rigorous process, involving collecting data from different samples and verifying validity and reliability through extensive statistical testing. To compensate for this, some studies measure distinct loyalty categories and operationalize them by developing separate constructs. In this way, researchers isolate the influence of individual antecedents on various loyalty categories and determine the effects of each one on different outcomes.

For example, Chaudhuri & Holbrook (2001) consider two forms of loyalty, purchase and attitudinal, and show that loyalty and brand affection determine both purchase loyalty and attitudinal loyalty, but purchase loyalty generates greater effects on market share, while attitudinal loyalty leads to a higher relative price for the brand. Furthermore, Garnefeld et al. (2013) show that participation in a referral program directly affects the behavioral loyalty of recommenders, but has a significant and positive impact on attitudinal loyalty only when there are higher monetary rewards. Attitudinal loyalty has the same effect on behavioral loyalty. These examples show how the use of different loyalty constructs allows us to model the relationships between various loyalty categories and evaluate any mutual influences along the customer journey.

5.9 Focus on retail

Table 5.8 provides an overview of the results that emerged from applying the TCCM framework to retail-related studies (for more details, see Appendix A2.) The reason for this in-depth exploration is that retail appears to be the context most frequently investigated based on the analysis presented in Section 5.5.1. Thanks to its distinctive characteristics, retail represents a profitable field of study and application for understanding loyalty dynamics in greater depth.

At the theoretical level, there is a prevalence of economic and marketing theories that shed light on the implications of loyalty for corporate marketing strategies (Ailawadi et al., 2001; Herhausen et al., 2019; Lynch Jr. & Ariely, 2000), followed by psychological and behavioral theories (Brady et al., 2012; Otim & Grover, 2006) and management theories (Arnold et al., 2011; Maria Stock et al., 2017). Sociological and cognitive theories appear sporadically (Rapp et al., 2013; Villas-Boas, 2004).

The context analyzed most often is the grocery sector in the United States and Europe (Ailawadi et al., 2014; Demoulin & Zidda 2009; Ngobo, 2017). Non-grocery studies focus on electronics, clothing, books, and sporting goods (Baehre et al., 2022; Brakus et al., 2009; Koça' & Bohlmann, 2008). A high level of interest is

Table 5.8   Summary of the TCCM framework of loyalty studies in the retail sector

Elements of the TCCM framework	Examples
Theories	
Economic and marketing theories	Price dispersion, theory of marketing mix response, anticipated utility, information economics, transaction costs, diffusion of innovations theory
Psychological and behavioral theories	Self-expansion model, theory of reasoned action, equity theory
Management theories	Conservation of resources theory, organizational design, theory of information value
Other theories	Contagion theory, consumer learning theory
Contexts	
Food sector (grocery)	Prevalence of studies focused on supermarkets and grocery stores in the United States, Europe, and international contexts
Non-food sector (non-grocery retail)	Apparel, electronics, books, sporting goods among the most investigated sectors in U.S. and international contexts
Online and omnichannel sector	Impact of e-commerce and omnichanneling on loyalty; analysis of online browsing and shopping behaviors, customer journey segmentation
Multi-sector contexts	Cross-industry studies in international contexts
Characteristics	
Antecedents	Customer satisfaction and shopping experience, quality and perceived value, customer behavior, demographic characteristics, costs associated with the customer, trust relationships, intangible brand characteristics, promotions, private label, loyalty programs, CRM, marketing orientation, technology and online factors
Outcomes	Economic and financial performance, operational performance, sales growth, pricing strategies, price sensitivity, consumer behavior and preferences, customer relationships and engagement
Moderators	Customer price orientation, product categories, market characteristics, purchase channel, customer journey segments, store quality, price positioning strategies, employee support
Methodologies	
Quantitative	Structural equation models, regressions, experiments, ANOVAs
Mixed methods	Interviews or focus groups + models to structural equations, regressions, or experiments

Source: authors' elaboration.

directed to online and omnichannel. Studies in this area investigate the impact of the omnichannel experience on customer loyalty (Rahman et al., 2022), the role of trust in e-commerce (Harris & Goode, 2004; Mangus et al., 2020), advertising (Ngobo, 2017; Yang et al., 2022), website characteristics (e.g., design, privacy, security, service) (Wolfinbarger & Gilly, 2003), and the intensity of the relationship between satisfaction and loyalty in online and offline contexts (Hult et al., 2019).

An analysis of item characteristics in retail shows a variety of loyalty antecedents. These are mostly attributable to drivers such as customer satisfaction, shopping experience, and consumer characteristics (Koça' & Bohlmann, 2008; Villas-Boas, 2004). From a corporate perspective, variables such as promotions, private brands, and LP structure are crucial to effective loyalty management (Lewis, 2004). The literature points out that leveraging promotions is often effective in acquiring new customers, but it risks being a counterproductive approach to retention (Ailawadi et al., 2001; Dong et al., 2011b). Private labels, on the other hand, drive repurchases, particularly for customers who show a strong price orientation; this means PLs are the right route for pursuing store loyalty (Koll & Plank, 2022; Koschate-Fischer et al., 2014), although this risks negatively impacting brand relationships (Burton et al., 1998). CRM and marketing orientation are also essential for maintaining long-term customer relationships (Becker et al., 2009; Kirca, 2011).

The outcomes investigated in the articles in our review involve the firm's financial and operational performance (Baehre et al., 2022; Rapp et al., 2013; Yang et al., 2022), and the effects that loyalty generates on pricing strategies, consumer behaviors, and perceptions (e.g., price sensitivity) (Hozier & Stem, 1985; Koça' & Bohlmann, 2008; Lynch Jr. & Ariely, 2000) and brand relationships (Park et al., 2013). The main moderators involve product and market characteristics (e.g., level of competition) (Koschate-Fischer et al., 2014; Mangus et al., 2020), shopping channels (Hult et al., 2019), store brand quality (Seenivasan et al., 2016), and the role of employees (Becker et al., 2009).

Methodologically, the sample includes mostly quantitative studies (49 studies, 91%), consistent with previous evidence; exceptions are some research supported by combining quantitative and qualitative methods (5 studies, 9%). Note the absence of purely qualitative studies.

The table in Appendix A3 provides an in-depth look at Likert scales and items used to measure loyalty in the retail sector. From the sample analysis, 33 applications of Likert scales emerge. Research applied to retail predominantly uses mixed scales (10) (Mangus et al., 2020; Rapp et al., 2013; Srinivasan et al., 2002) and scales attributable mainly to affective loyalty (9) (Demoulin & Zidda, 2009; Maxham III et al., 2008; Wolter et al, 2022) and behavioral loyalty (7) (Brady et al., 2012; Donthu & Cherian (1994; Rahman et al., 2022), while a small number of contributions employ scales to measure conative (4) (Hult et al., 2019; Jones & Reynolds, 2006) and cognitive (1) loyalty (Harris & Goode, 2004). In two cases, the approaches are not assimilated to any loyalty category because the authors do not specify the items or operationalize loyalty along with other constructs as a proxy for a broader concept (Hozier & Stem, 1985; Swaminathan

& Bawa, 2005). Some contributions (4) directly assign the reference category of loyalty to scales (Demoulin & Zidda, 2009; Harris & Goode, 2004; Steinhoff & Palmatier, 2016; Wolter et al., 2022), making explicit which interpretation of loyalty they are examining.

Some authors address developments in the study of e-commerce and digital contexts in retail, with scales designed to incorporate the digital dimension (Srinivasan et al., 2002; Wolfinbarger & Gilly, 2003) or implementing generic scales in digital contexts (Harris & Goode, 2004; Herhausen et al., 2019; Rapp et al., 2013). These studies focus on various influencing factors, such as purchasing channels (websites), products/services, and social media. All Likert scales used in digital contexts are mixed in nature, employing items attributable to different loyalty categories. The only exception is Harris & Goode (2004), who propose scales that measure diverse configurations of loyalty.

Authors tend to adopt scales that are already validated and previously used in the literature, readjusting them to their research contexts. In this case, some relevant contributions emerge more frequently than others. For example, the scale of Zeithaml et al. (1996) is adopted in subsequent studies (e.g., Brady et al., 2012; Herhausen et al., 2019; Rahman et al., 2022; Srinivasan et al., 2002; Wolfinbarger & Gilly, 2003), and the scale of Palmatier et al. (2007) is taken up by Stock et al. (2017) and Rapp et al. (2013). In a few other cases, however, the authors develop their own operationalization of the constructs (e.g., Steenkamp, 2024; Maxham III et al., 2008).

5.10 Conclusions and future research directions

This review has several research objectives:

1. to identify the evolutionary trajectory of the loyalty literature and current trends;
2. to determine the most widely adopted theories, contexts, characteristics, and methodologies in loyalty research;
3. to identify prevailing loyalty categories and their measurement methods; and
4. to detect gaps in the literature and develop proposals to guide future research directions.

In response to these objectives, this SLR notes that the focus on loyalty over the years has broadened to encompass elements such as the customer experience (including the emotional dimension), the diverse nature of interactions across touchpoints, interpersonal relationships as well as those on the brand-customer axis, personalization, and strategic management of loyalty through CRM-based approaches. Moreover, big data and AI can help develop more accurate, complex models to predict retention more accurately. In sum, loyalty is a concept that spans wide boundaries. This is evidenced by the fact that multiple theories are being applied to research on loyalty, which has now gone global, including numerous studies set in the Americas, Europe, Asia, and Oceania. However, from our literature review, some gaps also become apparent that require future research to be filled. Below we describe the most relevant.

- From the study of theories applied to loyalty, some gaps emerge that may represent directions for future studies. For example, stakeholder theory, legitimacy theory, and agency theory could find application in analyzing how companies can manage their stakeholder relationships to strengthen customer loyalty, or how perceptions of corporate legitimacy impact customer loyalty in crisis contexts. There is also a dearth of theories related to innovation and competitiveness. This is a promising path for future research given the recent introduction of disruptive technological innovations. Theories on innovation and competitiveness can frame studies on the influence of dynamic pricing and technology adoption on loyalty. Finally, corporate governance theory and stewardship theory can offer perspectives on the internal management of organizations and how governance decisions influence loyalty.
- To fill the gaps that have become apparent from the analysis of the contexts relative to loyalty studies, future research could focus on expanding into the online retail sector by investigating the loyalty dynamics specific to this channel in greater depth. In addition, it is crucial to explore the distinctive loyalty dynamics in offline and online channels, as only a few studies have currently drawn this comparison. Further research is also needed in the B2B sphere, a context rarely investigated in loyalty studies, to better clarify how loyalty dynamics develop. Finally, cross-industry and cross-country studies are essential to obtain generalizable results and contribute to a more comprehensive and integrated understanding of loyalty.
- From the analysis of the characteristics of the studies we identified, there is a need for more research around the intersection of loyalty and new technologies. With the advancement of digital technologies, such as AI and big data, there is a growing need to investigate how these tools can be integrated into LPs to improve their effectiveness. For example, research could focus on how AI can help to personalize the customer experience, predict customer needs, and incentivize sustainable purchasing behaviors.

In addition, it seems relevant to define how elements such as sustainability and CSR are implemented in LPs. Potential research questions could aim to discover how to make sustainability central in LPs; such efforts can be traced back to how to incentivize consumers to purchase sustainable products by offering rewards or incentives.

- Analyzing the characteristics of measurements applied to loyalty, there is a need to identify effective measurements that can be applied to the field of sustainability/CSR and loyalty. Indeed, despite the increasing importance of sustainability and responsible business practices in corporate strategies, there are still significant limitations in measuring their effectiveness in terms of loyalty. Future research should move toward developing reliable, valid metrics that can capture the impact of sustainability initiatives on customer loyalty. These measurements could include both quantitative and qualitative indicators that can reflect the influence of sustainable practices on consumer perception and behavior.

  In addition, the literature can advance in the area of defining and measuring loyalty constructs, which is not a monolithic concept but is composed of several dimensions. Future research should focus on exploring multidimensional constructs to better understand how each dimension affects consumer behavior and business performance. This approach would help inform more targeted, effective loyalty strategies that consider the customer loyalty journey in its entirety.

  In particular, it appears that the literature does not monitor the different stages of loyalty with equal scrutiny, paying more attention to affective and behavioral loyalty and neglecting cognitive loyalty. This is a major issue, considering that the comparative evaluation of product characteristics is the first stage of customer loyalty formation. Therefore, future research could fill this gap through a more specific focus on cognitive measurements. In the scope of this paper, more insights on loyalty measurement will be provided in Chapter 6, along with a structured analysis of loyalty KPIs and LPs, as well as the processes underlying their development, from the perspective of retailers and manufacturer brands.

- By examining the methodologies applied in the studies in our review, we reveal a significant lack of qualitative studies that look at the processes underlying purchase decisions and loyalty. Although quantitative studies provide valuable data, there is a growing need to develop qualitative studies that explore the psychological and behavioral processes that drive customer preferences and purchase decisions. Such research could reveal cause-and-effect links between intangible aspects, such as emotions, personal values and perceptions, and loyalty, offering a deeper understanding of how to build and maintain customer loyalty over time. In addition, there is an absence of qualitative studies focused on analyzing the business processes that lead to the adoption of loyalty policies. This point is relevant when considering that such investigation could improve our knowledge of the relevant variables according to managers' mindsets, business priorities, and sense-making mechanisms that define modes and goals, as well as the underlying rationale for LPs.

• The focus on retail highlights several sector-specific gaps. From a theoretical perspective, sociological and cognitive theories, currently underutilized, could explore how social dynamics (social groups or cultural norms) and cognitive processes (risk perception or decision-making) influence consumer loyalty in retail, especially in emerging contexts such as omnichannel and e-commerce. Analyzing the contexts for the papers in our review, there is also a paucity of research focused on the luxury sector. In addition, many studies focus on developed markets, such as the United States and Europe, leaving a knowledge gap in emerging markets.

From the characteristics of the papers we analyzed, it appears that the drivers and moderators we reviewed so far do not extensively consider any dynamics arising in the online context, such as the role of reviews, social media, or virtual communities. In addition, the impact of emerging technologies, such as AI and augmented reality, on consumer loyalty is still understudied in retail. Finally, looking at methodologies, qualitative approaches are lacking. These would be useful to investigate, for example, new dimensions of consumer behavior in retail through in-depth interviews, digital ethnographies, or analysis of social media activities. Chapter 6 attempts to partially remedy this situation by focusing on how retailers and industries measure loyalty and define its underlying processes.

CHAPTER 6
RESEARCH ON MEASURING LOYALTY
[Lara Penco, Ginevra Testa]

6.1 Background: the empirical analysis within the overall research design

The exploratory phase of our work, conducted on opinion leaders in the retail sector (Chapter 3), highlighted the relevance of loyalty measurement in relation to the various themes we address. What unequivocally emerges is the importance of this topic from a managerial perspective. The idea is to improve business performance (McManus & Guilding, 2008) by integrating loyalty into marketing information systems and linking it to control systems via other marketing indicators. Indeed, according to Kumar & Shah (2004), loyalty programs (LPs) must be associated with profitability to avoid implementing inadequate or ineffective initiatives. For example, resorting to loyalty measures that are overly focused on the past may risk not properly considering the future potential of customers (Reinartz & Kumar, 2003). As the meta review in Chapter 4 revealed, there are still numerous gaps to be filled (Grace et al., 2018) regarding the conceptualization and measurement of loyalty. Indeed, loyalty is a multidimensional construct combining attitudes, intentions, and behaviors that can help companies outperform their competitors. As such, it is not always readily measured (Belli et al., 2022). Therefore, several different scales have been proposed in the literature which are mainly oriented toward measuring how loyal the customer turns out to be.

Thanks to the systematic literature review presented in Chapter 5, we now know the progress made up till now on measuring loyalty. The review showed that the key performance indicators (KPIs) used to measure the success of loyalty initiatives are numerous and heterogeneous. Metrics refer to customer value, purchase frequency, retention, penetration, and customer satisfaction (Cooil et al., 2007; Hult et al., 2019; Lewis, 2004; Narayandas, 1998). These indicators, which serve to clarify how effective LPs are in creating customer value, allow companies to assess how well their loyalty initiatives can maintain their customer base and increase the number of loyal customers. Therefore, based on these considerations, we need to explore which KPIs managers use to measure loyalty, and how such information enables them to design successful LPs, that is, programs that can achieve certain goals in the long run and generate certain business performance.

There are still few qualitative studies that take a supply side viewpoint. This would serve to describe loyalty initiatives and measurement practices, not based on ex-post evaluation but aimed at creating new research perspectives and managerial applications. In addition, our analysis of the literature brought to light the need to investigate new profiles of loyalty, such as loyalty in the physical world (store loyalty) and in the digital world (e-loyalty); the search for LP initiatives that respond to customers' greater sense of social and environmental responsibility; a stronger association with customer attitudes and behaviors; and the evolution and diffusion of digital technologies capable of gleaning reams of data and information about customers, salient sources for mapping out business directions to pursue.

The focus on the retail world, as highlighted in the previous chapters, stems from several conditions that make this industry particularly dynamic and competitive: low profit margins, great customer volatility, high product variety, as well as the influence of "mass" flyer promotions (i.e. designed for the entire customer base), and poor differentiation of value propositions. All these aspects elicit interest in exploring the issue of loyalty within this context. In addition, we must consider how, in retail, multidimensional indicators are not always utilized. Such parameters are suitable for assessing the different dimensions of loyalty (Belli et al., 2022), but they often remain too anchored in measuring the impact of individual campaigns (Jacoby & Kyner, 1973) and fail to be properly integrated into business strategies. As a result, their explanatory effectiveness in terms of value creation is very limited (Schmitt et al., 2011).

To broaden the research context, our study also integrated the perspective of retail brands/manufacturers to highlight any differences and similarities around customer loyalty. The industry perspective allows us to explore how manufacturers and retailers collaborate to build a synergistic loyalty experience across the value chain. Based on this concise premise highlighting the overall course of our research journey, Chapter 6 seeks to answer the following question: *How do retailers measure loyalty?*

This chapter is the product of the previous phases of our study, incorporating the need for research on measuring loyalty, which emerged from Chapter 3; the gaps in the literature in its conceptualization and measurement, highlighted by Chapter 4; and the different profiles of loyalty and the need for strategic insights into the construct, described in Chapter 5. The present chapter will outline the methodology we followed in conducting our empirical research, and then describe our main findings, elaborated in the aggregate, from the interviews we conducted with a group of managers from retail and manufacturing industries who are very active in the sphere of loyalty.

Finally, we delineate the main implications for management and marketing, identifying directions for future development, giving due consideration to the evolution of the competitive and macro-environmental framework dictated by new technologies, such as Artificial Intelligence (AI), and new consumer trends, such as rising demand for sustainability.

6.2 Methodology for the empirical research

To comprehend the different measurements of loyalty and their relevance in the context of business strategies, we applied a qualitative method through in-depth interviews, allowing us to collect numerous insights, data, goals, and beliefs from our informants. Thanks to qualitative research, we can achieve a holistic understanding of the phenomenon under investigation, considering the different forces at play to extract interesting intuitions (Corbin & Strauss, 2008). To gather practical evidence, qualitative methods of analysis can better address the need to find answers to complex questions (Finfgeld-Connett, 2014).

We collected data through an interview protocol which we created based on the literature that emerged in Chapters 4 and 5. The decision to adopt this methodology stemmed from:

1. the research scope, centering on loyalty and measuring this construct, versus business strategy;
2. the company type, specifically large retailers and manufacturers. These considerations oblige us to take different approaches that are difficult to integrate within the scope of quantitative research.

As regards this research scope, the case study methodology is consistent with answering research questions based on "how" and "why." Indeed, multiple case studies offer a detailed picture of a phenomenon (Eisenhardt, 1989; Eisenhardt & Graebner, 2007), adding the comparative dimension that strengthens the generalizability and rigor of results. Qualitative research is consonant when emphasis is placed on developing a conceptual framework and identifying critical factors and other key variables. Moreover, thanks to qualitative approaches based on prior scientific knowledge and processing and interpreting research data, we can build new theories (Patton, 2014).

Regarding company typology, only qualitative research conducted through in-depth interviews adequately evidences similarities and differences between the kinds of organizations that do business in different industries (i.e. retail and manufacturing). As the framework evolves, including in terms of servitization, increasingly customer-focused orientations are being adopted.

Therefore, the study aims to expand and elaborate on existing literature streams from field interviews. Considering that companies often tend to avoid disclosing strategic and organizational information on the topic of loyalty measurement, direct contact with practitioners in the field was crucial to an in-depth understanding of these profiles. The research was conducted according to the guidelines and suggestions provided by established literature for qualitative methodologies. The steps we took to define the research design are illustrated in Figure 6.1.

Figure 6.1   The research design

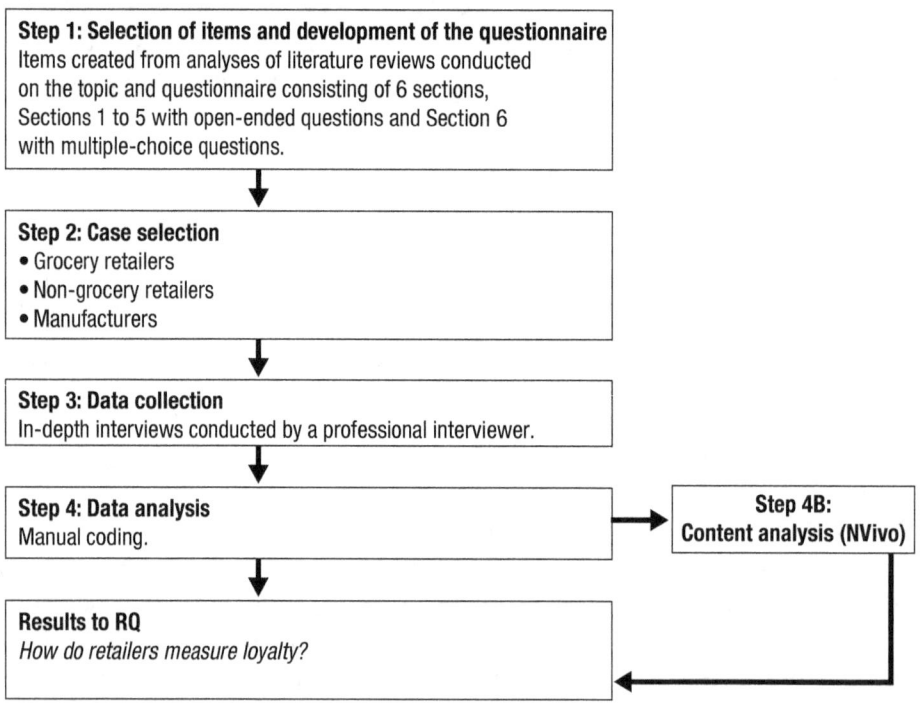

Source: authors' elaboration.

6.2.1 *Phase 1: Research design*

We selected the variables for our empirical research through an in-depth analysis of the literature review on the topic of loyalty and how it is measured. Specifically, to identify and systematize key elements, we were guided by the research question cited above: *How do retailers measure loyalty?* Therefore, the variables we identified focus on elements that prove crucial to effectively measuring LP outcomes and the different stages of the customer loyalty journey. For data collection, we mainly used a semi-structured questionnaire consisting of six sections that we developed based on the preliminary stage of the research and the literature reviewed in Chapter 4.

The structure of the questionnaire includes open-ended questions (Sections 1-5) and closed multiple-choice questions (Section 6, the survey). The former is intended to give respondents the chance to freely express their thoughts on adopting loyalty policies. The multiple-choice questions have a complementary role, namely, to collect "coded," easily comparable information.

Section 1, *"Measuring loyalty KPIs,"* is divided into questions designed to explore the indicators that companies adopt that are consonant with measuring loyalty (e.g., *1A. What KPIs do you use to measure loyalty?* and *1D. What technologies and tools do you use?*). In this section, we also explored how often these indicators are utilized, any processing that serves to simplify data interpretation, and segmentation practices.

Section 2 covers *"Structuring, implementing and measuring loyalty programs and promotions."* This stage identifies the different types of LPs implemented by the company (e.g., short collection, instant win, community programs, catalogs, etc.), specifying structure, reward content, reward delivery or frequency of LP promotions and what channels are used, and how long programs last. In this section, respondents are also asked to mention highly successful or unsuccessful loyalty initiatives to highlight best practices and mistakes made (e.g., *2C. In your history, what was the most successful loyalty initiative?* and *2D. In your history, what was the loyalty initiative that disappointed you the most?*).

Section 3 introduces the topic of *"Specific KPIs for store loyalty and online loyalty (e-loyalty)"* to determine whether organizations' conception of e-loyalty differed from loyalty in the physical store. We explore the concept of e-loyalty in behavioral terms, considering, for example, the intention to revisit the store, to make a purchase there, or to spread positive word-of-mouth. In particular, this section seeks to ascertain whether there are differences in terms of measuring the impact of loyalty initiatives between online and offline channels. In case differentiations are made, this section delves into the specific measurements that are adopted regarding e-loyalty (e.g., *3C. What specific measurements do you use to measure e-loyalty? Do you employ different methodologies for analyzing store loyalty or e-loyalty?*).

Section 4 focuses on *"Determinants and Expected Effects of Loyalty,"* in particular, underscoring the factors attributed to loyalty and the desired effects in terms of the goals of LPs (e.g., *4A. What are the main determinants (antecedents) of customer loyalty?* and *4B. What are the expected effects (outcomes, goals) of a successful loyalty program?*). Connected to this is Section 5, which looks at *"Future Developments,"* emphasizing upcoming goals, innovations, and how companies plan to measure these new developments in LPs (e.g., *5A. Are you working to implement new measurements beyond the ones you currently use?*).

As we anticipated, Section 6, *"KPIs and loyalty categories,"* was structured differently from previous sections as it contains closed-ended questions. A link was sent to informants to an online questionnaire, which they completed with the guidance of the interviewer. The aim here was to discover, based on the categories provided in the literature (cognitive, affective, conative, and behavioral dimensions of loyalty), whether at least one corresponding loyalty indicator is applied. For each category of loyalty, participants were how often they used it, starting from "Yes always and continuously," "Frequently," "Rarely, only on special occasions," "Never, but interesting to experiment with," to "Never used, does not apply."

In addition to this, responses were solicited on measurement in terms of business performance, and cognitive and affective drivers. The objective was to ascertain, through the questionnaire, whether respondents were monitoring the entire *customer loyalty journey*, covering all relevant aspects. Section 6, therefore, supports and complements the content that emerged from Question 1A, focusing on understanding whether and how different companies measure various loyalty categories using specific KPIs. For this reason and given the high logical consistency between Question 1A and the survey, the results will be presented after the open-ended responses on KPIs and frequency of loyalty measurements.

In compiling our questionnaire, we scrupulously structured it to collect meaningful data. To incorporate the perspective of brands/manufacturers too, we developed an additional questionnaire specifically for them. The latter was based on the model we already applied to retailers, keeping the structure and key questions essentially unchanged to ensure consistency, comparability, and integrability between the two perspectives. However, we added specific questions to reflect the peculiarities of the industry and the dynamics of the relationship between manufacturer and retailer, with the aim of better understanding the collaboration between the two parties and fostering the creation of a consistent and synergistic loyalty experience across the entire value chain. This provides an integrated view that can potentially help optimize loyalty initiatives at the market level.

From a methodological standpoint, we were careful to avoid bias that could influence participants' responses in the different sections of the questionnaire. Section 6, the last part of the survey, was critical, as the cognitive load accumulated by respondents toward the end of the questionnaire could increase the likelihood of biased responses. To mitigate this risk, we took several precautions, such as randomization of the order of questions and response options. This approach limited biases such as the distraction effect and the order effect, helping to improve the quality and reliability of the data we collected. The full semi-structured interview protocol is provided in Table A4.1 in Appendix 4.

6.2.2 *Step 2: Case Selection*

As anticipated, after validating our interview protocol with a small sample of industry experts and professionals, we collected data through semi-structured interviews with top managers of retail and manufacturing companies. The context of our study focused on businesses operating in these industries as they are particularly attentive to loyalty. As underscored in academic studies and well-established in the literature, a *purposive sampling method* (Campbell et al., 2020; Patton, 1990) is appropriate for in-depth investigation of a given phenomenon. Such sampling allowed us to select cases that were particularly salient to the topic at hand. For our purposes, this included specialists with extensive expertise in terms of loyalty and how it can be measured. Following this approach, we chose leaders from retail and manufacturing who could provide accurate insights into the performance of loyalty micro-practices.

Therefore, the study included a sample consisting of 36 executive managers at major retail groups and in large-scale organized distribution in the areas of marketing, sales, and loyalty management. Previous studies have suggested that this is a sufficient number, given that the value of qualitative samples depends on the ability of respondents to provide relevant information, as experts and representatives of broader contexts, e.g., economic sectors (Patton, 2014).

The retail cases we selected constituted a representative sample in terms of market share for Italy. Specifically, we chose the companies involved in the first phase of the research (see Chapter 3), and then added other individuals, representatives of retail companies and brands/manufacturers, who were interested in the research topic but, for organizational reasons, had not been able to participate in the first phase of our work. Informants were recruited by identifying particularly focused and loyalty management-oriented positions within the corporate structure (e.g., marketing director, loyalty manager, membership manager, etc.).

Manufacturing cases were selected not because they constitute a representative sample in statistical terms, but because they can provide meaningful insights into loyalty issues with a view to comparison with retailers.

6.2.3 *Step 3: Data collection*

Overall, semi-structured interviews were conducted involving 36 informants, 25 operating in retail (divided into grocery and non-grocery) and 11 in manufacturing. To maintain anonymity, participants' data were blacked out, and each one was given a numerical code. Table 6.1 provides a description of the target industry and corporate position of the informants interviewed in the process.

In the data collection phase, telephone or e-mail contact was made with the target companies, and a follow-up appointment was arranged. Semi-structured interviews were held online between July 2024 and September 2024 using the Microsoft Teams platform. Each session, lasting approximately 45 minutes on average, was conducted by an experienced interviewer to eliminate subjectivity issues that might have biased the research team members, following the previously defined protocol.

Interviewees were informed about the purpose of the research and assured that ethical considerations would be respected, and personal details would not be discussed (Priporas et al., 2017). Before the session began, each respondent was told that participation would be voluntary and that the purpose of the research was to learn only about his or her views on the topic of loyalty and how it is measured. The resulting data would be reported anonymously, aggregated, and used only for statistical purposes, as explained to participants.

The interviewer encouraged managers to respond freely, and no replies were coerced. To avoid confining respondents to a set of predetermined answers, we introduced general, open-ended questions to encourage them to reflect on the various topics and share more information. For each section, general questions were followed by more specific questions to hone the discussion in on the relevant areas of the study.

The interviews, with the informant's permission, were recorded and then transcribed verbatim. When necessary, a follow-up was done with the company via online meetings, e-mail, or telephone to track down colleagues from specific departments to flesh out some of the responses, which were not always provided

Table 6.1   **Case descriptions**

Informant number	Informant's role	Company Type	Classification
Informant 1	Head of Operational Marketing, Loyalty and Innovation	Retailer	Grocery
Informant 2	Marketing Director	Retailer	Grocery
Informant 3	Marketing Director	Retailer	Non-Grocery
Informant 4	Marketing Director	Retailer	Grocery
Informant 5	CRM and Loyalty Manager	Retailer	Grocery
Informant 6	Head of B2B and Strategic Partnership	Manufacturer	Manufacturer
Informant 7	Customer Engagement & Loyalty Manager	Manufacturer	Manufacturer
Informant 8	Go To Market Leader	Manufacturer	Manufacturer
Informant 9	Head of Omnichannel Marketing & Retail Media	Retailer	Non-Grocery
Informant 10	Marketing and Business Development Assistant	Manufacturer	Manufacturer
Informant 11	Marketing Director	Retailer	Grocery
Informant 12	CEO	Manufacturer	Manufacturer
Informant 13	Marketing Director	Retailer	Grocery
Informant 14	Communication and Marketing Manager	Retailer	Non-Grocery
Informant 15	Marketing Director Optical Retail Italy	Manufacturer	Manufacturer
Informant 16	Board of Directors	Retailer	Non-Grocery
Informant 17	Head of Digital & Marketing Services	Manufacturer	Manufacturer
Informant 18	Head of Marketing and Sales	Retailer	Non-Grocery
Informant 19	Director	Retailer	Grocery
Informant 20	Head of Marketing	Retailer	Grocery
Informant 21	Retail Manager	Manufacturer	Manufacturer
Informant 22	Head Of Corporate Sales	Manufacturer	Manufacturer
Informant 23	Sales Manager	Retailer	Non-Grocery
Informant 24	CEO South Europe	Retailer	Non-Grocery
Informant 25	Super Sales Manager	Retailer	Grocery
Informant 26	Head of Loyalty	Retailer	Non-Grocery
Informant 27	Senior Advisory Consultant	Manufacturer	Manufacturer
Informant 28	Loyalty Manager	Retailer	Non-Grocery
Informant 29	Communication and Marketing Manager	Retailer	Grocery
Informant 30	CRM & Loyalty Manager	Retailer	Grocery
Informant 31	Head of CRM & Loyalty	Retailer	Non-Grocery
Informant 32	Commercial Director	Manufacturer	Manufacturer
Informant 33	Digital, Marketing CB, Big Data & AI Director	Retailer	Non-Grocery
Informant 34	Marketing & Loyalty director	Retailer	Grocery
Informant 35	Marketing Director	Retailer	Grocery
Informant 36	Director Co-Brand, Partnerships, CRM, Membership Rewards	Retailer	Non-Grocery

in full by a single informant. Once data saturation was reached, that is, when additional information no longer furthered our understanding of the phenomenon, we considered the process complete (Corbin & Strauss, 2008).

6.2.4 *Step 4: Data Analysis*

We then conducted textual analysis, with the complete transcripts of the open-ended questions in the interviews (Section 1-5) as our main data source. From this wealth of material, we pulled out the most interesting verbatim and tallied absolute and relative frequencies with respect to each question on the main topics.

The first items in each section of the interview protocol were the most illustrative questions. On these, we ran a content analysis, which is a flexible tool that can shift from collecting impressions to systematically analyzing textual data (Hsieh & Shannon, 2005). These qualitative methods are useful for systematizing, integrating, interpreting, and rigorously synthesizing results (Finfgeld-Connett, 2014). The choice to conduct content analysis stems from the desire to analyze a rich, voluminous body of unstructured textual data that would otherwise be difficult to read, visualize, and interpret (Seuring & Gold, 2012).

More specifically, considering the multiplicity of questions submitted to the informants, we decided to adopt an inductive approach, starting by studying the data we collected, making inferences on the evidence we found, and organizing the recurring themes into codes. In this process, a crucial step is reading the transcripts and reflecting on the results to establish the codes (Elo & Kyngäs, 2008). Once the data are processed into different codes, they can be grouped together to form a set of broader categories. Reflective approaches involve subsequently generating themes created by the codes (Braun & Clarke, 2019). Therefore, researchers must analyze and interpret the data, a highly time-consuming activity, considering the need to scrutinize the individual sentences reported in the transcript, at times repeatedly, to gain a fuller comprehension of the underlying meaning. The reflexive approach, which we applied to our analysis, usually follows several stages, such as familiarization, coding, initial theme generation, theme revision and development, theme refinement, and writing (Braun & Clarke, 2021). These steps are repeated until the coding of all extracted data is complete to achieve a manageable synthesis of the results.

For our study, we did the coding manually to generate richer categories and themes, which are difficult to track with automated coding. Multiple researchers compared codes, categories, and themes that emerged with the aim of curtailing subjectivity resulting from data interpretation. In doing so, we minimized any cognitive bias. To facilitate the process of aggregating and organizing the codes, categories, and themes, NVivo 14 software was utilized, which allows for great flexibility in categorizing the results, and produces highly readable, impactful graphical displays that bring out the main trends in the coded data (Bazeley & Jackson, 2013). Considering the numerosity and complexity that emerged from the first question in each section, this methodology was adopted for those items. As for the subsequent questions, more specific and detailed manual coding was done using Excel.

6.3 Measuring loyalty

6.3.1 *KPIs for measuring loyalty*

The first section of the interview protocol was guided by a foundational re-search question (Question 1A), namely, *What KPIs do you use to measure loy-alty?* Verbatim analysis is utilized to discern the orientation of the informants. The results were convergent for the retailers overall, although there were some appreciable differences in the scope of the survey between grocery and non-gro-cery retailers. Among them, we found discrepancies between cooperatives and non-cooperatives.

Companies tend to identify two types of loyalty activities: short-term and long-term (Informant 5). Short-term loyalty is related to competitive activities, short collections, and spend-and-get promotions, initiatives that are developed primarily to boost frequency and engagement. Long-term loyalty, on the other hand, is based on the study of the consumer, aimed at identifying *Customer Lifetime Value* (CLV) and the creation of a *Unique Customer View* (UCV), i.e., a complete, unified profile of a customer based on integrating different kinds of data into a single record. Informant 34, as far as the significance of loyalty for his company, stated that *"loyalty is marketing, it's our business,"* expressing a strongly strategic, long-term perspective. Along the same lines, with reference to measurement, is Informant 2's statement, *"What you don't realize is that by now, monitoring the promo plan and shelf prices allows you to track just one piece of the marketing strategy, but it directly targets the company's loyal customers."*

This premise highlights the fact that loyalty has strategic value and, therefore, measurements should be increasingly geared toward this purpose. However, re-tail grocery companies continue to be very oriented toward monitoring classic transactional, economic KPIs, such as incremental sales generated by LP ac-tivities, to define the profitability of the initiative in terms of incremental ROI.

This is a short-term measurement, which directly relates to the relative investment. The antecedents of measuring investment profitability are related to economic/behavioral factors (i.e., incremental net sales, average receipt, the average amount spent, private label penetration), and pure behavioral factors, (such as redemption, the number of participating customers (including new members), rewards collected, and frequency of in-store visits). In terms of tools, short collections tend to engage the already loyal average consumer, augmenting *share-of-wallet* (Informant 2).

It is crucial, through tools like loyalty cards and descriptive, behavioral customer profiling, to identify clusters and monitor long-term loyalty (Informant 5). Resulting information allows the company to estimate the CLV by cross-referencing data. The careful study of the customer proves to be the prerequisite for creating a customer-centric orientation, i.e., a business strategy that places the customer at the center of all company decisions and activities. As we all know, in the process of shifting to *customer centricity*, creating solid, lasting relationships with customers (loyalty) turns out to be one of the foundational pillars, underpinned by the activation of positive affective and cognitive mechanisms in the customer.

For cooperative-based enterprises, *"all this analysis is done on members because they are the ones we have all the information on"* (Informant 1). In addition, membership card data allows us to identify the most attractive customer clusters, as there are customers who, although they represent only 30% of the population *"make up 80-85% of the sales"* (Informant 2). What becomes a useful KPI, then, is the migration process *"that exists between low-spending and high-spending clusters."* For retailers, especially for stores with a wide assortment, even of non-grocery products, monitoring *"cross-category purchases"* is strategic. In this sense, the segmentation related to the clusters labeled *"Super Premium, Premium, Shared, Polygamous, Opportunists and Infidels"* (Informant 29, 30) identifies loyal customers, not only the high spenders but the ones who get all their needs fulfilled at the same store (food and non-food). Equally, branded products prove to be relevant for understanding customer loyalty.

Behavioral segmentation is facilitated using new technologies that replace the physical card with an app. *"Through the app, customer behavior is not only monitored in real-time, but [customers are] also prompted in real time to change their behaviors: reminders are sent, callbacks are made, and challenges are launched to accumulate additional points, for example, on fresh and 'everyday low price' items"* (Informant 11). To capture more long-term loyalty, some companies are trying to consider customer behaviors in a predictive way to prevent customer abandonment: *"meanwhile, we've been developing, for two and a half, almost three years, even a predictive algorithm that works on anti-churn"* (Informants 29, 30).

The loyalty trend is happening in large-scale retail grocery, and organized distribution is a strategic lever in this context. To varying degrees, among different players, this is the case for discounters, which have always followed the principle that *"promotions are good for everyone, first-timers or repeat customers"* (Informant 13). Yet, in the face of more intense competition, discounters are also realizing that loyal customers are more profitable than non-loyal ones. In fact, despite being "the new kids on the block," so to speak, discounters have implemented more innovative, digital, and *customer-centricity*-oriented loyalty policies and tools.

The pharmaceutical cluster, for example, measures the construct in question based on loyalty card data, referring to card transactions and rewards spending. The difficulty at the cluster level in monitoring loyalty stems from the fact that spending on non-grocery drugs cannot be accounted for, nor can data from a person's national health card. In addition, retail partners in the network often adopt different information and management systems.

For non-grocery retail, customer loyalty becomes a strategic objective, not just a measurement. It is assessed, in addition to ROI and CLV, also in terms of *"frequency of interaction with the brand,"* which *"includes all the moments when a user – consumer or not – so a resident or a consumer, interacts with my brand"* (Informant 26). Here, we must remember that for "investment" goods (white and brown electronics, IT, furniture, etc.), purchase frequency is often very limited. We clearly see that players are increasingly considering the relevance of evaluating customer behavior, as well as the affective and emotional components concerning the brand.

Looking at these indications through a more synthetic lens, by implementing the content analysis with NVivo 14 software and taking up the four dimensions of loyalty mentioned in Chapters 4 and 5 (cognitive, affective, conative, and behavioral loyalty), it appears that informants mainly detect behavioral, transactional, and initiative participation-related KPIs and affective KPIs. The first three are broken down further by considering both a short-term perspective related to individual initiatives and a long-term perspective. The managerial evidence we collected shows no indicators related to conative loyalty, such as purchase intentions, or cognitive loyalty, such as perceived costs and benefits. Figure 6.2 shows the KPIs most frequently found in the sample for measuring loyalty, the bigger the rectangle, the more common the indicator.

Figure 6.2 shows that the indicators mainly mentioned by informants fall in the category of transactional KPIs related to a specific initiative, e.g., average receipt, incremental sales, and purchase frequency. In the second category ranked by frequency there are KPIs related to participation in the initiative, e.g., the

Figure 6.2   KPIs used to measure loyalty

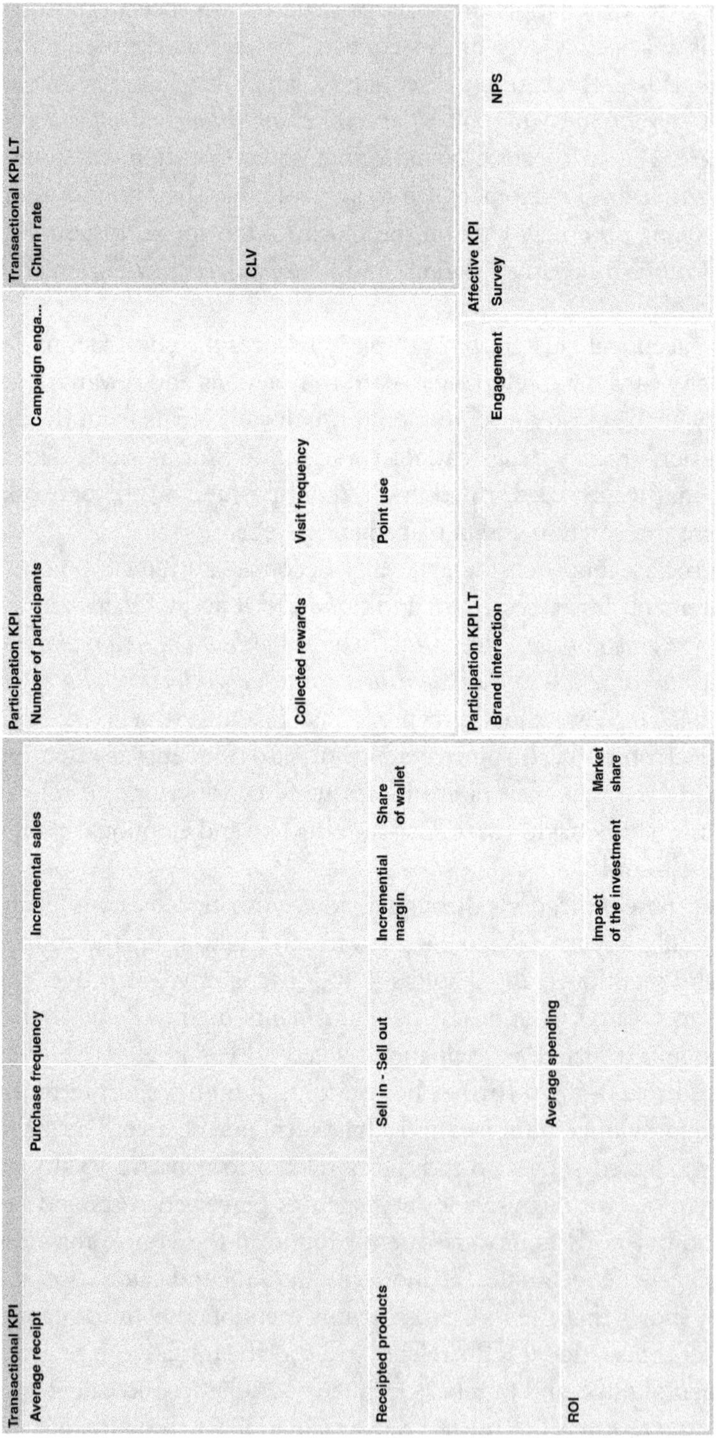

Transactional KPI				Participation KPI				Transactional KPI LT	
Average receipt	Purchase frequency	Incremental sales		Number of participants		Campaign enga...		Churn rate	
		Sell in - Sell out	Incremential margin	Share of wallet	Collected rewards	Visit frequency			CLV
Receipted products						Point use			
	Average spending	Impact of the investment	Market share	Participation KPI LT				Affective KPI	
				Brand interaction		Engagement		Survey	NPS
ROI									

Source: Data processing by NVivo 14.

number of people who take part, the number and attractiveness of prizes, and customer engagement in the campaign. KPIs measuring long-term transactions and participation appear to be utilized less often by informants than the two respective short-term indicators mentioned previously. Similarly, affective KPIs where evaluations are found regarding Net Promoter Score (NPS) appear to be residual, as do surveys focused on measuring the level of consumer satisfaction.

6.3.2 *Frequency in measuring loyalty*

Data management systems (Question 1B) are updated almost in real-time (see Informant 26, for example, *"our dashboard, which was created with all the loyalty indicators, updates daily."*). What's more, data can be extracted quite frequently, even on demand. Players choose to monitor data (mainly referring to sales and redemptions) either daily (Informant 7), weekly (Informants 4, 13, 15, 21, 29, & 30), or monthly (Informants 3, 32, & 36). Notably, annual monitoring is the prevalent measurement frequency among brands/manufacturers (Informant 6) in the B2B context. Even so, to evaluate the effectiveness of any investment in loyalty, companies can also take measurements *"when each initiative is deployed"* (Informant 17). Therefore, through manual coding, we can see convergence at the level of measurement frequency, with data and dashboards updating very quickly: daily for 23.53% of respondents and weekly for 20.59% (Table 6.3; Table A4.2 in Appendix 4).

Timely updating of data allows for effective tracking of the progress of initiatives, enabling quick interventions when necessary. In the medium term, however, monitoring and reporting are done for the rest of the organization. Verification takes place monthly for 44.12% of respondents, between periods (i.e., before and after an initiative) for 20.59%, and weekly for 14.71%. Once the trend is verified and transmitted to the rest of the organization, corrective actions are implemented. Some indicators also need to be evaluated according to their seasonality, as far as product category, or by events, such as Black Friday.

Table 6.2   **Frequency of measurement of loyalty KPIs**

Frequency	Absolute frequency	Relative frequency
Monthly check	15	44.12%
Daily update	8	23.53%
Weekly update	7	20.59%
Comparison between two periods	7	20.59%
Weekly check	5	14.71%

6.3.3 *KPIs and loyalty categories*

To complement the qualitative approach of the open-ended questions on KPIs and how they are measured, the interview included a survey. By analyzing and comparing structured quantitative data, it was possible to obtain more detailed information on measuring loyalty categories, such as identifying the most frequently measured categories based on the relevant KPIs for each one (Table A4.3 in Appendix 4). The results show that overall, the loyalty KPIs most often used are those pertaining to business performance by sales (all informants say they use transactional data with a high frequency; 97% say they always, continuously measure it) and profitability (90.9%; 75.8% always, continuously). The most frequently measured categories of loyalty include behavioral loyalty as far as spending (93.9% say they measure this very frequently), purchase quantity (87.9%), and purchase/visit frequency (87.9%).

The last category of loyalty we measured concerns cognitive drivers, referring to the customer's perceived economic costs. Only 15.2% of informants use KPIs attributable to this loyalty category with high frequency. In addition, a gap emerges in assessing the affective drivers of loyalty. Specifically, 51.5% of participants do not measure the perceived psychological benefits of LPs, or they do so only rarely or on special occasions (30.3%), while about 79% of informants say they do not use KPIs to detect perceived fairness or frustration resulting from LP participation (or do so only rarely).

Moreover, when analyzing the retail grocery, retail non-grocery, and manufacturing industries separately, no significant differences in the measurement frequency of the different loyalty categories emerge. This means that, regardless of the context of reference, the companies in our sample tend to assess the same loyalty categories very frequently and continuously, while neglecting to monitor the others or doing so rarely or only on special occasions in a non-continuous manner over time.

Even though there is substantial alignment in the measurement practices for loyalty categories, we can still see cross-sectoral differences in some of them. For example, perceived economic benefits (cognitive drivers) are measured regularly by 71.4% of non-grocery operators, compared to only 25% of grocery retailers. The same is true for perceived psychological benefits (affective drivers), regularly utilized by 35% of manufacturers but never mentioned by the grocery retailers in our sample. The retail industry (grocery and non-grocery) uses KPIs attributable to affective drivers more frequently than manufacturers to measure perceived status, equity, and frustration resulting from LP participation. One possible explanation for this finding may lie in the more complex structures

(tiers) of LPs in the retail sector. In general, it is important to specify that the non-application of certain loyalty KPIs could sometimes be attributable to the specific nature of LPs, which makes certain indicators more suitable than others.

6.3.4 *Loyalty information sources*

What emerged from Question 1C is that the loyalty card is still the primary source of data. But thanks to digitization, there is a tendency to use additional supplementary sources to create broader data warehouses that cross-reference information about the customer from different sources (surveys, panels, demographic profiling, data from the Italian National Institute of Statistics, etc.). The aim here is to study the customer more closely from various perspectives. Informants stated that they implement surveys with varying periodicity and, in some cases, quite frequently. Informant 2 described how transactional NPS is measured immediately after the purchase experience; perceptions of convenience and evaluation of company policies about every two months. In addition, this individual's company surveys a panel of customers annually. The goal of these assessments is to create an information base to support *customer centricity*.

Management and CRM systems become both sources and collectors of data. Informant 7 said his company has invested in an integrated system as a strategic priority to *"bring together all the feedback that comes in from surveys, customer satisfaction, reports on customer care, all the online sentiment part that goes from social media to Google, to Google My Business tabs."* The need is to integrate economic data with sentiments about the individual store, the individual item, and the entire digital and customer care world. With the implementation of Salesforce, Informants 29 and 30 said they are creating UCV. To enrich customer knowledge, some companies are turning to outside consultants to obtain and analyze data (Informants 6, 3, & 13). Data protection appears to be very high, even though companies make use of external sources and support systems. For example, the surveys that some companies run allow them to collect shopper trends *"which give us customer clusters based on their loyalty, the number of times they make a purchase, and the average receipt value"* (Informant 13).

Summarizing the insights gathered at the level of data sources tapped to measure loyalty, Table 6.3 shows loyalty cards, whether physical or digital, ranked 41.18%. This is followed by data from surveys and CRM systems, 20.59% and 17.65%, respectively. Next comes check out information regarding the average receipt (14.71%) and input on app usage (11.76%). To a small extent, information about sentiment, customer feedback, and customer satisfaction are mentioned among the data sources (Table 6.3; Table A4.4 in Appendix 4).

Table 6.3 **Main data sources used for the collection of loyalty KPIs**

Data sources	Absolute frequency	Relative frequency
Loyalty card	14	41.18%
Survey	7	20.59%
CRM	6	17.65%
Average receipt	5	14.71%
App	4	11.76%

Surveys include market research conducted to reveal *shopper trends* which are helpful for discovering what's new with consumers. Data sources go hand in hand with privacy concerns, as there is a need to ensure that consumers have adequate protection for the data and information they share. The various sources mentioned above show a shift from the use of primarily transactional data to more qualitative feedback related to the interactions between organizations and customers, which allows multiple pieces of information to be cross-referenced across the consumer lifecycle.

6.3.5 *The tools and technologies for measuring loyalty*

The question referring to the technologies and tools utilized by participants shows different case histories, but all reveal the same need (Question 1D). Companies invest in standard management tools, such as SAP and SIAC (Informant 1), to implement technological infrastructures that integrate different data (Informant 2). What emerges unequivocally is that there is not always a dedicated technology system for loyalty. However, Business Intelligence dashboards (Informants 4, 29, & 30) and data warehouse systems (Informant 9) are queried from time to time. This exposes a gap, namely the need for the tech consulting world to offer solutions that enable the creation of CLV and UCV, which are seen as strategic elements in the generation of a "customer contribution margin."

Regarding the technologies and tools used for measurement, our sample shows great heterogeneity (Table A4.5 in Appendix 4). The platforms mentioned by respondents include, for example, Salesforce, MicroStrategy, and Google My Business, in addition to those listed above. Some informants show interest and commitment to achieving greater centralization of data and tools, while others prefer the combination of multiple types of software, both internal and external to the organization. Excel continues to be very popular. Data are often entered into dashboards to synthesize the large volume of information that serves to guide strategic business decisions. Participants show a growing interest in conducting increasingly automated analyses, using SQL queries and direct queries to extract valuable information from the large pool of available data.

As for Business Intelligence tools mentioned by informants as useful for developing interactive dashboards and enabling real-time decisions, Power BI is cited (Informant 20), while the implementation of algorithms and Generative AI is still underdeveloped. The combination of different tools allows for greater monitoring of the many variables that can come into play in today's competitive market, aiding in predictive analysis.

6.3.6 *How loyalty variables are processed*

Questions 1E and 1F are geared toward figuring out whether "crossover" processing is carried out among the variables and if so, how (i.e., the main methodologies). Respondents say that they cross-reference variables to conduct behavioral analyses on each customer profile, with long-term effects. Cross-referencing variables in different management systems and data warehouses serve to "*interpret these data to understand what behaviors are related to their profile*" (Informant 1). An example of this approach is analyzing the effectiveness of a loyalty campaign in stimulating "low frequenters" to augment store visits with an eye to boosting expected sales. To cross-reference different data, as we saw earlier, "*you try to bring together all this information and the strategies of these activities that converge on loyalty*" (Informant 2) through calculations based on cross-tabulation, for example (Informant 5). The unifying element is CRM, which makes it possible to evaluate engagement activities and prepare correctives to improve loyalty initiatives.

Retail companies, having a territorial dimension, try to explore the effectiveness of loyalty campaigns by cross-referencing data on customers in the territory and querying management systems and data warehouses for in-depth analytical needs (Informants 4 & 34). The data, which often also come from databases and different sources, are numerous to say the least, especially for retail grocery companies. Consequently, the "query" logic can be traced back to established models in consumer behavior analysis, such as RFM (which aims to very clearly identify the high/low spenders, high/low frequenters, and "others"), CLV, and the Churn Model: "*These three models then give us the indices that we need to go and manage [the business] and be able to derive from these mega data clusters, obviously which we then go and reflect on*" (Informant 26). New data processing methodologies may need to be adopted, as rudimentary systems are still sometimes used. More innovative, sophisticated systems could be explored, for example utilizing regression analysis and structural equation models that are not always applied. Geomarketing data processing is being activated (Informant 27 & 28).

To monitor sales growth, the companies we surveyed use time series methods and control groups, without much variance for the different categories of businesses (question 1G). What would be interesting to ascertain are the effects. In other words, not only what emerges from a before-and-after comparison, or between customers who took advantage of the promotion or the ones who didn't, but also through follow-up analysis: "*What does this kind of activity leave behind? What's left in terms of behavior in a medium- to long-term perspective?*" (Informant 1). For respondents, control groups are generally set up *ex-ante*, when they roll out CRM and direct marketing initiatives (Informants 12, 29, & 30), deliberately excluding a portion of customers and instead counting the ROI of those who accept the invitation to participate. In contrast, for mass initiatives, control groups are defined *ex-post* (Informant 4): "*one-to-many activities, you communicate them to everyone and so it's hard to set up control groups. You should take stores where you don't do these activities, but it is quite difficult to isolate stores as control groups*" (Informant 11). Among the comparison variables are frequency of purchase, receipt value, and average expenditure, which is gauged with the question: "*the delta I was able to generate through this type of activity*" (Informant 7).

In an attempt to summarize all this, the various methods described above to process data are aimed at gaining greater control and awareness of what's happening in order to course-correct when need be. Among our informants, there is still little emphasis on regression or predictive analyses. Regressions, for example, are implemented to evaluate the effectiveness of a communication campaign by identifying the channels that achieved the best results. At the same time, predictive models are mainly applied to weigh the likelihood that certain customer segments may be on the verge of leaving the company; this serves to implement strategies designed to retain them.

The most common method of data processing (Table A4.6 in Appendix 4), about 20.59% of the total, is customer profile analysis. Specifically, comparisons are drawn between high- and low-spending customers and high- or low-frequenters to target LPs to meet their needs. In addition to consumer profiles, customer trends over time are also evaluated (new, growing segments, or declining segments) to understand how customers move overall. Comparisons with variables are made to verify campaign performance (8.82%), for example, by assessing the products that favored certain promotions, the number of promoted products, and the use of branded products (5.88% respectively). However, to obtain interesting data from a strategic point of view, it is crucial to carry out appropriate processing; this can be done by constructing synthetic indices, for example.

Table 6.4   **Most widely used methodologies to measure the increase in sales compared to a given loyalty campaign**

Methodologies	Absolute frequency	Relative frequency
Comparison between control groups	16	47.06%
Time comparison	12	35.29%
Segmentation	5	14.71%
Comparison of product sales	3	8.82%
Comparison of initiatives	2	5.88%

Overall, as far as methodologies are concerned (Table 6.4; Table A4.7 in Appendix 4), the control group comparison appears to be the one most often implemented (47.06%). The objective of this methodology is to highlight the variation between the target group and the control group (that was not invited to participate) to verify the effectiveness of the activity in question. For example, respondents mentioned control groups involving engaged and unengaged consumers.

Results can also be compared by initiative (5.88%) and by product (8.82%), rather than over time (35.29%). For example, temporal comparisons include time series or analysis based on seasonality. Having a benchmark derived from the previous initiative is very useful to monitor the performance of the current promotion.

6.3.7 *Loyalty and segmentation*

Of particular interest is understanding the relationship between loyalty and segmentation practices (Question 1H). First, both retailers (grocery and non-grocery) and manufacturers are increasingly oriented toward segmentation methods that are not strictly descriptive but behavioral as well. These relate to the benefits the company wants to pursue and are based on exploring affective and cognitive aspects. This very strong orientation, which we often found, is facilitated by CRM, the multiplicity/variety of data and sources, as well as the growing sophisticated of digital data warehouse systems. In this sense, the most widely applied segmentation, also as a basis for CRM activities, is RFM (Informants 5 & 34).

For cooperatives, cluster analysis-based criteria are evaluated referencing RFM buying behavior and spending amount and frequency (Informant 2: platinum, gold, silver, no spenders, occasional, frequent, habitual). Other variables are added as well, namely the regularity of purchases and the weight of fresh food or other specific departments, that can justify the assumption that the customer feels affection toward the store and the retail brand (Informant 5). For some cooperatives, there also needs to be a return to *"segmentation by age: we should work on that more because we have a problem with the age of our members; we need to lower it"* (Informant 17). Efforts and investments "to do more" are sizeable, but so are the difficulties encountered in implementing more refined segmentation systems aimed at creating true customer centricity (Informant 1: *"We also have to be grounded...in our story, we might look like an advanced structure from the point of view of business intelligence and CRM; actually we're trying to build our model, a concept of analysis"*).

So the goal of retailers should be to move beyond the typical concepts of "raw" segmentation to develop more refined criteria, culminating in the definition of *buyer personas*, i.e., representations of customer profiles based not only on descriptive but also behavioral variables, along with psychographic analyses related to values, personality, motivations, and trust. The purpose here is to create increasingly personalized offerings that affect long-term relationships. By compiling personas, companies can formulate a differentiated UCV per individual customer. This appears to be a strategic goal, paving the way to the customer centricity that becomes the cornerstone of long-term value creation. Data mining techniques using loyalty cards, cross-referenced with other variables, make it possible to identify segments and profiles of buyer personas based on consumption, interests, and passions. Starting from these, big grocery retailers design targeted campaigns, for example, for pet lovers, or for personas strongly linked to specific lifestyles, such as those related to healthy food.

This approach to detailed segmentation and the creation of personas is also applied in the non-grocery industry, where buyer personas are defined by customers' interests in certain themes and passions (e.g., books). The endpoint, as far as segmentation techniques/criteria, is to arrive at *"marginality segmentation per customer"* (Informants 29 & 30), making it possible to combine an economic and a long-term perspective. However, respondents pointed out the difficulties in intersecting data to show the return on CRM investments per customer. Our findings seem to show that this is only being done in one company at this point. Measured up against all the techniques that see buying behavior, and therefore sales, from the customer's point of view, this segmentation criterion based on buyer personas is *"the one that comes out a little bit more from the classic routine patterns and really gives us another level of depth and understanding of investments"* (Informants 29 & 30).

Even for non-grocery retailers, the RFM criterion is the basis for segmentation (Informants 7, 9, & 14). However, in this case, given the complexity of certain purchases of durable goods, segmentation is also done on the *consumer journey* and the level of interaction with different touchpoints (Informant 7). Loyalty campaigns are developed by monitoring loyalty-card-holding customers and analyzed in terms of activity, frequency, and purchases concerning the brands/products sold (Informant 14). These campaigns are predominantly promotional, although new strategies are being adopted, such as creating a need through a service (e.g., providing recipes) and then delivering the relative communication. In addition, the companies in our sample carry out predictive segmentation, not based on existing customers, but rather on external sources (such as zip codes, Italian National Statistics Institute data, etc.) to identify potential customer segments to target, for example, at new openings (Informant 9). In the non-grocery world, some companies do segmentation based on "benefits pursued," tracking previous purchases (Informant 15), but also pinpointing clusters of interactions based on spending thresholds and reactions to campaigns on specific products. For pharmaceutical retailers, the segmentation process is very firmly linked to loyalty cards and demographic/descriptive profiles.

Thanks to information systems, our informants also stated that they significantly improved the process of acquiring information about purchases in general and particular types of purchases specifically. This enables them to carry out campaigns *"on specific segments of users or consumers, people who purchased those categories most often,"* through direct marketing supported by text messages, newsletters, etc. (Informant 3).

Regarding segmentation, Table 6.5 (Table A4.8 in Appendix 4) shows that certain socio-demographic variables related to age, gender, geolocation, ethnicity, or household composition are crucial to achieving better segmentation (47.06%). In addition to the RFM model mentioned earlier, segmentations related to lifestyles and purchasing behavior can also be highlighted, according to 8.82% of our sample.

In light of our findings, segmentation should also be explored from a long-term perspective to highlight different buying needs. Moreover, proper segmen-

Table 6.5   **Main segmentation practices**

Segmentation	Absolute frequency	Relative frequency
Socio-demographic variables	16	47.06%
Product	7	20.59%
Frequency of purchase	6	17.65%
RFM	5	14.71%
Lifestyles	3	8.82%
Behavioral segmentation (purchasing behaviors)	3	8.82%

tation should lead to the definition of suitable buyer personas to convey initiatives and promotions that align with the interests of the target customers.

6.3.8 *Integrating and interpreting data*

With regard to how data are interpreted (Question 1I), informants make use of reporting "*by human intelligence*" (Informant 5). The role of human intelligence in querying systems and interpreting data is critical. Data extraction must be done to answer a strategic marketing question, and the resulting data must be leveraged to drive strategic marketing decisions (Informant 34). This is why information systems management is directed by marketing in terms of objectives and functionality and not by data scientists. Future challenges will arise as far as exploring the potential of AI in facilitating effective data integration and interpretation (Informant 35).

Queries are complex elements, as loyalty data tend to be highly integrated into certain business metrics to create UCV and CLV (Question 1J). This is true for all companies: "*Loyalty is at the heart of the company's strategy, so it's cross-referenced with all data. It impacts almost all business parameters*" (Informant 26); "*loyalty is marketing*" (Informant 34); "*loyalty is customer relationship intensity, [it's] multidimensional*" (Informant 35). Given the strategic nature of loyalty, outside agencies and data providers are sometimes hired, but this practice is limited, especially among large grocery and non-grocery retailers. Instead, systems integration regularly happens, combining loyalty data with internal management control data. Moreover, this process is increasingly marketing driven. The information inherent to loyalty is integrated with business metrics such as sales, margin, profit, turnover, and costs. The reason is precisely because loyalty, which lies at the heart of strategy and impacts several performance parameters and business departments, needs to be properly integrated and cross-referenced with all business data.

This aspect also emerges from the next item (Question 1K), referring to the structure of the analytics team, whether outsourced or in-house. Respondents say that they set up internal teams in the company, for the most part, creating "spot" and "on-demand" relationships with external vendors. As regards the loyalty focus, internal professionals with different backgrounds and competencies are involved, working together to integrate complementary skills.

Informant 1 says that the different internal competencies that "have to do with the customer" tend to be connected, i.e., "*the loyalty network with their special initiatives, the people who handle CRM and the digital side, the people in charge of CFM, the social activities, the e-commerce area, the app.*" For Informant

4, too, loyalty management is mainly managed by a multidimensional internal team, but they often resort to external support: *"when we need to evolve our models and techniques, we turn to external consulting to bring new methods in-house, and then we continue independently."* Informant 11 also states that there is a marketing intelligence team *"that takes care of the whole customer database, analytics, forecast models and also handles external market research, customer satisfaction, brand awareness, image, etc."* In-house teams are enriched with new skills and knowledge around loyalty data analytics; this upgrades levels of innovation and fosters continuous experimentation. Even manufacturers, given the strategic relevance of loyalty, tend to manage this issue internally (Informant 6). Most interviewees emphasize the development of in-house analytical skills, while external consulting firms are used in a residual and complementary way. Neuroscience/communication specialists, as well as data mining and collaboration with external parties, are seen as important aspects of establishing CLV and UCV. This is true in both grocery retail (Informant 11) and non-grocery retail (Informant 7). In conclusion, loyalty is dealt with directly by all players: external specialists are called on to tap into skills that are not available internally and/or to create learning effects.

6.4 Structuring, implementing, and measuring loyalty programs and promotions

6.4.1 *Implementing various LPs*

This section is geared toward understanding the different LPs, moving on to identify the salient success and failure factors and how they are measured. Beginning with identifying LPs (question 2A), multiple initiatives are launched by organizations simultaneously, e.g., short collections, point collection, cashback, contests, and others that are developed over different time periods. The companies interviewed in our sample tend to specify the time horizon of an LP as a discriminating variable. The scheduling of loyalty promotion activities typically takes place on an annual basis (Informant 1), as do infra-annual point collection activities (Informant 4). More continuous actions related to experiences (solidarity projects, cultural experiences, community participation) and short-term actions offering material rewards (short collections or very short-term initiatives) are also planned in this time frame (Informant 2). Very short-term actions like personalized couponing (Informant 33, 34) are profiled by consumption styles. Alternatively, point doubling is done in some stores that need the support, either because they are newly opened, restructured, or have turnover problems (Informant 11). The limitation here is that all these LPs are focused on turnover and pursue transactional KPIs.

To go beyond merely transactional projects, retail grocery brands also create point collection programs in which rewards are initiatives involving sports teams, community organizations, and school associations (Informants 1, 2, & 32). This extends the role of the customer, in collaboration with the retailer, contributing to society and collective welfare (Informants 1, 12, 5, & 17). From a long-term perspective, companies also seek to use loyalty campaigns to create churn redemption (Informant 4) through CRM activities and contests.

New technologies, in addition to enabling continuous customer tracking, serve to create personalized loyalty systems, including gamification and challenges (Informant 11). Apps are instrumental in stimulating additional customer promotions, typically through immediate rewards; specifically, promo apps follow the timing of flyers, which are short-term initiatives (Informant 13).

As for non-grocery retail, LPs are strongly oriented toward the long-term and customer-centricity. The beauty care segment, for instance, focuses on providing personal services (e.g., "*hairdressing, massage, hair removal,*" Informant 24) that are loyalty-enhancing by creating programs that foster "*emotional loyalty, based on interaction with the brand.*" A membership-based model, "*moving from transactional to emotional loyalty*", a long-term tactic, is based on a somewhat broader concept of brand interaction (Informant 26).

In TELCO services, where competition is very dynamic, continuous rewarding programs are created; these are not related to short collections but connected instead to cashback options. Several LPs provide benefits based on privileged weekly discounts for which "*the main KPI was engagement*" (Informant 33). But if engagement is based on economic benefits, it is easily imitated.

At the comprehensive level, Figure 6.3 shows that the most frequent initiatives are point collections with the possibility of discounts or physical, experiential, or even value-based rewards. Concerning point collection, innovations include the dynamic physical rewards catalog, whereby rewards can also be changed during the initiative. In addition to physical rewards and experiential rewards, value rewards have been added lately as well. These can respond to new consumer preferences, from the point of view of sustainability, but also in terms of support and advocacy to their community. Beyond point collection, which has a long-term horizon (usually annual) short collections are also very popular, (which logically run on a short-term horizon).

Memberships allow consumers to enjoy several exclusive benefits that augment their interaction and engagement with the organization. However, mem-

Figure 6.3   **Most common loyalty programs**

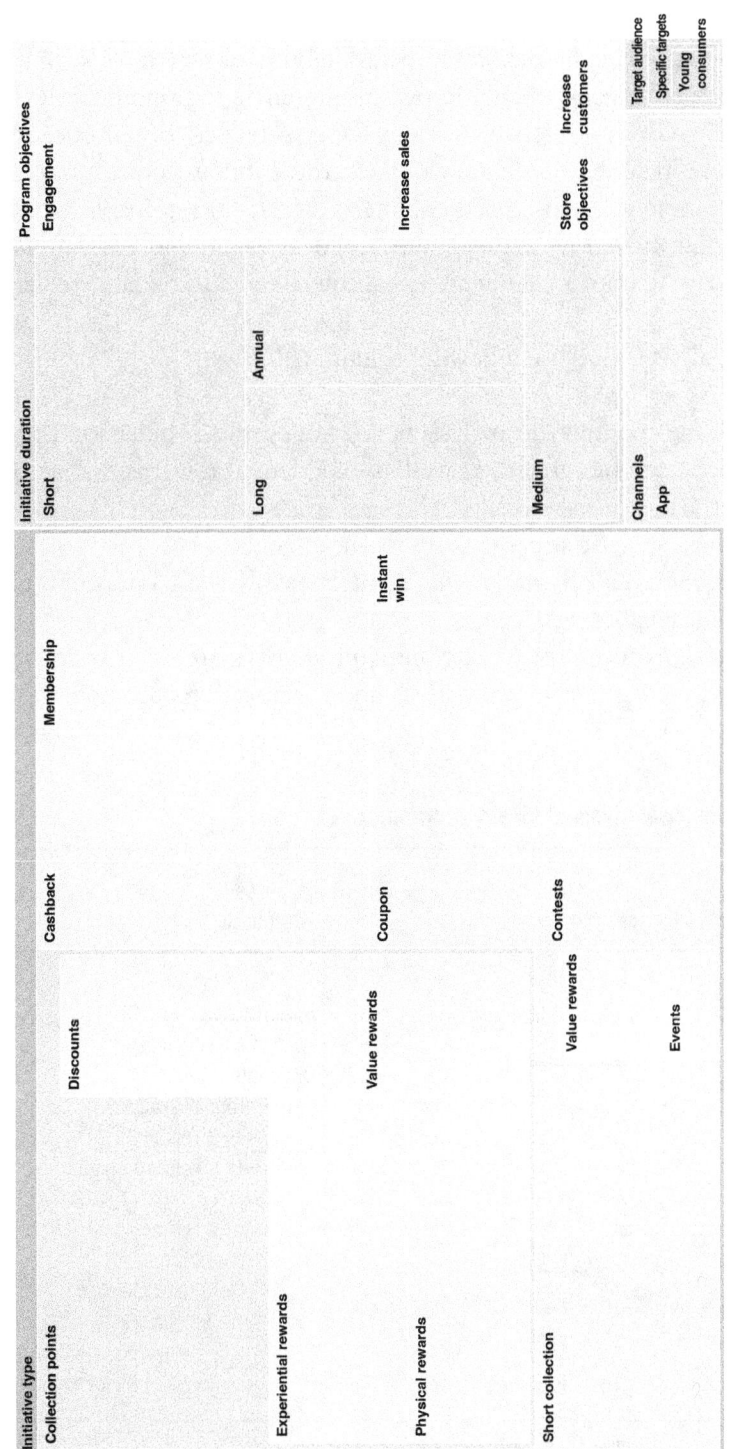

Source. Data processing by NVivo 14.

berships, cashback, and coupons appear to be less common, while instant wins and contests are only sporadic. With the availability of new tools such as apps, LPs and the relative goals of such programs are changing significantly. In fact, during point collection initiatives, many aspects related to gamification and storytelling are included on digital channels; these innovations promote a shift from more transactional loyalty to enhanced emotional loyalty. Therefore, the goals still include boosting customer numbers or sales, but more and more often, companies strive to improve audience engagement and consolidate greater brand attachment.

Cluster analysis shows the following (Figure 6.4):

1. Thanks to the app and the analysis of relative customer behaviors, personalized coupons can be offered, as well as experiential rewards that are consistent with the customer's profile.
2. Contests help specific stores achieve financial goals.
3. Point collection, usually on an annual basis, involves discounts and physical prizes, in most cases.
4. As for the short term, the most common initiatives are short collections. At the same time, instant win initiatives and memberships promote brand engagement.

Figure 6.4   Cluster analysis of loyalty programs

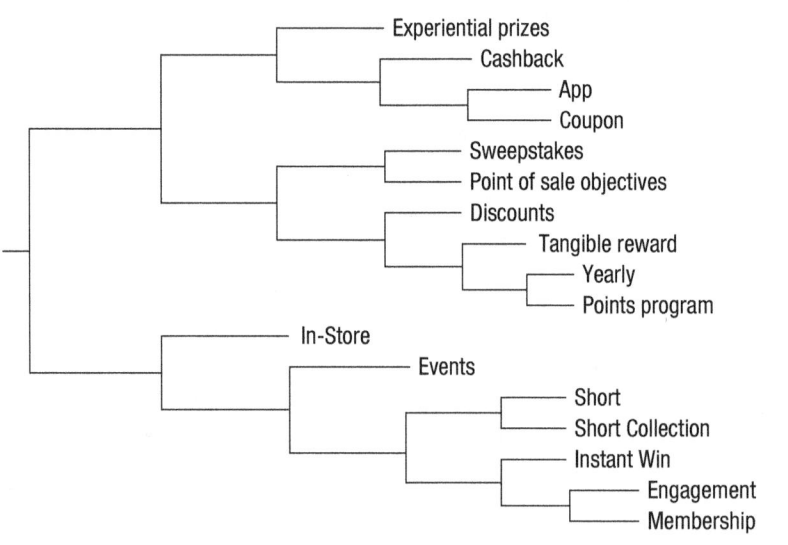

Source: Data processing by NVivo 14.

6.4.2 *Cases of LP success and failure*

Next, we asked our participants about their most/least successful initiatives (Questions 2C & 2D). The most successful (Table A4.9 in Appendix 4) were the ones that allowed consumers to enjoy exclusive services, such as access to experts, consultants, or famous individuals. These initiatives create a powerful sense of belonging and exclusivity in the consumer, generating extremely positive feedback and culminating in higher sales (cross-selling and up-selling). Aspects of success are also related to the attractiveness of the prize, the level of innovation embedded in the initiatives, the respect for values, the promises made by the brand, and the generation of promotions tailored to certain target consumers (e.g., pet lovers). Similarly, continuity in activities and initiatives makes it possible to retain and maintain the relationship with the customer in the long run.

On the contrary, unsuccessful initiatives (Table 6.6; Table A4.10 in Appendix 4) included activities aimed at consumer segments (e.g., younger consumers, sustainability-conscious consumers, etc.) that produced excessively narrow segmentations which did not generate an adequate return on investment (17.65%). Likewise, activities targeting specific products or contests with unattractive prizes were found to be unsatisfactory and not particularly appreciated by the public.

Table 6.6   Aspects that led to the failure of initiatives

Disappointing initiatives	Absolute frequency	Relative frequency
Activities targeting specific segments	6	17.65%
Activities aimed at a specific product	2	5.88%
Competition (unappealing products)	2	5.88%
Discounts	2	5.88%
Technological aspects (bit-com)	1	2.94%

Some campaigns can also flop in the face of dramatic shifts in consumer preferences, difficulty in boosting purchase frequency for certain product categories, and overly technological initiatives for certain customer segments. In addition, companies should avoid overdoing discounting, which can seriously erode customer loyalty by triggering opportunistic behavior. Considering the big changes that consumers are experiencing, it is more vital than ever to understand the advantages that they now want to find in the organization. This can be done by leveraging the wide range of information available about their consumption habits and behaviors. In sum, the keys to success could be continuously experimenting and identifying satisfactory solutions that are relevant to the target audience.

Table 6.7   **The use of loss leaders/accelerators products**

Sponsored products	Absolute frequency	Relative frequency
Incremental sales	4	11.76%
Loss leader/accelerator products	3	8.82%
Extensive basket of goods	2	5.88%
Product integration with store	2	5.88%
Own-brand products	1	2.94%

Table 6.7 (Table A4.11 in Appendix 4) shows how the use of loss leaders or accelerators allows companies to reach a threshold of incremental sales (11.76%), especially when this involves more ample basket of products, for example, a category of products of a certain brand, instead of an individual item.

To ensure a successful campaign, our respondents emphasized the importance of spotlighting the product in the store and implementing suitable communication to publicize it. When the product is perfectly integrated into the communication and the campaign, there will be better results in terms of incremental sales. Companies also need to consider feedback coming directly from the public about the desire for a certain product and the difficulties in finding it, aspects that can guide them in assembling the right assortment. In addition, accelerators must be consistent with corporate positioning to avoid creating a value mismatch.

6.5 Measuring loyalty with specific KPIs for store loyalty and e-loyalty

6.5.1 *Informants' assessments of the relationship between store loyalty and e-loyalty*

New digital technologies emerge as almost universal drivers among all participants, regardless of industry, for improving LP management. The effects of these technologies on LPs warrant further investigation. The first question in Section 3 on this issue centered on understanding whether (and what) differences exist between the virtual and physical worlds, i.e., whether respondents conceived of e-loyalty differently than store loyalty, and whether divergences in shopper behavior existed between online and in-store channels (Question 3A).

For all the companies we surveyed (grocery retail, non-grocery retail, as well as brands/manufacturers), the concept of omnichannel has now become a defining element of business strategy. As a result, the divergences between the physical and virtual worlds become less significant, and the points collected online and in the physical store essentially carry the same weight.

For retail grocery, there is typically no such thing as an online-only customer; in fact, online customers also visit the physical store. Instead, in-store customers might only use this channel (Informants 17 & 34). Moreover, *"It is empirically and scientifically proven that the customer who buys from [the company's name] and uses multiple sales channels spends more on average. Period. Therefore, he or she carries more value for the company"* (Informants 29 & 30). This is precisely why there is a tendency to create seamless loyalty policies between channels: for example, *"95% of the coupons we send out are valid on both in-store and online. The goal is the omnichannel concept: everything that is valid in the physical store is valid online too"* (Informant 5).

Despite the orientation toward an omnichannel value proposition, the online segment is considered strategic. This channel must be monitored so that retailers can analyze and compare customer behaviors online and in-store: *"We do several specific surveys on certain items for our analysis, and we do two dedicated customer satisfaction surveys per year, where in addition to the whole satisfaction side, we measure the customer effort score, assortment, something on e-commerce, the single NPS of e-commerce, intention to repurchase, along with the classic KPIs"* (Informant 5). It's interesting to see how adopting the app moves the needle on customer behavior indicators toward the digital side of the interaction, even if there is no e-commerce channel (Informant 11).

To promote online sales, some retailers are trying to activate specific campaigns with additional point collections or dedicated CRMs (Informant 4). Online has loyalty mechanisms that don't directly play into long-term loyalty (Informant 2) but that reward loyalty in terms of frequency and receipt value, offering an additional discount if a certain amount is spent. In the non-grocery sector, different orientations emerge. In some cases, the online channel acts as a precursor for "drive to store" (*"the online channel is not about selling but about driving to the store"* Informant 14), with the goal of enticing customers to visit the store, where they can get personalized advice to find the best solution for them. The online channel can also become an "extra shelf" for items that aren't available in the store (Informant 31). Phygital solutions allow companies to give advice and to listen to customers, responding to their needs, especially when the product is a complex one. A very important issue emerges here: retailers tend not to make any distinction between e-loyalty and store loyalty, but where marketplaces are used, loyalty measurement doesn't exist or, at any rate, doesn't reflect the extent to which a third party might intervene.

Digitization also impacts rewards, which sometimes dematerialize. The success of these initiatives is mixed. For example, retail customers didn't show much appreciation for digital awards. For Informant 1: "*It was an activity that applied to both the physical store and e-commerce, where there was no physical prize, but with the receipt. You could go to a platform and download a game, a video game.*" Instead, when the prize is tied to a game that allows customers to earn points on spending (the concept of gamification), this proves to be a constructive solution for creating engagement (Informant 11).

In summary, companies' commitment to integrating loyalty in the offline and online worlds, with a view to omnichannel presence and complementarity, is highlighted in Figure 6.5. Such an approach follows consumer evolutions in this direction and aims to further streamline the *customer journey*, both between online channels and offline stores, to reduce problems or interruptions during purchase. The individual who moves along multiple business touchpoints brings greater value to the organization than the customer who only take advantage of one specific channel. In other words, greater value is generated by cross-channel customers.

According to our findings, attention is specifically placed on e-loyalty to reinforce consumers' online behaviors. Several initiatives are also introduced to incentivize the use of these digital channels, for example, by offering additional free services such as home delivery. Therefore, several actions are done exclusively and specifically for online channels, involving awarding additional points or making specific products available to encourage their utilization.

However, when specific initiatives are deployed or products and made available in several channels, integrating the resulting customer data becomes complex.

Figure 6.6 highlights the construction of specific clusters related to:

1. store loyalty;
2. the difficulty in integrating consumer data when implementing channel-differentiated initiatives, such as offering different products online;
3. implementing specific initiatives to emphasize e-loyalty and the use of digital channels; and
4. designing loyalty from an omnichannel perspective to make the consumer experience more and more continuous and integrated, creating more value.

6.5.2 *Differentiations among LPs*

As regards Question 3B, focused on differentiating between dedicated LPs for online shoppers and in-store shoppers and defining dedicated KPIs for the two different channels, the responses were fairly convergent for grocery retail. Om-

Figure 6.5   **Store loyalty vs online loyalty**

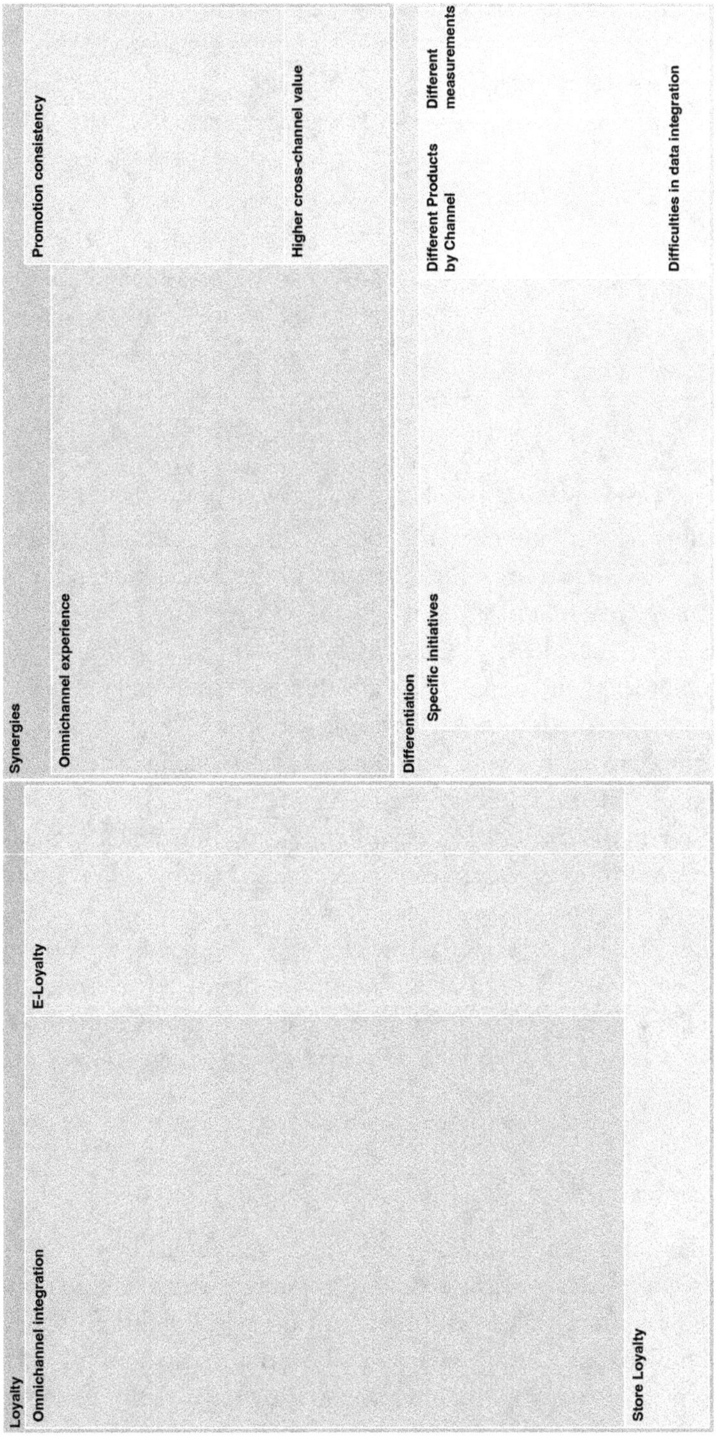

Source: Data processing by NVivo 14.

Figure 6.6 Cluster analysis reflecting store loyalty and e-loyalty

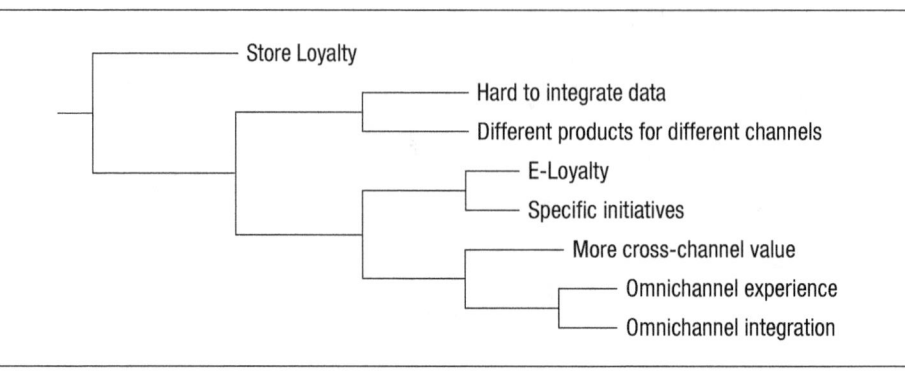

Source: Data processing by NVivo 14.

nichannelness is a strategic goal that helps create *customer centricity*. As a result, specific e-loyalty programs are rare and not very often "sponsored": points accumulated in-store and online are equivalent, and cashback points tend to be *"the same for everyone"* (Informants 29 & 30).

A relevant aspect of e-loyalty concerns home delivery. Of course, specific promotions are created and pegged to the value per "shopping cart" of online customers. The marketing information system, through CRM, can help segment this target audience to learn more about the customers who use the online channel (Informant 1). The non-grocery sector also tends to converge toward the unification of the two channels (Informant 26) but with a greater focus on certain aspects related to engagement rate and click-to-rate, which are typical of virtual commerce. In non-grocery, customers are mapped more to the digital world regardless of their use of the online channel. As a result, the non-grocery sector tends to adopt a variety of KPIs specific to the digital channel, such as conversions, clicks, new users and newsletter sign-ups (Informant 10), *"engagement rate, click-to-rate, click-through, and for sales, traffic, volume, and value top line"* (Informant 15).

6.5.3 *Different measurements for loyalty and e-loyalty programs*

The development of digital channels raises questions about the use of specific measurements aimed at assessing e-loyalty, possibly differentiated from those used for store loyalty or purchases in the physical world (Question 3C). Despite the focus on omnichannel, interview results show that companies take different approaches to measuring e-loyalty, often integrating online and offline metrics to gain a comprehensive view of customer behavior. Assessing online receipt value is crucial for understanding whether economies of scale are being achieved in distribution approaches. As we all know, e-commerce for grocery is, in fact, a service and not a source of profit, at least in the short/long term. Consequently, retailers need to push for high average receipts to achieve the business objectives of optimizing logistics costs and studying their territorial distribution (Informants 2, 3, 7, & 21).

Some specific metrics relate to voucher redemption, i.e., tallying how many vouchers were sent out, how many were redeemed and where (online or in the store). This helps clarify whether e-commerce is diverting sales from the physical store to online or augmenting overall sales for the retailer: *"If I do e-commerce, am I shifting sales from in-store to online? Am I increasing sales? Or am I doing something else?"* (Informant 1). The two channels are not substitutes for one another, but complementary or "promotional." In other words, although store customers can become online customers, typical customers only do their shopping in the store. *"Sometimes you have a gradual increase in online sales and sometimes e-commerce consumers start to learn about the physical store as well"* (Informant 1).

For the non-grocery sector, it is important to evaluate the online experience by measuring, for example, *"dwell time"* (Informant 24), *"exit rate"* (Informant 22), and *"other indicators that show how the customer interacts with the online channel"* (Informant 7). No distinction is made in terms of multichannel, but the concept of omnichannel is explored comprehensively (Informants 29 & 30). Interaction is disconnected from channel: *"The user doesn't distinguish between e-commerce, physical store, or other channels, but interacts with the brand in an integrated way. The main metric is how the user interacts with the brand, regardless of the channel"* (Informant 7).

Specific measures for e-loyalty mentioned by informants regarding digital channels such as e-commerce include CTR (11.76%), conversion rate (8.82%), shopping cart abandonment, CPM, and dwell time (5.88%). Other aspects include adding products to the shopping cart, opening DEMs, or measurements such as NPS on online channels (Table 6.8; Table A4.12 in Appendix 4). This

Table 6.8   **Specific KPIs for e-loyalty**

Specific KPIs	Absolute frequency	Relative frequency
Click-through rate (CTR)	4	11.76%
Conversion	3	8.82%
Shopping cart abandonment	2	5.88%
Cost per thousand impressions (CPM)	2	5.88%
Time spent on the site	2	5.88%

additional information allows for a greater understanding of consumer online behavior. Although these measurements are specific to e-loyalty, our informants prefer applying consistent and uniform metrics regarding overall loyalty.

6.6 The antecedents and effects of loyalty

6.6.1 *Factors that build loyalty*

If loyalty is a strategic goal, it's essential to pinpoint the antecedents (Question 4A) and outcomes (Question 4B) that lead to building a climate of mutual loyalty. As emphasized by Informants 29 and 30 (and a very relevant aspect in comprehending the strategic nature of the concept), loyalty should not be considered instrumental to achieving certain business goals. Instead, loyalty should be a constituent element of what the company is and what the company does.

Accordingly, the first factor we identified in our research pertains to *trust*, a fundamental value that must be cultivated and preserved over time. Trust stands as an antecedent that is built over the medium- to long-term (Informant 1). The literature on the topic highlights the multidimensionality of the construct: trust is what the customer accords not only to the company, but also to the staff, the organization of the store (*"the most important thing is that in the store, the assortments are put together just so; the courtesy of the staff is fundamental"* (Informant 5) and, last but not least, the private label. This last item is considered a pivotal factor in the trust-oriented relationship, such that a visit to the store may be motivated precisely by the availability of a branded product that is trusted for quality, respect for the supply chain, and value for money (Informants 17 & 20).

Private labels are critical levers. *"84% percent of customers surveyed say they come to [company name] because the private label is there, and the moment you get loyalty to the private label, it becomes loyalty to the brand, no longer to the store. So, one of the important determinants is the private label. The other thing we are working on is a customer care concept"* (Informant 2).

But loyalty also depends on very basic, utilitarian determinants related to the concept of physical proximity and attractiveness, understood in terms of the convenience of the store (*"consistently low prices,"* Informant 4), a given discount, or the usefulness and exclusivity of a reward, which are *"crucial factors in differentiating oneself and attracting both loyal and non-loyal customers."*

There is a high rate of infidelity in grocery (*"The customer is increasingly nomadic,"* Informant 11), and "fly-by-night promotions" are still applied in an undifferentiated way. Given this, companies need to keep many levers under control. These relate not only to the product's value for money (VFM) but its extended VFM, which touches on *"the in-store shopping experience, which is a very important element. Then there's the ability to monitor all signals, even weak ones, concerning changes in customer behavior and the ability to target them immediately with quick actions"* (Informant 4).

Informant 11 reflects on the significance of brand equity and customer satisfaction, in other words, attachment to the brand: *"you build it with lots of little parts, such as the operations of the store, the quality of the store, the price, which is about* value *for money, not just price"* (Informant 11). It follows that quality of service, reasonable prices, and the overall store experience become key elements. Customer loyalty is seen as a branding tool, with an emphasis on inclusiveness and the ability to cater to customers at different income levels. Customer fit is considered an essential element, as *"the shelf must be inclusive for everyone"* in terms of spending capacity (Informant 11). Some discounters are gaining market share even though they do not market industrial brands (Informant 13) because they offer simplicity and reliability, that is, they do what they promise.

Moving on, there is also an interpretation of loyalty anchored in the relationship between the company and the customer, and the company's role in society. This perspective is pursued by cooperative-type businesses in particular: *"the member becomes part of the cooperative; the whole social side goes beyond just shopping"* (Informant 5). A connection is established, and the customer tends to identify with the values expressed by the company, which creates a real emotional bond (Informant 20, *"the customer's affinity with certain core values"*).

Especially with retailers such as pharmacies, where the main antecedent of loyalty is *proximity*, offering specific products and services to loyalty card holders is what helps create a direct bond between the retail brand and the consumer. These elements, combined with effective business strategies and quality customer service, can contribute significantly to building and maintaining customer loyalty.

Non-grocery retailers rely heavily on the concept of personalized advice, which in some cases also touches on aspects of an emotional nature (Informant 24). For manufacturing companies, on the other hand, the focus is mainly on product quality and a customer-centric approach, developing reliable products based on customer needs (Informant 10). In addition, B2B services take on special importance, partly due to the network of retailers that support interaction with the final customer (Informant 23). When the product is a reward for a loyalty campaign, it's the brand and the product that create added value for retailers and final customers (Informant 6).

Relating the antecedents of loyalty to the macro categories identified in our literature review (Chapter 5), Figure 6.7 shows the predominance of brand-re-

Figure 6.7 **Loyalty antecedents**

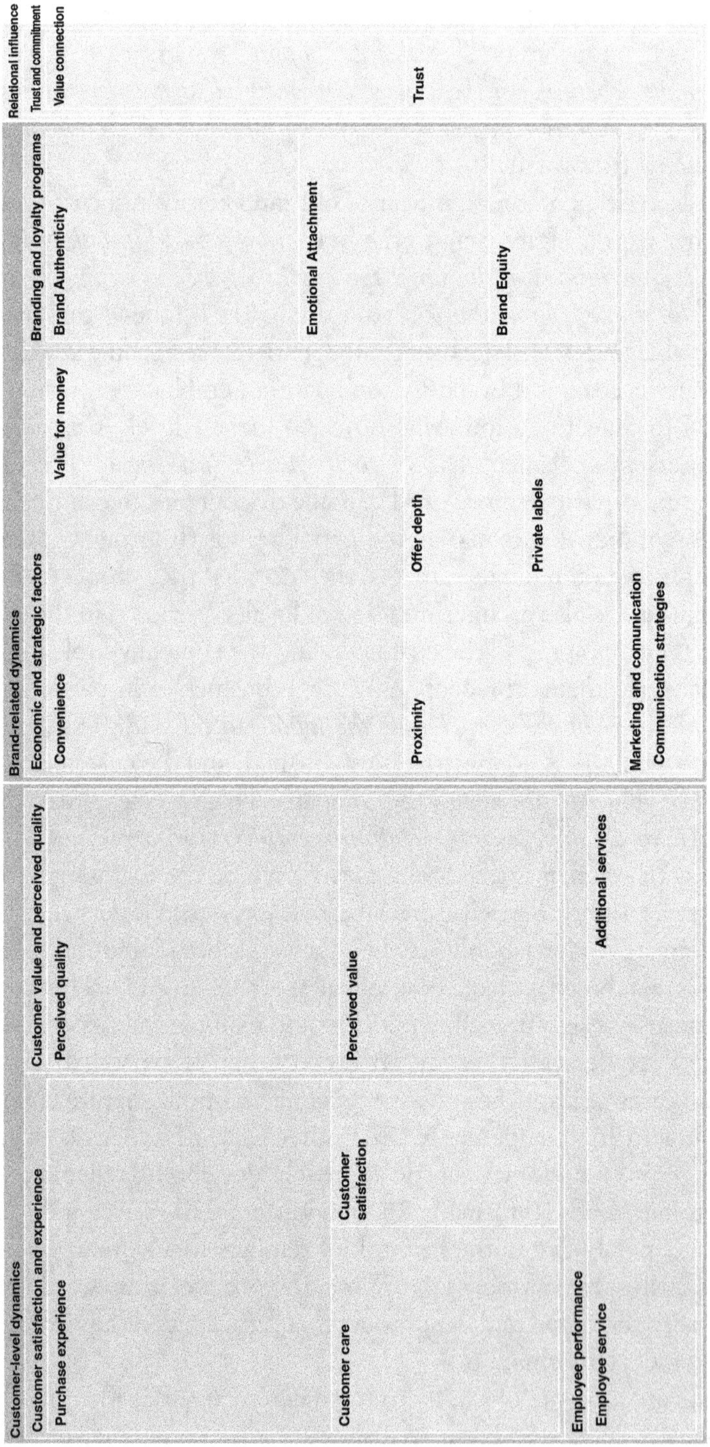

Source. Data processing by NVivo 14.

lated dynamics and customer-related dynamics. To a more marginal extent, we find relational influences; environmental forces are absent entirely. For brand-related dynamics, the prominent role of economic and strategic factors, brand, and communication emerges, while for customer-level dynamics, customer satisfaction comes to the fore, followed by perceived quality and employee performance.

Figure 6.7 highlights the shift from a logic of supply-side convenience to one that centers on the connection and value alignment between organization and consumer. Only by creating value on an economic, emotional, and consumer experience level can companies generate long-term loyalty. Initially linked to factors such as convenience, proximity, or services offered, consumer loyalty evolves during the customer experience toward more emotional aspects involving brand equity and authenticity.

6.6.2 *The outcomes of loyalty policies: the link to measurement*

Compared to the findings in the literature, which place great emphasis on the antecedents of loyalty, operators accentuate the expected effects and objectives of the initiatives they implement even more (Question 4B). From these objectives, we can draw a correlation with the initial research question, namely, how is loyalty measured. Many companies consider the transactional aspect and return on investment as a starting point, along with indicators of promotional campaign success. However, grocery retailers tend to go further, identifying long-term goals such as improving CLV, reducing churn rates, and expanding the base of new customers as relevant outcomes. For consumer cooperatives, moreover, a crucial aspect is membership (Informant 5). Very interestingly, attention also focuses on affective aspects: word-of-mouth becomes not so much a quantitative measure of NPS but a demonstration of attachment to the retail brand (Informants 29, 30, & 36). This can generate particularly significant long-term loyalty effects.

In terms of outcomes, the four macro categories outlined in our literature review (Chapter 5) are all present. In order of frequency, we identify engagement and relationships, financial and operational performance, marketing and strategy, and, finally, consumer behavior (Figure 6.8).

In addition to the relevance in hitting certain financial and operational goals, such as boosting sales, reducing churn rates, and improving CLV, it is becoming more and more crucial for companies to achieve a set level of engagement, particularly in maintaining long-term relationships with their customers and generating positive word-of-mouth with other consumers.

Figure 6.8 Loyalty outcomes

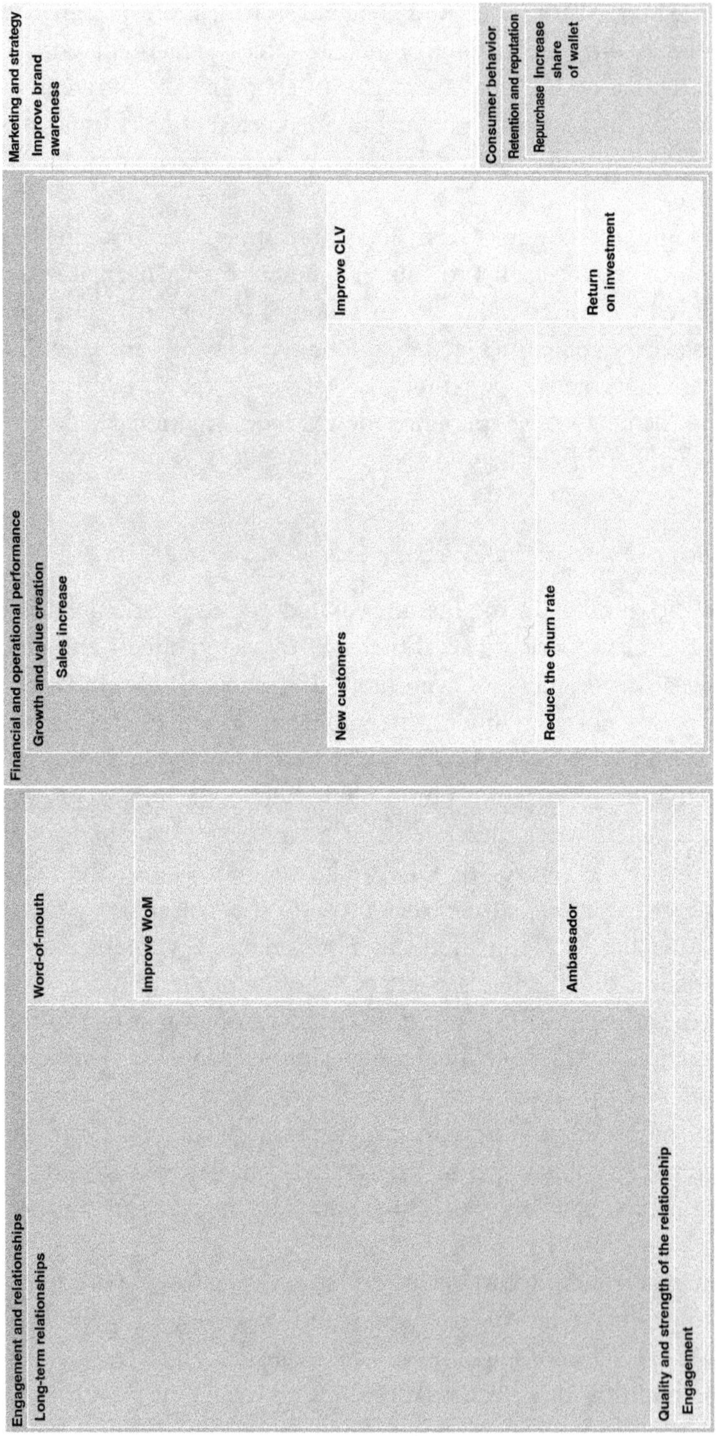

Source: Data processing by NVivo 14.

Figure 6.9   Clusters of loyalty antecedents and outcomes

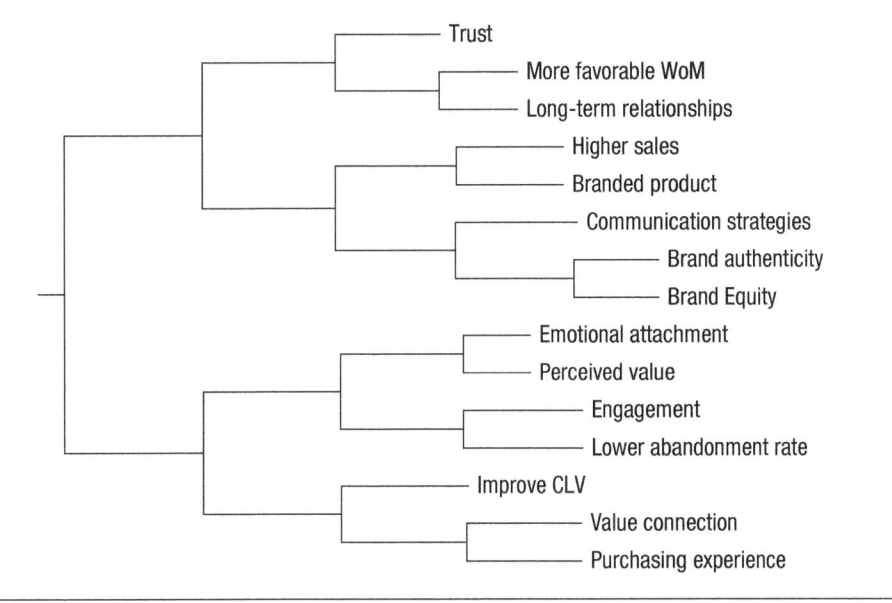

Source: Data processing by NVivo 14.

Figure 6.9 highlights the clusters resulting from the combination of antecedents and expected effects:

1. Trust in the organization enables the creation of long-term relationships that can improve word-of-mouth.
2. Communication strategies, if they effectively convey brand authenticity and brand equity, can incentivize sales.
3. Perceived value enables the generation of emotional attachment, enhanced engagement, and a lower abandonment rate.
4. Asatisfying shopping experience and a strong value connection between the consumer and the brand can result in higher CLV.

6.7 Corporate strategies and policies for the future development of loyalty and loyalty measurements

The results of this section identify the DNA of different companies. The question specifically asked of the informants concerns whether their companies are working to implement new measurements in addition to the ones they're currently utilizing (Question 5A). In some cases, we note the need to develop novel loyalty indicators as future implementations, going beyond the traditional profiles related to the transactional aspect (Informant 7). According to Informant 20, *"the goal is certainly from a measurement point of view to continue to refine and develop measurements that are increasingly effective and predictive in a certain sense."* Also, according to Informant 21, *"the KPIs will expand…the basis is the quantitative data, I'm sure though there could be some interesting qualitative analysis. The proper use of AI can be directed toward the qualitative side."*

A common refrain is the need to enhance different digital touchpoints (Informant 2) and apps, which prove to be not only tools for monitoring customer engagement, but also channels of communication, even interaction, i.e., creating an interactive two-way relationship (Informant 1, 5). This also emerges in the non-grocery sector, where digital would allow companies to *"create points of interaction with the customer that are not related to the purchase"* (Informant 7). Future developments will lead to a shift from classic short-term loyalty campaigns, which are mass market, to the study of the consumer in terms of CLV and UCV (Informant 11), using big data and AI (Informant 34) to personalize the offer, and by doing so, grow the *share-of-wallet* for the typical profile.

What emerges for all informants is the growing perspective of *customer centricity*, which must determine a real cultural change, up to and including greater interaction between business functions (e.g., marketing, sales, IT, and management control).

In this sense, the co-operative world faces the problem of *"thinking about communities"* (Informant 1), i.e. identifying communities of people who want to work on a project (e.g. school) or an interest (e.g. the BBQ community in the U.S.). Furthermore, consumer co-operatives are active in the provision of services to members (e.g. member loans, utilities, payment systems), which, however, are not always effectively communicated to the public.

For non-grocery retailers, the inclination is to change the relationship with the customer, shifting communication from promotion to value-based content, focusing on customer relevance and the creation of personalized pathways (Informant 27). Informant 26 even mentions a tendency to create a roadmap. Starting from strengthening the concept of membership, the aim here is to put the customer experience at the center of the different channels and then, finally, *"bring benefits to their real life."* In this way, the retailer aspires to become a partner in the different stages and occasions of the customer's life.

In conclusion, regarding future developments, we need to consider the importance of customer engagement, the relevance of measurement, and the role of new technologies. As Figure 6.10 highlights, as far as customer engagement,

Figure 6.10   **Future developments**

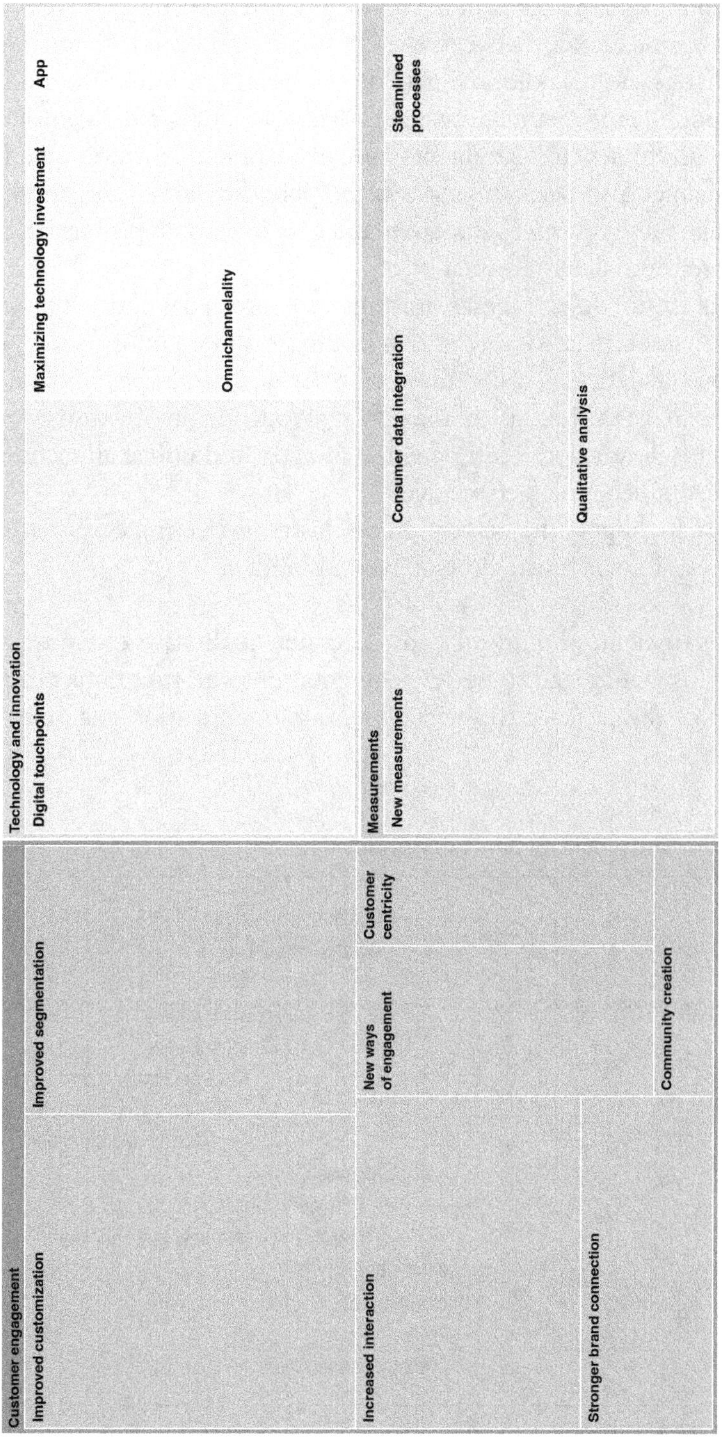

Source: Data processing by NVivo 14.

better segmentation is the key to personalizing value propositions more precisely and shoring up interaction between the consumer and brand. Companies can do all this thanks to the additional data on consumers collected from different offline and online touchpoints. Consumer data, when integrated appropriately, can generate useful new measurements for consideration. However, in addition to this, companies also need to work on the periodic monitoring and control phases to make these processes smoother and easy to read, to pick up on critical issues and interpret salient information.

In terms of future developments, informants expressed a desire for more automation, such as automated queries that can extract more information and enable predictive analytics. A broad discussion revolves around technologies and innovations to make the best use of the different touchpoints, maximize technology investments, leverage the full potential of apps, and utilize all technologies in a seamless, omnichannel perspective.

Figure 6.11 highlights the generation of clusters reflecting corporate strategies and policies for the future development of loyalty:

1. New measurements should take into account qualitative consumer information. This would lead to better segmentations and programs tailored to the needs of the target customers to elevate organization-customer interaction.

Figure 6.11   Clusters reflecting future developments

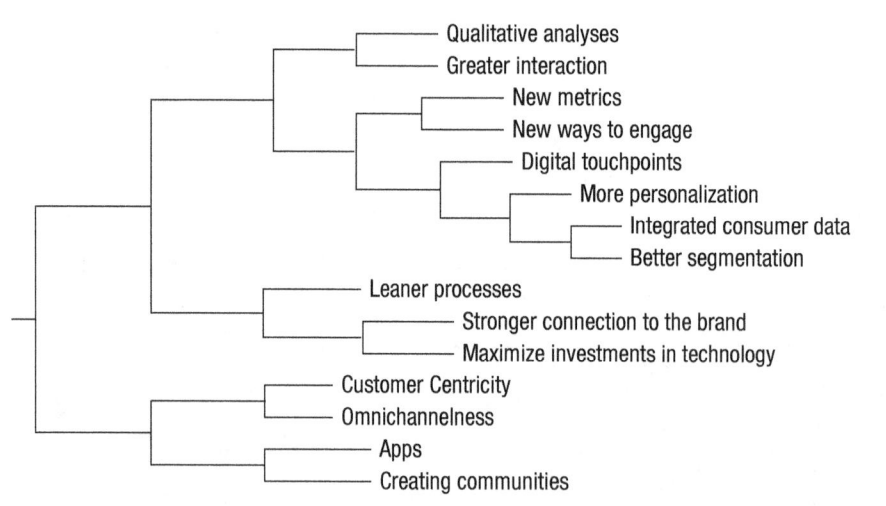

Source: Data processing by NVivo 14.

2. Technology investments in software and applications should be maximized to make monitoring processes faster and smoother, quickly identifying critical issues and strengthening the connection with the organization.
3. Fostering consumer omnichannelness can achieve customer centricity, providing a deeper understanding of the customer.
4. Better use of apps can enhance a sense of community between organizations and consumers.

6.8 Conclusions

From the interviews we analyzed, we discern various loyalty measurement practices in terms of KPIs, and the mode and frequency of monitoring by different companies in retail, grocery and non-grocery, and manufacturing. On the one hand, the focus is still more on short-term KPIs related to specific initiatives, such as incremental sales, average receipt value, and visit frequency. In addition to these, however, there are several longer-term measurements based on more sophisticated metrics such as CLV, which assesses the entire customer lifecycle, and methods such as UCV, which offers a unified view of the customer through better integration of behavioral and transactional KPIs.

The measurements and initiatives undertaken by companies in our sample reflect the evolution of LPs, which are moving away from a straightforward transactional bent to embrace more complex, customer-centered approaches (*customer centricity*). LPs, in fact, no longer simply offer rewards or discounts in exchange for frequent purchases but aim to create an emotional and relational bond with the customer. This approach is also made possible by digital tools such as apps, which allow companies to monitor and interact with customers in real time, soliciting purchasing behavior through gamification mechanisms, challenges, or additional rewards.

Customer centricity, resulting from the integration of multiple data that can be achieved with new technologies, produces more detailed segmentation that enables companies to identify clusters of customers or more clearly define buyer personas with a variety of needs and behaviors. This empowers organizations to create targeted, personalized offerings that better meet consumer needs.

The quest for greater *customer satisfaction* goes beyond the logic of tangible rewards to include experiential rewards and value rewards to engender stronger brand attachment. However, initiatives are still rare that include rewards linked to social and environmental values in response to consumers' growing focus on social and environmental responsibility.

Another aspect to consider is omnichannel integration, i.e., the fact that consumers today expect a seamless loyalty experience across different sales channels, whether physical or digital. As a result, companies are investing in creating seamless LPs, where points and rewards are valid regardless of the channel. This approach enhances the complementarity between different business touchpoints, demonstrating the importance of a unified, consistent customer experience.

In summary, companies are striving to design increasingly customer-centric LPs by adopting innovative measurements and integrating new digital tools. Moreover, businesses recognize that customer loyalty can no longer be measured only in transactional terms but must be based on a long-term view that considers relational, value-based, and behavioral elements. This shift in perspective marks a major transition in the way companies manage their loyalty strategies, moving the focus from transaction to interaction, relationship maintenance, and emotional customer engagement.

CHAPTER 7
CONCLUDING CONSIDERATIONS
AND MANAGERIAL IMPLICATIONS

[Emanuele Acconciamessa, Bruno Busacca, Generoso Branca, Sandro Castaldo, Andrea Ciacci, Alice Mantovani, Lara Penco and Ginevra Testa]

7.1 Introduction

This volume provides a comprehensive overview of customer loyalty, analyzing the topic from different angles to integrate the academic perspective with business practice, highlighting gaps and opportunities. Chapter 1 introduces the competitive environment and the concept of loyalty, defined as a critical resource for businesses, highlighting its different forms and dimensions. Chapter 2 explores challenges and trends for retailers, emphasizing the crucial role of loyalty in a context marked by increasing economic uncertainty and complexity. Chapter 3 investigates relevant scenarios for large-scale retailers, affirming the importance of loyalty measurement and digital transformation for Italian players, and presents the results of qualitative research conducted on a sample of managers at large-scale Italian retail companies. In Chapter 4, we delve into the main conceptualizations and measurements of loyalty. Chapter 5 provides a systematic literature review, highlighting the most recent evolutions of loyalty, particularly in the omnichannel and digital context, loyalty antecedents and outcomes, and possible future research directions. Finally, based on interviews conducted with retail and industry managers and practitioners, Chapter 6 brings out relevant insights about the current status of loyalty and loyalty programs (LPs). The unique feature of this survey is that it adopts the retailer's perspective, taking a snapshot of initiatives, measurements, major critical issues, and expected future developments. Preliminary analysis of the literature has shown that existing research is essentially customer-focused, with mainly quantitative survey-based studies whose purpose is to measure the antecedents and/or effects of loyalty based on psychometric theoretical approaches. The corporate approach, on the other hand, involves a "perspective reversal" of sorts, investigating in more detail the

LPs used and the measurements made by companies to better understand how the concept of loyalty relates to corporate management. From this, several key macro-directions emerge, which we will briefly address.

7.2 The evolution of strategic relevance of loyalty

Grocery retailers are pioneers in implementing loyalty programs, and there are a few different reasons for this. First, in industry-distribution competition, retailers have traditionally had to counterbalance brand loyalty toward producers by strengthening store loyalty; consequently, all initiatives aimed at creating attachment to the retailer and the store (including store brand policies) were instrumental in securing an advantage in this vertical competition.

In horizontal competition between retail chains, creating an ongoing relationship with the same customer turns out to be a strategic factor that ensures continuity and profitability in the long run. Overinvesting in undifferentiated promotions based on price and flyers drums up traffic, but it is more "opportunistic" traffic: cherry pickers who migrate from one store to another in search of the best price, fueling price wars that erode corporate profitability.

In light of all this, grocery retailers have realized that customer-relationship building shifts the axis of competitor comparison from price to other factors that are difficult to imitate or compare. Whereas in the past, these companies focused on short-term transactional KPIs (which are limited to evaluating the profitability of the investment, in terms of average receipt and incremental sales, for instance), a growing trend is emerging that looks at loyalty from a strategic, long-term perspective. In this regard, we find that businesses are using indicators such as CLV along with methods for building customer databases, including a variety of different KPIs. Integrating multiple perspectives is a way to understand the needs, preferences, and values that motivate customers in their purchase choices.

Loyalty has gradually come to the fore as a driver for changing the competitive approach, placing loyalty-innovative retailers in a kind of "competitive isolation." As they know, short-term KPIs must be properly balanced with long-term ones, which require a more integrated approach to foster long-term relationships.

Moreover, from a historical perspective, consumer cooperatives, constitutionally recognized organizations that have developed in Italy, have founded their business models on member loyalty. They offer special programs that go beyond the incentive of "exclusive" discounts and rewards, aiming to elicit engagement with the world of cooperatives based on shared values, characteristic of the most advanced stages of trust.

Our analysis also highlights another interesting situation: discount brands. These retailers have unequivocally understood that a loyal customer is a more profitable one. What is more, facing elevated competition from traditional retail (with articulated LP architectures spanning the first price to the premium range), discounters have discovered that relying only on the concept of convenience is a limiting factor that progressively erodes their positioning. A common refrain from grocery retailers – *"Loyalty IS the business"* - makes it the priority value lever on which to build competitiveness and profitability.

7.2.1 *Main approaches to loyalty measurement*

As regards loyalty measurement categories, a clear bias emerges toward using behavioral data (economic and non-economic) and in part affective data. Conative loyalty, which does not appear appreciably, is used in a limited fashion. Retailers, with their near real-time behavioral monitoring, identify in behavior the true *"intention to be loyal."* Considering the complexity and strategic nature of loyalty measurement, it is necessary to prepare a comprehensive set of indicators aimed at understanding all facets of the concept along the entire customer journey, going far beyond the pure act of purchasing. In addition to quantitative measures, qualitative data have become increasingly crucial, from sentiment to Net Promoter Score (NPS), consumer feedback to consumer trends: all this serves to correct and improve the effectiveness of LPs. The latter is mainly measured by cross-variables, summary indices, and comparisons with control groups.

7.2.2 *Customer centricity as a pillar for loyalty*

A common message from market opinion leaders is that more than ever before, they consider loyalty a strategic factor for all companies, retailers, and manufacturers. Taking on a strategic perspective means maximizing the value that customers can generate for a company throughout their relationship. This in turn leads to placing customers at the center by understanding their needs, expectations, desires, and behaviors. Consequently, customer centricity tends to involve offering products and services that are ever more responsive to consumers' needs. This approach to shoppers' preferences also includes activities related to environmental and social responsibility and, therefore, a move toward Corporate Social Responsibility (CSR).

Through various tools such as loyalty cards, apps, and CRM systems, companies can collect huge amounts of data that allow them to learn more about consumer behavior, predict it, and then segment demand into different clusters. Moreover, advanced segmentations enable companies to personalize offerings, responding more adequately to the needs of individual customers. Personalizing initiatives not only amplifies their effectiveness but also fosters high customer engagement, improving customer loyalty through a relational path that aims at intimacy.

We can observe how loyalty and customer segmentation (even to the point of defining buyer personas) have become increasingly interrelated. Responsiveness to LPs and the creation of long-term loyalty serve to delineate precise consumer segments (and buyer personas). Segment definition, in turn, serves to develop tailor-made, non-standardized loyalty programs capable of assimilating not only past behaviors but also customer values and perceptions. Therefore, investing in customer centricity is an effective strategy to ensure future competitiveness by realizing behavioral segmentation that aligns with consumer lifestyles. Furthermore, membership arrangements can offer consumers a range of services that make them feel the exclusivity of their relationship with the brand.

7.2.3 Omnichannel and customer journey

One of the crucial themes that emerged from our research is the omnichannel approach: integrating different business touchpoints to make the customer journey more fluid, to create seamless experiences, and to allow access to LPs across all customer touchpoints. This approach is particularly crucial in retail, where there is no longer a distinction between physical and online customers and where cross-channel customers bring more value. Companies that succeed in creating an uninterrupted, integrated customer experience, online and offline, can multiply the value generated by customers.

However, omnichannel integration presents significant challenges. One of these is precisely the difficulty in integrating data collected across different channels, an obstacle that causes real disruptions in customer knowledge production. Indeed, companies must be able to combine data from physical sales with data generated from online purchases to obtain a single, integrated view of the customer. This means that the distinction between online and offline experiences will continue to blur, offering consumers a seamless, connected customer experience across channels.

7.2.4 *Emotional loyalty and customer engagement*

As far as the elements that emerged from the research that should be further explored through future developments, we can include the measurement of the emotional effects of different LPs, which appear to be highly diversified in terms of type, duration, rewards, and target audience. Emotional loyalty and customer engagement represent increasingly crucial aspects of corporate loyalty strategies. Apps and digital tools can foster customer engagement by employing gamification and storytelling. Rewards, whether they be physical, experiential, or value-based, strengthen the emotional bond between the customer and the brand. Emotional loyalty is further reinforced when the organization and consumer share the same values. Companies that can elicit greater engagement and a strong emotional connection will benefit from deeper, longer-lasting relationships that can withstand competitive challenges. Moreover, when consumers have a strong attachment to an organization, they can be transformed into promoters thanks to brand advocacy activities, fueled by positive word-of-mouth mechanisms that are visible and measurable with NPS.

7.2.5 *Technological innovation*

Several new technological tools, such as Business Intelligence and Artificial Intelligence, can facilitate predictive analytics to identify customers at risk of abandonment (churn), incentivizing the adoption of customer retention initiatives. The development of capabilities and skills to automate data processing and interpretation enables companies to perform more sophisticated analyses that do not just look at the past but predict future customer behavior. This proves particularly useful when it comes to identifying patterns of behavior that may indicate a higher risk of churn or an opportunity to augment the value generated by certain customer segments.

Technological investment in CRM software and data dashboards is also a valuable resource to guarantee increasingly timely updating and tracking; these tools also serve to better interpret today's highly volatile competitive environment. Companies are adopting a variety of technology platforms to monitor the performance of their LPs and make data-driven decisions. However, not all companies are keeping up with this trend, as some businesses are still anchored to more rudimentary tools, hindering their ability to optimize and automate analytical processes. As a result, they are unable to amplify the opportunities identified by human intelligence, which still plays a major role in managerial processes.

7.3 Managerial implications and future research directions

From our analysis of the conceptualizations and measurements of loyalty identified in the academic literature (Chapters 4 and 5), and the findings of our empirical research conducted on manufacturers and distributors (Chapter 6), some interesting gaps have emerged, inspiring both recommendations for managers and suggestions on directions for future research in loyalty. If properly addressed, these challenges can lead to new practices and produce new knowledge, contributing to the alignment and joint advancement of theory and practice.

- **Loyalty is not just repeated purchases.**
  Customer loyalty is not embodied exclusively in repeat purchasing behavior. On the contrary, to capture all aspects of the construct, cognitive, attitudinal, and conative dimensions should also be examined. In promoting loyalty measurement practices, companies should make sure to implement specific KPIs to analyze the attitudinal (e.g., satisfaction) and behavioral (e.g., repeat purchases) aspects of loyalty distinctly and synergistically. In fact, the drivers of each loyalty category may vary, as well as the effects generated on customers' purchasing behaviors. However, with this fine-grained analysis, practitioners will be able to better understand what factors contribute to the different loyalty categories and how these factors impact business performance. In addition, using attitudinal and behavioral measurements in a complementary way has been shown to enhance the explanatory power of analysis models, providing more accurate insights into the effects produced by loyalty in terms of relevant business outcomes.

- **Loyalty is not just a short-term concept.**
  Loyalty should be seen as a long-term strategic goal, not limited to obtaining immediate results. While it is true that short-term initiatives, such as discounts and promotions, can generate immediate behaviors and traffic, only more personalized strategies can turn consumers into loyal customers and relationships into lasting bonds. Consequently, LPs should move from a short-term approach focused on transactional KPIs (such as incremental sales or visit frequency) to a long-term view (such as CLV) that integrates behavioral data with relational elements. This transition reflects a more customer-centric approach, to build lasting, emotional relationships, moving beyond the logic of material rewards and embracing personalized, value-based experiences. For example, although a physical reward always finds some appreciation, the trend is to create new LPs that also include inherently emotional prizes, de-

signing interactions based on service delivery and one-to-one communications (e.g., podcasts, recipes, reward points for reviews).

- **Loyalty is not only about marketing.**
  Loyalty should no longer be considered simply a part of the retailing mix;
  instead, it should enter fully into strategic marketing and corporate strategy.
  Moreover, loyalty measurement should be strongly integrated into the company's overall strategy. To be successful in this context, retailers and manufacturers need to invest in technological innovations, experimental approaches, and
  the development of internal expertise, creating multidisciplinary teams, and
  integrating marketing knowledge, data analysis, and technology. All business
  functions should collaborate to improve loyalty. Only through a holistic, integrated view of loyalty will it be possible to meet future challenges and seize the
  emerging opportunities of an increasingly competitive and volatile market.

- **Understand the *why*, not just the *what*.**
  It also seems necessary to integrate behavioral analyses with qualitative insights and studies to explore in more detail the psychological and relational
  dynamics that drive loyalty. Such an approach can help deepen our understanding of the decision-making processes underlying purchase decisions
  and repeat behavior from a loyalty perspective. Approaches such as in-depth
  interviews, digital ethnographies, or analysis of social media activities can
  reveal crucial insights on how to make LPs more attractive.

- **Set clear goals for effective loyalty strategies.**
  Loyalty strategies should be modulated according to the tools-goals nexus.
  For example, if the goal is to incentivize word-of-mouth, the focus should be
  placed more on investing in attitudinal loyalty, since this reflects customers'
  willingness to recommend the brand, regardless of the constraints that influence their purchasing behaviors. Therefore, before allocating resources,
  companies need to carefully consider whether their customer loyalty is more
  attitudinal or behavioral. A customer with high attitudinal loyalty may have a
  high NPS, but without appropriate behavioral loyalty, the effect on business
  performance may be limited.

- **Monitor all stages of the customer loyalty journey.**
  The customer loyalty journey is multifaceted and complex, which gives rise
  to the need to implement different strategies and measurements depending
  on the level of customer loyalty. Loyalty practitioners, experts, and scholars

should implement loyalty measuring strategies that consider each stage of the customer journey, including the following aspects: cognitive (appreciation of product/service features and functionality), attitudinal (perceptions and opinions), conative (purchase intention), and behavioral (actual purchase actions). This approach lets us get a better grasp on how customers develop their loyalty so we can effectively intervene at each stage of the funnel to maximize the impact of our loyalty strategies. To have a holistic view, regardless of the channel employed, organizations should focus on solid technology infrastructure, introduce effective data management practices, and implement a well-defined strategy for measuring and evaluating customer behavior in a consistent, omnichannel way. An integrated view of data enables timely strategic and marketing decisions, as well as the resolution of any critical issues.

- **Align values and strengthen relationships.**
  LPs can be the go-to architecture for promoting greater value alignment between the company and the customer. Such programs should not only include short-term incentives but also focus on long-term strategies that build strong relationships based on commitment, trust, and satisfaction. For example, by integrating sustainability-related incentives into LPs with rewards for customers who purchase sustainable products, companies can encourage more conscious purchasing behaviors. In addition, implementing digital technologies makes it possible to personalize the customer experience, improving the effectiveness of LPs and the emotional connection between the customer and the company, establishing stronger loyalty relationships over time.

- **Remember the importance of trust for data-driven approaches.**
  Among the challenges practitioners face, there is the issue of privacy protection, skepticism, and public resistance to sharing personal information. Inspiring trust about the proper use of data, while respecting sensitive information, incentivizes the client to consent to data processing. Adopting virtuous practices in data management is a key part of building a corporate reputation. If customers perceive trustworthiness, they may be more likely to share personal data, based on assumptions driven by that trust. In this way, practitioners can expand their customer base and promote more accurate segmentation and personalization of value propositions.

- **The benefits of an LP evolve based on the loyalty that it generates.**
  Very often LPs suffer from an appreciable level of staticity, manifesting little flexibility in adapting to different types of customers, who in turn present

heterogeneous levels of trust and loyalty to the retail brand. While in the initial part of the retailer-customer relationship, it may be sufficient to invest in price promotions aimed at strengthening rational trust, in the later steps of the trust-building process, these are no longer enough. To shore up relational trust and subsequently value-based trust, different tools must be deployed, capable of strengthening the relationship (e.g., gamification) and shared values (e.g., participation in CSR-related initiatives). The presence of heterogeneous customer segments should be reflected in differentiated benefits for each cluster. The one-size-fits-all approach that offers so many (often untargeted) alternatives to customers should give way to a tier-based loyalty proposition aimed at truly rewarding them, making them special, and also reinforcing the desirability of higher tiers.

- **Measure the effectiveness of sustainability initiatives on loyalty.**
  At the intersection of sustainable practices and their measurement in terms of loyalty, a consistent gap emerges. Conceptually, it is not always clear what the link is and whether sustainability is an effective vehicle in determining loyalty dynamics. A better understanding of the relationships between these two concepts and their benefits is essential to achieve effective alignment. Furthermore, to assist in the proper implementation of these strategies, it is essential to develop reliable metrics, to measure the impact of sustainable practices on loyalty. These measures should combine quantitative and qualitative indicators to reflect customer behavior and perceptions of the company's efforts.

- **Use loyalty promotions instead of undifferentiated price cuts.**
  After the pandemic, promotional price pressure increased significantly, returning to pre-COVID-19 levels for some distribution formats. As reiterated repeatedly in this volume, undifferentiated price promotions risk fueling opportunistic behavior by demand, discriminating against loyal customers, and creating negative impacts on corporate profits and the stability of the customer base. In contrast, developing approaches to reward loyal customer behaviors and customer loyalty in general is proven to be effective in both studies and management practice. So, it takes courage to curb undifferentiated price promotions, which absorb sizeable economic resources from distribution and industry, and multiply loyalty promotions, boosting the long-term value of the customer base.

7.4 Academia and business together generate value

Retail and manufacturing businesses have vast amounts of data and direct access to their customers, but these organizations may not have the scientific expertise, the structure, or the resources in-house to make the most of these assets. In an environment of resource scarcity, very often the use of data is functional to target short-term actions, neglecting deep consumer knowledge, which may require more time and information to generate and manage. On the other hand, academia possesses the most advanced scientific knowledge and research methodologies, but often accessing data and reaching customers directly is difficult. Close collaboration between these two realities can generate mutual value, allowing businesses to improve their strategies and academia to apply relevant knowledge to real-world contexts, leading to advances in research and practice, and enriching both worlds. We must be willing to take bold steps both in academia, by innovating research and making it relevant and useful for management, and in business, by supporting research and giving researchers access to valuable data. In short, we need to have the courage to break down the walls often erected between the ivory towers of academia and the world of management practice, building bridges and engaging in ongoing dialogues instead. This research project represents a concrete step in this direction.

For this, too, we are extremely grateful to TCC, which pioneered the first study on the topic of loyalty promotions more than 30 years ago, and to all the managers who have patiently supported us in carrying out the Loyalty Promotion Monitor research summarized in this text. We are confident that they will provide us with their support in the future as well, to evolve the dialogue between academia and business and foster the advancement of knowledge and the growth of competitiveness of our distribution system.

Part Two
CORPORATE EXPERIENCE

CHAPTER 8
LOYALTY MANAGEMENT AND MEASUREMENT ACCORDING TO TCC: A DATA-DRIVEN APPROACH

[Generoso Branca, Andrea Ciacci, Damien Katris and Yana Rubashkina]

8.1 Introduction

In the current competitive landscape, the ability to measure and optimize loyalty campaigns has become a critical strategic asset for retailers. However, in Italy, the adoption of advanced loyalty management and measurement practices is heterogeneous, with many companies still at the preliminary stage. In fact, against a huge wealth of data and information, the number of industry players approaching such processes according to purely data-driven logic is undersized. This chapter explores the approach of TCC Global (henceforth TCC), showing how the most advanced methodologies and strategic use of data can profoundly influence the performance of loyalty campaigns.

8.2 TCC

TCC is a global leader specializing in designing loyalty programs and innovative marketing solutions. Founded to help businesses build lasting and meaningful relationships with their customers, the company has an international presence with offices and operations in several countries worldwide. Indeed, its vision is to become a global reference partner. By focusing on innovation and operational excellence, TCC aspires to revolutionize the loyalty landscape, creating programs that are both rewarding for consumers and profitable for business partners, and generating positive impacts on the lives of consumers, their families, and communities through retail.

The company's mission is to create value for its clients through effective, innovative loyalty solutions. TCC is committed to deeply understanding the consumers' needs and motivations, offering experiences that not only encourage repeat purchases but also build genuine and lasting loyalty toward the brand.

TCC offers a wide range of services to enhance customer engagement and increase brand loyalty. For years, the company has worked closely with retailers and other businesses to develop customized campaigns aimed at stimulating desired purchasing behaviors and strengthening the emotional connection between consumers and the brand.

TCC's main activities include:

- **Developing loyalty programs.** The company designs and implements tailored loyalty programs to drive buyer engagement, purchase frequency, average spending, penetration, and loyalty card usage, using rewards and incentives suitable for target audiences.
- **Designing integrated marketing solutions.** TCC offers multichannel marketing campaigns that combine traditional and digital elements to maximize the reach and impact of promotional initiatives.
- **Analyzing customer data and insights.** Using advanced data analysis tools, TCC helps businesses better understand consumer behaviors and preferences, enabling more informed, customer-oriented strategic decisions.

8.3 TCC's approach to loyalty

Data lies at the core of TCC's actions, which are deployed by taking a holistic and data-driven approach to designing and executing loyalty campaigns based on three fundamental pillars:

1. customized campaign design
2. performance monitoring and optimization
3. post-campaign analysis

Every stage of the campaign lifecycle is supported by rigorous data analysis aimed at maximizing both return on investment (ROI) and return on emotion (ROE) for retailers.

8.3.1 *Campaign design*

The first step in designing an effective loyalty campaign is the data collection and analysis phase before the campaign is launched. Using various sources, such as transactional data from loyalty card programs, weekly sales, or spending brackets, TCC develops tailored strategies for each client. Customer segmentation is crucial at this stage as it helps identify the most relevant target groups and establish a reference baseline. With advanced predictive models, the company can accurately forecast campaign performance in terms of participation, units sold, and redemption, supporting the sales process and overall campaign development, while ensuring retailers can optimally manage investment levels.

8.3.2 *Performance monitoring*

During the campaign, TCC employs a set of operational, commercial, and behavioral KPIs to constantly monitor performance. This monitoring occurs periodically and includes omnichannel solutions, integrating data from online media, in-store media, and gamification initiatives. Such an approach allows project teams to intervene promptly, optimizing the campaign in real-time by adjusting parameters and initial projections, ensuring a rapid response to any deviations from the original design.

8.3.3 *Post-campaign analysis*

Once the campaign is over, the focus shifts to measuring and analyzing the results. This phase involves a comprehensive evaluation of the campaign's impact on relevant KPIs: customer loyalty, return on emotions, sales growth, purchase frequency, loyalty card acquisition and penetration, scan rate, churn rate, massification (i.e., the percentage of customers who used a coupon in a month), repeat shoppers, market share, and NPS (as detailed in Section 8.4). TCC employs advanced analytics to assess the evolution of customer behavior during the campaign and determine its overall outcome. These insights are then integrated into the company's ecosystem to improve future projections and optimize upcoming campaigns.

8.3.4 *The lifecycle of a loyalty campaign*

The approach described above is reflected in the process illustrated in Figure 8.1. The foundation for developing this process is the availability of information: the more detailed and comprehensive the data used, the more effective and impactful the process will be.

   In summary, the lifecycle of a loyalty campaign is characterized by several key stages:

- **Campaign design.** The first involves designing the loyalty campaign, which means deciding on the campaign's mechanics and the offer, identifying target segments, and establishing a baseline.
- **Forecasting and projections.** The second phase focuses on forecasting and projections, detecting patterns and trends, defining the campaign's characteristics, and managing investments.
- **Campaign monitoring.** Once the campaign is launched, continuous monitoring ensures that the objectives are being met and allows for timely action in case of unforeseen issues or deviations from the original design.
- **Optimization and forecasting.** Weekly performance monitoring enables projections to be adjusted based on actual performance, ensuring maximum efficiency of the investment.
- **Post-campaign analysis.** Once the campaign is completed, the process moves to post-campaign analysis and measurement, which covers a comprehensive dashboard of KPIs relevant to the retailer. This phase allows for outlining the campaign's performance and developing stronger future campaigns.

Figure 8.1　**The steps of a loyalty campaign**

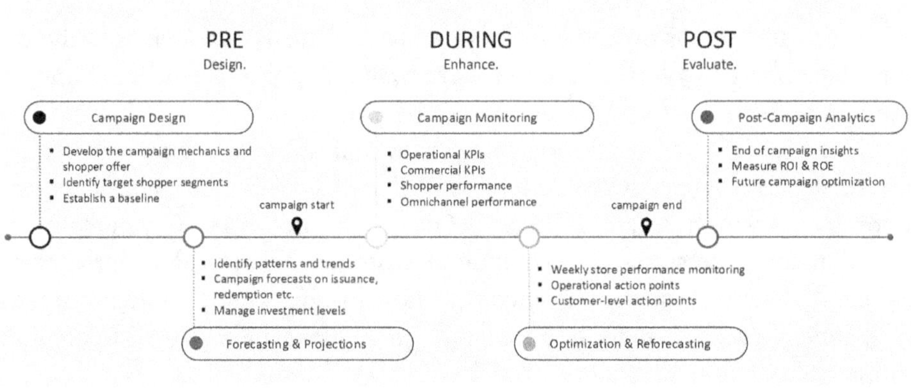

8.4　Depth in data analytics

TCC's portfolio of activities in terms of data analytics reflects the approach and processes described so far, as summarized in Figure 8.2.

- **Market insight** includes sector analysis, changes in preferences, and economic trends that influence purchasing behavior.

Figure 8.2   **TCC's portfolio of activities, in terms of data analytics**

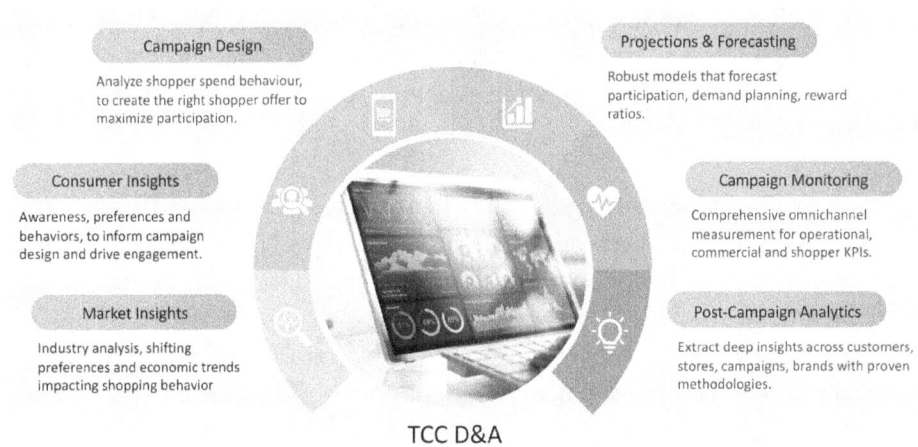

Campaign Design

Analyze shopper spend behaviour, to create the right shopper offer to maximize participation.

Projections & Forecasting

Robust models that forecast participation, demand planning, reward ratios.

Consumer Insights

Awareness, preferences and behaviors, to inform campaign design and drive engagement.

Campaign Monitoring

Comprehensive omnichannel measurement for operational, commercial and shopper KPIs.

Market Insights

Industry analysis, shifting preferences and economic trends impacting shopping behavior

Post-Campaign Analytics

Extract deep insights across customers, stores, campaigns, brands with proven methodologies.

TCC D&A

- **Customer insight** covers consumer awareness, preferences, and behaviors, aimed at guiding campaign design and building engagement.
- **Campaign design** involves analyzing buyer spending behavior to create the right offer that maximizes participation in loyalty campaigns.
- **Forecasting and projections** include developing reliable models to predict campaign participation, plan demand, and manage reward ratios.
- **Campaign monitoring** refers to the comprehensive omnichannel measurement of operational, commercial, and behavioral KPIs.
- **Post-campaign analysis** involves extracting detailed insights on customers, stores, campaigns, and brands using established methodologies.

8.5   The value of data and KPIs

TCC employs diverse methodologies for measuring loyalty, which go beyond simple sales KPIs and embrace a more complex, multifaceted analysis of loyalty campaign performance. The use and analysis of data follow three fundamental principles:

- **value**, to assess the full effects of the campaign and its impact on the business;
- **optimization**, to monitor the campaign, fine-tuning it to achieve set KPIs; and
- **understanding**, to gain detailed insights into business activities and customer behavior.

A comprehensive loyalty measurement extends beyond simple sales metrics. This approach instead builds additional value by shifting from traditional loyalty KPIs (such as basket size, purchase frequency, sales growth, NPS, or market share) to a broader set of indicators, including penetration rate, number of shoppers, churn, and so forth. TCC monitors a wide spectrum of KPIs that fall into three macro-areas:

- **Reach** measures the campaign's ability to generate awareness and engagement (i.e., marketing activation) using operational and social media data. KPIs in this area are omnichannel awareness, in-store execution, ad impressions, and clicks, among others.
- **Reward** evaluates the conversion of awareness into participation, based on reward redemption rates, participation, and sales. Key KPIs include participation rate, issuance rate, demand forecasts, and reward popularity.
- **Return** analyzes the campaign's impact on short- and long-term ROI, customer loyalty, and brand value, using both transactional data and qualitative research. Some typical KPIs here are ROI, ROE, shopper segments, NPS, and market share.

8.5.1 *Measurement tools*

TCC's holistic approach is characterized by the use of various measurement tools.

Figure 8.3   **The main categories of KPIs**

Control group

The most robust method is control group analysis. This approach involves creating groups of customers who participate in the campaign (redeemers) and similar groups who do not (non-redeemers) based on criteria such as spending, purchase frequency, and shopper type. By comparing these groups, it is possible to isolate the campaign's effect on purchasing behaviors, providing an accurate measure of increases in sales and purchase frequency and calculating ROI. This methodology is distinctly quantitative, as measurement relies on big data tools and techniques, with a strong statistical foundation that allows the company to manage millions of transactions (typically covering periods from six months to two years).

This methodology was developed in collaboration with the Universidad Carlos III of Madrid – IbiDat (Banco Santander Institute of Big Data).

Figure 8.5 below gives an example of how ROI is measured. The control group, made up of customers who don't participate in the loyalty program (non-redeemers), shows very similar behavior to those who do (redeemers) in terms of spending and purchase frequency before the campaign begins. But when it does, we see a net difference between the two groups, as evidenced by the divergence in the behavior curve.

This indicates that the loyalty initiative has a positive impact on redeemers compared to non-redeemers.

Figure 8.4   **The control group methodology**

Objective

Establish a group of redeemers and a "look-alike" group of non-redeemers based on spend, frequency and typology to examine the campaign's impact on shopper behaviour (spend & frequency).

→ Measurement based on Big Data techniques and technology, using robust mathematical and statistical foundations.

→ Manage millions of transactions from retailers using "R" software.

→ Methodology developed in partnership with University Carlos III Madrid – IBiDat (Banco Santander Institute of Big Data).

500k redeemers   250k control group
                                  (non-redeemers)

Figure 8.5   **The economic return on the loyalty campaign**

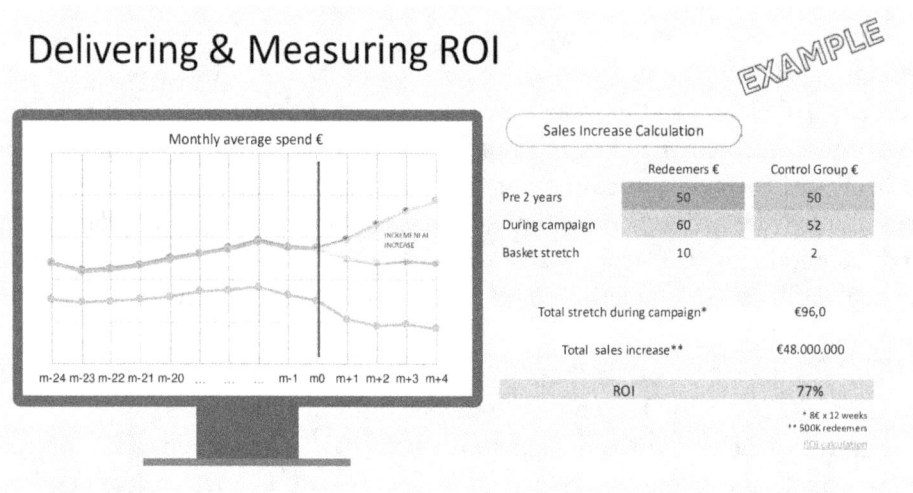

Shopper insights (panel)

TCC employs additional techniques to enrich the understanding of loyalty dynamics. This approach consists of focus groups (qualitative method) and surveys (quantitative method), often conducted in collaboration with third-party partners. These analyses provide insights into behavioral changes and the campaign's impact on brand perception, adding an emotional dimension to loyalty measurement.

Like-for-like (L4L) stores

Another approach is comparing the sales performance of similar stores during the campaign period against the same period in the previous year. This method allows for a quick evaluation of the campaign's local impact, though it offers less granularity compared to the methods described earlier.

8.6 Enhancing loyalty and sales with data: a success story

TCC collaborated with a North American grocery retailer to design, implement, and measure the impact of an in-store loyalty campaign offering high-perceived-value dinnerware as rewards. The campaign provided customers with a strong incentive—a 90% discount off the retail price—making it a compelling offer. By collecting digital stamps through the retailer's loyalty app and redeeming them for dinnerware, customers were encouraged to use their loyalty cards more frequently.

The objectives were clear: to increase sales and purchase frequency while boosting loyalty card registration, scan rates, and penetration. This dual approach targeted both customer loyalty and commercial KPIs. To support these efforts, the campaign was heavily promoted both in-store and online. In fact, customers were exposed to the campaign everywhere, from in-store posters to digital displays, social media, and the retailer's mobile app, which offered digital stamps, coupons, and personalized deals. Through the app, customers could easily scan their loyalty cards and collect and redeem stamps for rewards, simplifying the entire experience.

Throughout the campaign, data was the key to verifying its impact. TCC collected transaction and loyalty card data to evaluate how well the campaign performed against its KPIs. The results were excellent: loyalty card penetration ticked up by 5%, and the campaign attracted numerous new high-spend customers, driving significant sales volume.

While the overall redemption rate of stamps was 32%, the average participant redeemed about 2.5 rewards. Redeemers, who represented 20% of those who collected stamps, accounted for 37% of total sales and shopped 40% more frequently than the average customer during the campaign.

To further understand shopper behavior, TCC used RFM (Recency, Frequency, and Monetary) analysis to segment participants and track their movements across groups during the campaign (Figure 8.6). The results were extremely interesting: most "champions" (high-value customers) remained in their segment, while many loyal customers moved up to this higher level by augmenting their spending and purchase frequency. Additionally, there was a net increase of 8% in new customers, demonstrating the campaign's success in driving growth. Thanks to these insights, retailers were able to strategically target new customers with personalized offers after the campaign, with the goal of retaining them as champions before the next promotion.

The data also revealed a strong correlation between reward redemption and loyalty card penetration. The more stamps customers collected, the more frequently they scanned their loyalty cards, which is a key KPI for all retailers. The upturn in card scans provided valuable customer data, underscoring the importance of the campaign in promoting both engagement and actionable insights. To further evaluate the campaign's impact, TCC compared the behavior of redeemers with a control group of non-redeemers. The results showed a clear divergence in spending and purchase frequency, with redeemers exhibiting con-

Figure 8.6   **The shift in customer clusters**

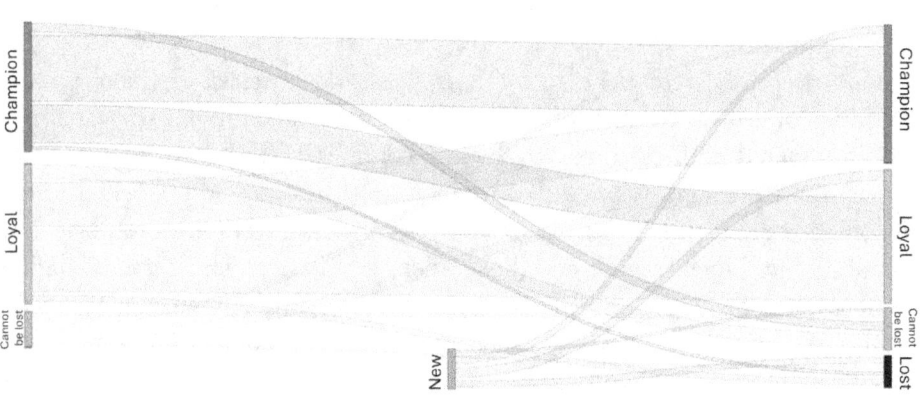

siderably higher engagement. The analysis also highlighted an upturn in overall sales of 4.2% among loyalty cardholders, demonstrating the campaign's effectiveness in driving both revenue growth and shopper participation.

Operational KPIs, particularly stock management efficiency, were also closely monitored. TCC analyzed the redemption curve alongside delivery data, ensuring that forecasts and inventory levels were well balanced. Throughout the campaign, inventory was efficiently managed, and real-time adjustments were made to meet demand. At the SKU level, performance was measured to pinpoint the items that performed above or below expectations, allowing for a quick adjustment of the offer.

The standardized, automated measurement methods used by TCC made the entire process highly efficient. By reducing manual effort and streamlining workflow, TCC provided the retailer with valuable insights into customer behavior, enabling that company to tailor post-campaign communications and retain newly acquired customers.

In conclusion, the campaign not only boosted sales and loyalty card penetration but also provided the retailer with valuable data to refine future strategies, solidifying TCC's role as a trusted partner in maximizing customer engagement and long-term loyalty.

8.7 Conclusions

TCC's approach to loyalty measurement exemplifies what retailers can achieve by adopting a data-driven strategy. Beyond enhancing campaign performance, this approach enables retailers to gain detailed insights into customer behavior, optimize marketing strategies, and increase customer loyalty. Access to more comprehensive data and the willingness of retailers to share this information are essential in fully leveraging the potential of loyalty campaigns, bridging the technological and analytical gap, and significantly improving market performance and competitiveness.

BIBLIOGRAPHY

Aflaki, S., & Popescu, I. (2014). Managing retention in service relationships. *Management Science*, *60*(2), 415-433.

Ailawadi, K. L., Gedenk, K., Lutzky, C., & Neslin, S. A. (2007). Decomposition of the sales impact of promotion-induced stockpiling. *Journal of Marketing Research*, *44*(3), 450-467.

Ailawadi, K. L., Lehmann, D. R., & Neslin, S. A. (2001). Market response to a major policy change in the marketing mix: Learning from Procter & Gamble's value pricing strategy. *Journal of Marketing*, *65*(1), 44-61.

Ailawadi, K. L., Neslin, S. A., Luan, Y. J., & Taylor, G. A. (2014). Does retailer CSR enhance behavioral loyalty? A case for benefit segmentation. *International Journal of Research in Marketing*, *31*(2), 156-167.

Ailawadi, K. L., Pauwels, K., & Steenkamp, J. B. E. (2008). Private-label use and store loyalty. *Journal of Marketing*, *72*(6), 19-30.

Andaleeb S. S., (1996), An Experimental Investigation of Satisfaction and Commitment in Marketing channels: The role of trust and dependence. *Journal of Retailing, 72(1),* 77–93

Andaleeb, S.S., (1992). The Trust Concept: Research Issues for Channel of Distribution, in J.N. Sheth (a cura di) *Research in Marketing*, Vol. 11, Jai Press Inc., 1-34.

Arens, Z. G., & Rust, R. T. (2012). The duality of decisions and the case for impulsiveness metrics. *Journal of the Academy of Marketing Science*, *40*, 468-479.

Arnold, T. J., (Er) Fang, E., & Palmatier, R. W. (2011). The effects of customer acquisition and retention orientations on a firm's radical and incremental innovation performance. *Journal of the Academy of Marketing Science*, *39*, 234-251.

Ascarza, E., Iyengar, R., & Schleicher, M. (2016). The perils of proactive churn prevention using plan recommendations: Evidence from a field experiment. *Journal of Marketing Research*, *53*(1), 46-60.

Ascarza, E., Netzer, O., & Hardie, B. G. (2018). Some customers would rather leave without saying goodbye. *Marketing Science*, *37*(1), 54-77.

Baehre, S., O'Dwyer, M., O'Malley, L., & Lee, N. (2022). The use of Net Promoter Score (NPS) to predict sales growth: insights from an empirical investigation. *Journal of the Academy of Marketing Science*, *50*(1), 67-84.

Batra, R., Ahuvia, A., & Bagozzi, R. P. (2012). Brand love. *Journal of Marketing*, 76(2), 1-16.

Bazeley, P., & Jackson, K. (2013). *Qualitative data analysis with NVIVO*. Los Angeles, CA, Sage.

Becker, J. U., Greve, G., & Albers, S. (2009). The impact of technological and organizational implementation of CRM on customer acquisition, maintenance, and retention. *International Journal of Research in Marketing*, 26(3), 207-215.

Bell, D. R., Ho, T. H., & Tang, C. S. (1998). Determining where to shop: Fixed and variable costs of shopping. *Journal of Marketing Research*, 35(3), 352-369.

Bellenger D.N., Steinberg E., & Stanton WW. (1976). The Congruence of Store Image and Self-Image, *Journal of Retailing*, 52 (Spring), 17-32.

Belli, A., O'Rourke, AM., Carrillat, F.A., Pupovac, L., Melnyk, V., & Napolova, E. (2022). 40 years of loyalty programs: how effective are they? Generalizations from a meta-analysis. *Journal of the Academy of Marketing Science*, 50, 147–173.

Beltagui, A., & Candi, M. (2018). Revisiting service quality through the lens of experience-centric services. *International Journal of Operations & Production Management*, 38(3), 915-932.

Berry, L.L. (1969). The Components of Department Store Image: A Theoretical and Empirical Analysis, *Journal of Retailing*, 45(1), 3-20.

Borle, S., Boatwright, P., Kadane, J. B., Nunes, J. C., & Galit, S. (2005). The effect of product assortment changes on customer retention. *Marketing Science*, 24(4), 616-622.

Brady, M. K., Voorhees, C. M., & Brusco, M. J. (2012). Service sweethearting: Its antecedents and customer consequences. *Journal of Marketing*, 76(2), 81-98.

Brakus, J. J., Schmitt, B. H., & Zarantonello, L. (2009). Brand experience: what is it? How is it measured? Does it affect loyalty?. *Journal of Marketing*, 73(3), 52-68.

Braun, V., & Clarke, V. (2019). Reflecting on reflexive thematic analysis. *Qualitative research in sport, exercise and health*, 11(4), 589-597.

Braun, V., & Clarke, V. (2021). Can I use TA? Should I use TA? Should I not use TA? Comparing reflexive thematic analysis and other pattern—based qualitative analytic approaches. *Counselling and psychotherapy research*, 21(1), 37-47.

Briggs, E., & Grisaffe, D. (2010). Service performance—loyalty intentions link in a business-to-business context: The role of relational exchange outcomes and customer characteristics. *Journal of Service Research*, 13(1), 37-51.

Burnham, T. A., Frels, J. K., & Mahajan, V. (2003). Consumer switching costs: A typology, antecedents, and consequences. *Journal of the Academy of Marketing Science*, 31, 109-126.

Burton, S., Lichtenstein, D. R., Netemeyer, R. G., & Garretson, J. A. (1998). A scale for measuring attitude toward private label products and an examination of its psychological and behavioral correlates. *Journal of the Academy of Marketing Science*, 26, 293-306.

Busacca B. & Bertoli G. (2024). *Customer Value. Soddisfazione, Fedeltà, Valore (4a ed.)*, Egea, Milano.

Busacca B. & Castaldo S., (2002), La Customer Loyalty: Definizione, Misurazione e Valore, in Castaldo, S., & Mauri, C. (a cura di). *Il loyalty management nella distribuzione moderna*, Egea, Milano.

Busacca, B., (1990). *Analisi del consumatore*, Egea, Milano.

Campbell, C., Sands, S., McFerran, B., & Mavrommatis, A. (2023). Diversity representation in advertising. *Journal of the Academy of Marketing Science*.

Campbell, S., Greenwood, M., Prior, S., Shearer, T., Walkem, K., Young, S., ... & Walker, K. (2020). Purposive sampling: complex or simple? Research case examples. *Journal of research in Nursing*, 25(8), 652-661.

Cardozo R.N. (1974). How Image Vary by Product Class, *Journal of Retailing*, 4 (Winter), 85-98.

Castaldo, S. (2002). *Fiducia e relazioni di mercato*. Il Mulino, Bologna.

Castaldo, S. (2010). *Go to Market*. Il Mulino, Bologna.

Castaldo, S., & Mauri, C. (1993). *Promozioni-fedeltà nella distribuzione moderna. Un'indagine empirica*, Egea, Milano.

Castaldo, S., & Mauri, C. (2002). *Il loyalty management nella distribuzione moderna*, Egea, Milano.

Castaldo, S., & Molteni, L., (1992). Il posizionamento dell'impresa commerciale: un'evidenza empirica. *Economia & Management, 2*, 28-40.

Chaudhuri, A., & Holbrook, M. B. (2001). The chain of effects from brand trust and brand affect to brand performance: the role of brand loyalty. *Journal of marketing*, 65(2), 81-93.

Chaudhuri, M., Voorhees, C. M., & Beck, J. M. (2019). The effects of loyalty program introduction and design on short-and long-term sales and gross profits. *Journal of the Academy of marketing science*, 47, 640-658.

Chen, Y., Mandler, T., & Meyer-Waarden, L. (2021). Three decades of research on loyalty programs: A literature review and future research agenda. *Journal of Business Research*, 124, 179-197.

Chitturi, R., Raghunathan, R., & Mahajan, V. (2008). Delight by design: The role of hedonic versus utilitarian benefits. *Journal of Marketing*, 72(3), 48-63.

Cooil, B., Keiningham, T. L., Aksoy, L., & Hsu, M. (2007). A longitudinal analysis of customer satisfaction and share of wallet: Investigating the moderating effect of customer characteristics. *Journal of Marketing*, 71(1), 67-83.

Coop (2023), Rapporto Coop.

Corbin, J., & Strauss, A. (2008). Basics of qualitative research: Techniques and procedures for developing grounded theory (3rd ed.). Tousand Oaks, CA: SAGE.

Costabile M. & Marzocchi G. (1995). L'analisi e la misurazione della customer satisfaction nelle banche, *Micro & Macro Marketing, 3,* 401-424.

Costabile, M. (2000). Un modello dinamico di customer loyalty. *Working Paper Ossevatorio di Marketing*, 57, inverno, SDA Bocconi.

Costabile, M. (2001). *Il capitale relazionale*, McGraw Hill, Milano.

D'Aveni, R.A. (2016). *Commodity Trap*, Franco Angeli, Milano.

Daryanto, A., de Ruyter, K., Wetzels, M., & Patterson, P. G. (2010). Service firms and customer loyalty programs: a regulatory fit perspective of reward preferences in a health club setting. *Journal of the Academy of Marketing Science, 38,* 604-616.

Davies, G., & Brooks, J. (1989). *Positioning strategy in retailing,* Paul Chapman Publishing, London.

Deighton, J., & Grayson K. (1995). Marketing and Seduction: Building Exchange Relationship by Managing Social Consensus. *Journal of Consumer Research,* 660-676.

Demoulin, N. T., & Zidda, P. (2009). Drivers of customers' adoption and adoption timing of a new loyalty card in the grocery retail market. *Journal of Retailing, 85*(3), 391-405.

Diversity Brand Index (2024).

Dixon, M., & Verma, R. (2013). Sequence effects in service bundles: Implications for service design and scheduling. *Journal of Operations Management, 31*(3), 138-152.

Dong, S., Ding, M., Grewal, R., & Zhao, P. (2011a). Functional forms of the satisfaction–loyalty relationship. *International Journal of Research in Marketing, 28*(1), 38-50.

Dong, X., & Chintagunta, P. K. (2016). Satisfaction spillovers across categories. *Marketing Science, 35*(2), 275-283.

Dong, Y., Yao, Y., & Cui, T. H. (2011b). When acquisition spoils retention: Direct selling vs. Delegation under CRM. *Management Science, 57*(7), 1288-1299.

Donthu, N., & Cherian, J. (1994). Impact of strength of ethnic identification on Hispanic shopping behavior. *Journal of Retailing, 70*(4), 383-393.

Doyle, P., & Fenwick, I. (1974), How Store Image Affects Shopping Habits in Grocery Chains, *Journal of Retailing, 50*(4), 39.

Dwayne Ball, A., & Tasaki, L. H. (1992). The role and measurement of attachment in consumer behavior. *Journal of Consumer Psychology, 1*(2), 155-172.

Dwyer, F.R., Schurr, P.H. and Oh, S. (1987) Developing Buyer-Seller Relationships. *Journal of Marketing,* 51, 11-27.

Echambadi, R., Jindal, R. P., & Blair, E. A. (2013). Evaluating and managing brand repurchase across multiple geographic retail markets. *Journal of Retailing, 89*(4), 409-422.

Eisenhardt, K. M. (1989). Building theories from case study research. *Academy of management review,* 14(4), 532-550.

Eisenhardt, K.M., & Graebner, M.E. (2007). Theory building from cases: Opportunities and challenges. *Academy of Management Journal,* 50(1), 25–32.

Elo, S., & Kyngäs, H. (2008). The qualitative content analysis process. *Journal of advanced nursing,* 62(1), 107-115.

Finfgeld-Connett, D. (2014). Use of content analysis to conduct knowledge-building and theory-generating qualitative systematic reviews. *Qualitative research,* 14(3), 341-352.

Fink, A. (2009). *Conducting research literature reviews: From the internet to paper* (3rd ed.). Sage, Thousand Oaks, CA.

Fishbein M.A, & Ajzen I. (1975). *Belief, Attitude, Intention and Behaviour: An Introduction to Theory and Research,* Addison-Wesley, Reading, MA.

Fontenot, R.J., & Wilson, E.J. (1997). Relational Exchange: A Review of Selected Models for a Prediction Matrix of Relationship Activities. *Journal of Business Research*, *39*, 5-12.

Ford D. (1980). The Development of Buyer-Seller Relationships, *European Journal of Marketing, vol. 14*, 339-354.

Fullerton, G. (2003). When does commitment lead to loyalty?. *Journal of Service Research*, *5*(4), 333-344.

Ganesan, S. (1994). Determinants of Long-Term Orientation in Buyer-Seller Relationships, *Journal of Marketing*, *58*, 1-19.

Gao, L., de Haan, E., Melero-Polo, I., & Sese, F. J. (2023). Winning your customers' minds and hearts: Disentangling the effects of lock-in and affective customer experience on retention. *Journal of the Academy of Marketing Science*, *51*(2), 334-371.

Garnefeld, I., Eggert, A., Helm, S. V., & Tax, S. S. (2013). Growing existing customers' revenue streams through customer referral programs. *Journal of Marketing*, *77*(4), 17-32.

Grace, D., Ross, M., & King, C. (2018). Brand fidelity: a relationship maintenance perspective. *Journal of Brand Management*, *25*(6), 577-590.

Grissemann, U. S., & Stokburger-Sauer, N. E. (2012). Customer co-creation of travel services: The role of company support and customer satisfaction with the co-creation performance. *Tourism Management*, *33*(6), 1483-1492.

Gronroos, C. (1990). *Service Management and Marketing: Managing the Moment of Truth in Service Competition*, Lexington Books, Lexington, Mass.

Gu, Z., Bapna, R., Chan, J., & Gupta, A. (2022). Measuring the impact of crowdsourcing features on mobile app user engagement and retention: A randomized field experiment. *Management Science*, *68*(2), 1297-1329.

Guadagni, P. M., & Little, J. D. (2008). A logit model of brand choice calibrated on scanner data. *Marketing Science*, *27*(1), 29-48.

Guatri, L. (1992), Relazione introduttiva al convegno *Valori di capitale economico e valori di mercato delle imprese: quali strumenti per attenuarne i divari?*, Università Luigi Bocconi, Milano.

Guo, L. (2023). Overage Charge or Loyalty Discount: When Should Extra Consumptions Be Penalized or Rewarded?. *Marketing Science*, *42*(3), 614-633.

Gupta S. & Zeithaml, V. (2006). Customer Metrics and Their Impact on Financial Performance. *Marketing Science*, *25*, 718-739.

Gutman, J., & Alden, S. (1985). Adolescents' Cognitive Structures of Retail Stores and Fashion Consumption: A Means-End Chain Analysis of Quality, in J. Jacoby, J. Olson (a cura di) *Perceived Quality. How Consumers View Stores and Merchandise*, Lexington Books, Lexington, Mass.

Hansen, K., & Singh, V. (2008). Research note—Are store-brand buyers store loyal? An empirical investigation. *Management Science*, *54*(10), 1828-1834.

Harrigan, P., Evers, U., Miles, M., & Daly, T. (2017). Customer engagement with tourism social media brands. *Tourism Management*, *59*, 597-609.

Harris, L. C., & Goode, M. M. (2004). The four levels of loyalty and the pivotal role of trust: a study of online service dynamics. *Journal of Retailing, 80*(2), 139-158.

Haumann, T., Quaiser, B., Wieseke, J., & Rese, M. (2014). Footprints in the sands of time: A comparative analysis of the effectiveness of customer satisfaction and customer–company identification over time. *Journal of Marketing, 78*(6), 78-102.

Herhausen, D., Emrich, O., Grewal, D., Kipfelsberger, P., & Schoegel, M. (2020). Face forward: How employees' digital presence on service websites affects customer perceptions of website and employee service quality. *Journal of Marketing Research, 57*(5), 917-936.

Herhausen, D., Kleinlercher, K., Verhoef, P. C., Emrich, O., & Rudolph, T. (2019). Loyalty formation for different customer journey segments. *Journal of Retailing, 95*(3), 9-29.

Hill, T., Canniford, R., & Eckhardt, G. M. (2022). The roar of the crowd: How interaction ritual chains create social atmospheres. *Journal of Marketing, 86*(3), 121-139.

Hillebrand, B., Nijholt, J. J., & Nijssen, E. J. (2011). Exploring CRM effectiveness: an institutional theory perspective. *Journal of the Academy of Marketing Science, 39*, 592-608.

Hirschman, A.O. (1970), *Exit. voice and loyalty. Responses to declines in firms, organizations and states,* Harvard University Press, Cambridge, Mass.

Hirschman, E.C., Greenberg, B., & Robertson, D.H., (1978). The Intermarket Reliability of Retail Image Research: An Empirical Examination, *Journal of Retailing, 54*(1), 3-12.

Hochstein, B., Voorhees, C. M., Pratt, A. B., Rangarajan, D., Nagel, D. M., & Mehrotra, V. (2023). Customer success management, customer health, and retention in B2B industries. *International Journal of Research in Marketing, 40*(4), 912-932.

Homburg, C., & Tischer, M. (2023). Customer journey management capability in business-to-business markets: Its bright and dark sides and overall impact on firm performance. *Journal of the Academy of Marketing Science, 51*(5), 1046-1074.

Homburg, C., Wieseke, J., & Hoyer, W. D. (2009). Social identity and the service-profit chain. *Journal of Marketing, 73*(2), 38-54.

Hozier, G. C., & Stem, D. E. (1985). General retail patronage loyalty as a determinant of consumer outshopping behavior. *Journal of the Academy of Marketing Science, 13*, 32-46.

Hsieh, H. F., & Shannon, S. E. (2005). Three approaches to qualitative content analysis. *Qualitative health research, 15*(9), 1277-1288.

Hsu, C. L., Chen, M. C., Chang, K. C., & Chao, C. M. (2010). Applying loss aversion to investigate service quality in logistics: A moderating effect of service convenience. *International Journal of Operations & Production Management, 30*(5), 508-525.

Hu, F., Teichert, T., Liu, Y., Li, H., & Gundyreva, E. (2019). Evolving customer expectations of hospitality services: Differences in attribute effects on satisfaction and Re-Patronage. *Tourism Management, 74*, 345-357.

Hult, G. T. M., Sharma, P. N., Morgeson III, F. V., & Zhang, Y. (2019). Antecedents and consequences of customer satisfaction: do they differ across online and offline purchases?. *Journal of Retailing*, *95*(1), 10-23.

Iacobucci, D., & Zerrillo P. (1997). The Relationship Life Cycle: A Network-Dyad-Network Dynamic Conceptualization, and the Application of Some Classic Psychological Theories to Its Management. *Research in Marketing*, *13*, 47-68.

Iyengar, R., Jedidi, K., Essegaier, S., & Danaher, P. J. (2011). The impact of tariff structure on customer retention, usage, and profitability of access services. *Marketing Science*, *30*(5), 820-836.

Jacoby, J., & Chestnut, R. (1978). *Brand Loyalty. Measurement and Management*, John Wiley & Sons, new York.

Jacoby, J., & Kyner, D. B. (1973). Brand loyalty vs. repeat purchasing behavior. *Journal of Marketing Research*, 10, 1-9.

Jai, T.C., Tong, X., & Chen, H.S. (2022). Building brand loyalty on social media: theories, measurements, antecedents, and consequences. *Journal of Brand Management*, *29*, 35-57.

James, D.L., Durand, R.M., & Drevees R.A. (1976). The Use of Multi-Attribute Attitude Model in a Store Image Study, *Journal of Retailing*, *52*(2), 23-32.

Jones, M. A., & Reynolds, K. E. (2006). The role of retailer interest on shopping behavior. *Journal of Retailing*, *82*(2), 115-126.

Kim, H. B., & Kim, W. G. (2005). The relationship between brand equity and firms' performance in luxury hotels and chain restaurants. *Tourism Management*, *26*(4), 549-560.

Kim, H., & So, K. K. F. (2024). Customer touchpoints: Conceptualization, index development, and validation. *Tourism Management*, *103*, 104881.

Kim, W. G., Lee, C., & Hiemstra, S. J. (2004). Effects of an online virtual community on customer loyalty and travel product purchases. *Tourism Management*, *25*(3), 343-355.

Kirca, A. H. (2011). The effects of market orientation on subsidiary performance: Empirical evidence from MNCs in Turkey. *Journal of World Business*, *46*(4), 447-454.

Koçaş, C., & Bohlmann, J. D. (2008). Segmented switchers and retailer pricing strategies. *Journal of Marketing*, *72*(3), 124-142.

Koll, O., & Plank, A. (2022). Do shoppers choose the same brand on the next trip when facing the same context? An empirical investigation in FMCG retailing. *Journal of Retailing*, *98*(4), 576-592.

Koschate-Fischer, N., Cramer, J., & Hoyer, W. D. (2014). Moderating effects of the relationship between private label share and store loyalty. *Journal of Marketing*, *78*(2), 69-82.

Kuehnl, C., Jozic, D., & Homburg, C. (2019). Effective customer journey design: consumers' conception, measurement, and consequences. *Journal of the Academy of Marketing Science*, *47*, 551-568.

Kumar, V., & Shah, D. (2004). Building and sustaining profitable customer loyalty for the 21st century. *Journal of Retailing*, *80*(4), 317-329.

Kunkel, J.H., & Berry, L.L. (1968). A Behavioral Conception of Retail Image, *Journal of Marketing*, *32*, 21-27.

Lander, M. W., Heugens, P. P., & van Oosterhout, J. (2017). Towards an integrated framework of professional partnership performance: The role of formal governance and strategic planning. *Human Relations*, *70*(11), 1388-1414.

Larivière, B. (2008). Linking perceptual and behavioral customer metrics to multiperiod customer profitability: A comprehensive service-profit chain application. *Journal of Service Research*, *11*(1), 3-21.

Larivière, B., Keiningham, T. L., Aksoy, L., Yalçin, A., Morgeson III, F. V., & Mithas, S. (2016). Modeling heterogeneity in the satisfaction, loyalty intention, and shareholder value linkage: A cross-industry analysis at the customer and firm levels. *Journal of Marketing Research*, *53*(1), 91-109.

Lee, D. J., Kruger, S., Whang, M. J., Uysal, M., & Sirgy, M. J. (2014). Validating a customer well-being index related to natural wildlife tourism. *Tourism Management*, *45*, 171-180.

Lemmink, J., & Mattsson, J. (1998). Warmth during non-productive retail encounters: the hidden side of productivity. *International Journal of Research in Marketing*, *15*(5), 505-517.

Lewis, M. (2004). The influence of loyalty programs and short-term promotions on customer retention. *Journal of Marketing Research*, *41*(3), 281-292.

Li, C., Swaminathan, S., & Kim, J. (2024). Point Redemption in Loyalty Programs: The Role of Customer Relationship Characteristics and Their Implications for Service Providers. *Journal of Service Research*, 10946705241246341.

Li, X. (2010). Loyalty regardless of brands? Examining three nonperformance effects on brand loyalty in a tourism context. *Journal of Travel Research*, *49*(3), 323-336.

Liang, Y., Huang, Z., & Su, L. (2023). Too time-crunched to seek variety: the influence of parenting motivation on consumer variety seeking. *Journal of Marketing Research*, *60*(4), 812-833.

Liao, H., & Chuang, A. (2004). A multilevel investigation of factors influencing employee service performance and customer outcomes. *Academy of Management Journal*, *47*(1), 41-58.

Lim, J., Currim, I. S., & Andrews, R. L. (2005). Consumer heterogeneity in the longer-term effects of price promotions. *International Journal of Research in Marketing*, *22*(4), 441-457.

Liu, J., & Ansari, A. (2020). Understanding consumer dynamic decision making under competing loyalty programs. *Journal of Marketing Research*, *57*(3), 422-444.

Lynch Jr, J. G., & Ariely, D. (2000). Wine online: Search costs affect competition on price, quality, and distribution. *Marketing Science*, *19*(1), 83-103.

Mangus, S. M., Jones, E., Folse, J. A. G., & Sridhar, S. (2020). The interplay between business and personal trust on relationship performance in conditions of market turbulence. *Journal of the Academy of Marketing Science*, *48*, 1138-1155.

Maria Stock, R., Jong, A. D., & Zacharias, N. A. (2017). Frontline employees' innovative service behavior as key to customer loyalty: Insights into FLEs' resource gain spiral. *Journal of Product Innovation Management*, *34*(2), 223-245.

Markets & Markets (2023). Loyalty Management Market.

Maxham III, J. G., Netemeyer, R. G., & Lichtenstein, D. R. (2008). The retail value chain: linking employee perceptions to employee performance, customer evaluations, and store performance. *Marketing Science*, 27(2), 147-167.

Mayer, R.C., Davis, J.H., & Schoorman, F.D. (1995). An integrative model of organizational trust. *Academy of Management Review*, 20(3), 709-734.

Mazodier, M., & Merunka, D. (2012). Achieving brand loyalty through sponsorship: The role of fit and self-congruity. *Journal of the Academy of Marketing Science*, 40, 807-820.

McCarthy, D. M., & Oblander, E. S. (2021). Scalable data fusion with selection correction: An application to customer base analysis. *Marketing Science*, 40(3), 459-480.

McDougall, G., & Fry, J.N. (1974). Combining Two Methods of Image Measurement, *Journal of Retailing*, 50(4), 53.

McManus, L., & Guilding, C. (2008). Exploring the potential of customer accounting: A synthesis of the accounting and marketing literatures. *Journal of Marketing Management*, 24(7-8), 771-795.

Miller, C. J., Wiles, M. A., & Park, S. (2019). Trading on up: An examination of factors influencing the degree of upgrade: Evidence from cash for clunkers. *Journal of Marketing*, 83(1), 151-172.

Moorman, C., Zaltman, G., & Deshpandè. R. (1992). Relationship Between Providers and Users of Market Research: The Dynamics of Trust Within and Between Organizations, *Journal of Marketing Research*, 29, 314-329.

Morgan, N. A., & Rego, L. L. (2008). Rejoinder—Can behavioral WOM measures provide insight into the net promoter© concept of customer loyalty?. *Marketing Science*, 27(3), 533-534.

Morgan, N. A., & Rego, L. L. (2009). Brand portfolio strategy and firm performance. *Journal of Marketing*, 73(1), 59-74.

Morgan, R.M., & Hunt, S.D., (1994). The Commitment-Trust Theory of Relationship Marketing, *Journal of Marketing*, 58, 20-38.

Morgeson III, F. V., Sharma, U., Schultz, X. W., Pansari, A., Ruvio, A., & Hult, G. T. M. (2024). Weathering the crash: Do customer-company relationships pay off during economic crises?. *Journal of the Academy of Marketing Science*, 52(2), 489-511.

Morhart, F., Malär, L., Guèvremont, A., Girardin, F., & Grohmann, B. (2015). Brand authenticity: An integrative framework and measurement scale. *Journal of Consumer Psychology*, 25(2), 200-218.

Narayandas, D. (1998). Measuring and managing the benefits of customer retention: An empirical investigation. *Journal of Service Research*, 1(2), 108-128.

Newman, J. W., & Werbel, R. A. (1974). Automobile brand loyalty. *Journal of the Academy of Marketing Science*, 2, 593-601.

Ngobo, P. V. (2017). The trajectory of customer loyalty: an empirical test of Dick and Basu's loyalty framework. *Journal of the Academy of Marketing Science*, 45, 229-250.

NielsenIQ. Top4Top 2.0 - Anno XX – n° 06 – Giugno 2024.

NielsenIQ. Top4Top 2.0 - Anno XXI – 2° Semestre 2023.

Oliver, R.L. (1999). Whence consumer loyalty? *Journal of Marketing*, 63 (4-suppl1), 33-44.

Otim, S., & Grover, V. (2006). An empirical study on web-based services and customer loyalty. *European Journal of Information Systems*, *15*(6), 527-541.

Ou, Y. C., Verhoef, P. C., & Wiesel, T. (2017). The effects of customer equity drivers on loyalty across services industries and firms. *Journal of the Academy of Marketing Science*, *45*, 336-356.

Page, M. J., McKenzie, J. E., Bossuyt, P. M., Boutron, I., Hoffmann, T. C., Mulrow, C. D., Shamseer, L., Tetzlaff, J. M., Akl, E. A., Brennan, S. E., Chou, R., Glanville, J., Grimshaw, J. M., Hróbjartsson, A., Lalu, M. M., Li, T., Loder, E. W., Mayo-Wilson, E., McDonald, S., … Moher, D. (2021). The PRISMA 2020 statement: An updated guideline for reporting systematic reviews. *Systematic Reviews*, 10(1), 89.

Palmatier, R. W., Dant, R. P., & Grewal, D. (2007). A comparative longitudinal analysis of theoretical perspectives of interorganizational relationship performance. *Journal of marketing*, 71(4), 172-194.

Papatla, P., & Krishnamurthi, L. (1996). Measuring the dynamic effects of promotions on brand choice. *Journal of Marketing Research*, *33*(1), 20-35.

Park, C. W., Eisingerich, A. B., & Park, J. W. (2013). Attachment–aversion (AA) model of customer–brand relationships. *Journal of Consumer Psychology*, *23*(2), 229-248.

Patton, M.Q. (1990). *Qualitative Evaluation and Research Methods*, (2nd ed), Newbury Park, CA, Sage.

Patton, M.Q. (2014), *Qualitative Research and Evaluation Methods: Integrating Theory and Practice*, Newbury Park, CA, Sage.

Paul, J., & Benito, G.R.G. (2018). A review of research on outward foreign direct investment from emerging countries, including China: What do we know, how do we know and where should we be heading? *Asia Pacific Business Review*, *24* (1), 90–115.

Paul, J., & Criado, A. R. (2020). The art of writing literature review: What do we know and what do we need to know?. *International business review*, 29(4), 101717.

Paul, J., & Rosado-Serrano, A. (2019). Gradual internationalization vs born-global/international new venture models: A review and research agenda. *International Marketing Review*, 36(6), 830-858.

Pena-Marin, J., & Wu, R. (2019). Disconfirming expectations: Incorrect imprecise (vs. precise) estimates increase source trustworthiness and consumer loyalty. *Journal of Consumer Psychology*, *29*(4), 623-641.

Petersen, J. A., Kumar, V., Polo, Y., & Sese, F. J. (2018). Unlocking the power of marketing: Understanding the links between customer mindset metrics, behavior, and profitability. *Journal of the Academy of Marketing Science*, *46*, 813-836.

Petrick, J. F. (2004). Are loyal visitors desired visitors?. *Tourism Management*, *25*(4), 463-470.

Petrick, J. F., & Backman, S. J. (2002). An examination of the construct of perceived value for the prediction of golf travelers' intentions to revisit. *Journal of Travel Research*, *41*(1), 38-45.

Priporas, C. V., Stylos, N., & Fotiadis, A. K. (2017). Generation Z consumers' expectations of interactions in smart retailing: A future agenda. *Computers in human behavior*, 77, 374-381.

Pritchard, M. P., Havitz, M. E., & Howard, D. R. (1999). Analyzing the commitment-loyalty link in service contexts. *Journal of the Academy of Marketing Science*, 27, 333-348.

Raassens, N., & Haans, H. (2017). NPS and online WOM: Investigating the relationship between customers' promoter scores and eWOM behavior. *Journal of Service Research*, 20(3), 322-334.

Rahman, S. M., Carlson, J., Gudergan, S. P., Wetzels, M., & Grewal, D. (2022). Perceived omnichannel customer experience (OCX): Concept, measurement, and impact. *Journal of Retailing*, 98(4), 611-632.

Rapp, A., Beitelspacher, L. S., Grewal, D., & Hughes, D. E. (2013). Understanding social media effects across seller, retailer, and consumer interactions. *Journal of the Academy of Marketing Science*, 41, 547-566.

Reinartz, W. J., & Kumar, V. (2003). The impact of customer relationship characteristics on profitable lifetime duration. *Journal of marketing*, 67(1), 77-99.

Reynolds, T., & Jamieson, L. (1985). Image Representations: An Analytic Framework, in J. Jacoby, J. Olson (a cura di) *Perceived Quality. How Consumers View Stores and Merchandise*, Lexington Books, Lexington, Mass.

Rossi, F. (2018). Lower price or higher reward? Measuring the effect of consumers' preferences on reward programs. *Management Science*, 64(9), 4451-4470.

Rumelt, R.P. (1984). Toward a strategic theory of the firm. In R. Lamb (ed.), *Competitive Strategic Management*, Prentice Hall, Englewood Cliffs, NJ, pp. 556-570.

Schmitt, P., Skiera, B., & Van den Bulte, C. (2011). Referral programs and customer value. *Journal of Marketing*, 75(1), 46-59.

Schmitz, C., Friess, M., Alavi, S., & Habel, J. (2020). Understanding the impact of relationship disruptions. *Journal of Marketing*, 84(1), 66-87.

Seenivasan, S., Sudhir, K., & Talukdar, D. (2016). Do store brands aid store loyalty?. *Management Science*, 62(3), 802-816.

Seuring, S., & Gold, S. (2012). Conducting content-analysis based literature reviews in supply chain management. *Supply chain management: An international journal*, 17(5), 544-555.

Shaalan, A., Agag, G., & Tourky, M. (2023). Harnessing customer mindset metrics to boost consumer spending: a cross-country study on routes to economic and business growth. *British Journal of Management*, 34(1), 442-465.

Shaffer, G., & Zhang, Z. J. (2002). Competitive one-to-one promotions. *Management Science*, 48(9), 1143-1160.

Shin, H., & Perdue, R. R. (2023). Developing a multi-dimensional measure of hotel brand customers' online engagement behaviors to capture non-transactional value. *Journal of Travel Research*, 62(3), 593-609.

Singson, R.L. (1975). Multidimensional Scaling of Store Image and Shopping Behavior, *Journal of Retailing*, 51(2), 38-52.

Sipilä, J., Alavi, S., Edinger-Schons, L. M., Dörfer, S., & Schmitz, C. (2021). Corporate social responsibility in luxury contexts: potential pitfalls and how to overcome them. *Journal of the Academy of Marketing Science*, *49*, 280-303.

Sirdeshmukh, D., Singh, J., & Sabol, B. (2002). Consumer trust, value, and loyalty in relational exchanges. *Journal of Marketing*, *66*(1), 15-37.

Sirohi, N., McLaughlin, E. W., & Wittink, D. R. (1998). A model of consumer perceptions and store loyalty intentions for a supermarket retailer. *Journal of Retailing*, *74*(2), 223-245.

Sprott, D., Czellar, S., & Spangenberg, E. (2009). The importance of a general measure of brand engagement on market behavior: Development and validation of a scale. *Journal of Marketing Research*, *46*(1), 92-104.

Srinivasan, S. S., Anderson, R., & Ponnavolu, K. (2002). Customer loyalty in e-commerce: an exploration of its antecedents and consequences. *Journal of Retailing*, *78*(1), 41-50.

Stahl, F., Heitmann, M., Lehmann, D. R., & Neslin, S. A. (2012). The impact of brand equity on customer acquisition, retention, and profit margin. *Journal of Marketing*, *76*(4), 44-63.

Steenkamp, J. B. E. (2024). What is holding private label back in the United States and in emerging markets?. *Journal of Retailing*, *100*(1), 56-69.

Steinhoff, L., & Palmatier, R. W. (2016). Understanding loyalty program effectiveness: managing target and bystander effects. *Journal of the Academy of Marketing Science*, *44*, 88-107.

Stock, R. M., & Zacharias, N. A. (2013). Two sides of the same coin: How do different dimensions of product program innovativeness affect customer loyalty?. *Journal of product innovation management*, *30*(3), 516-532.

Sutton, R. I., & Staw, B. M. (1995). What theory is not. *Administrative science quarterly*, 371-384.

Swaminathan, S., & Bawa, K. (2005). Category-specific coupon proneness: The impact of individual characteristics and category-specific variables. *Journal of Retailing*, *81*(3), 205-214.

Tamaddoni, A., Stakhovych, S., & Ewing, M. (2016). Comparing churn prediction techniques and assessing their performance: a contingent perspective. *Journal of Service Research*, *19*(2), 123-141.

Tankersley, C. B. (1977). Attitude and brand loyalty: a longitudinal study of multiattribute attitude models and intervening variables. *Journal of the Academy of Marketing Science*, *5*, 249-262.

Tarasi, C. O., Bolton, R. N., Gustafsson, A., & Walker, B. A. (2013). Relationship characteristics and cash flow variability: Implications for satisfaction, loyalty, and customer portfolio management. *Journal of Service Research*, *16*(2), 121-137.

Temerak, M. S., Micevski, M., Kadić-Maglajlić, S., & Latinovic, Z. (2024). Nuances of Sales–Service Ambidexterity across Varied Sales Job Types. *British Journal of Management*.

Toufaily, E., Ricard, L., & Perrien, J. (2013). Customer loyalty to a commercial website: Descriptive meta-analysis of the empirical literature and proposal of an integrative model. *Journal of Business Research, 66*(9), 1436-1447.

Tranfield, D., Denyer, D., & Smart, P. (2003). Towards a methodology for developing Evidence-Informed management knowledge by means of systematic review. *British Journal of Management, 14*(3), 207–222.

Van den Bulte, C., Bayer, E., Skiera, B., & Schmitt, P. (2018). How customer referral programs turn social capital into economic capital. *Journal of Marketing Research, 55*(1), 132-146.

van Doorn, J., Leeflang, P. S., & Tijs, M. (2013). Satisfaction as a predictor of future performance: A replication. *International Journal of Research in Marketing, 30*(3), 314-318.

Vanier, D. J., & Trippi, R. R. (1976). Consumer choice consistency in transportation decisions. *Journal of the Academy of Marketing Science, 4*, 617-630.

Vicari, S. (1980). *Le strategie di sviluppo dell'azienda commerciale*, Giuffrè, Milano.

Vicari, S. (1991). *L'impresa vivente. Itinerario di una diversa concezione*, Etas, Milano.

Vicari, S. (2024). *The Living Firm: A Journey into a Different Conception,* Amazon Publishing Agency, Sheridan, WY.

Vicari, S., & Troilo, G. (1997). Affrontare il Possibile: le mappe cognitive. Approcci di management in condizioni di incertezza. *Economia & Management, 1*, 93-109.

Vickery, S. K., Droge, C., Stank, T. P., Goldsby, T. J., & Markland, R. E. (2004). The performance implications of media richness in a business-to-business service environment: Direct versus indirect effects. *Management Science, 50*(8), 1106-1119.

Villas-Boas, J. M. (2004). Consumer learning, brand loyalty, and competition. *Marketing Science, 23*(1), 134-145.

Vlachos, P. A., Tsamakos, A., Vrechopoulos, A. P., & Avramidis, P. K. (2009). Corporate social responsibility: attributions, loyalty, and the mediating role of trust. *Journal of the Academy of Marketing Science, 37*, 170-180.

Walsh, G., & Beatty, S. E. (2007). Customer-based corporate reputation of a service firm: scale development and validation. *Journal of the Academy of Marketing Science, 35*, 127-143.

Wang, L., Gopal, R., Shankar, R., & Pancras, J. (2022). Forecasting venue popularity on location-based services using interpretable machine learning. *Production and Operations Management, 31*(7), 2773-2788.

Wang, S., Cheah, J.-H., Lim, W.M., Kumar, S., Lim, X.-J. and Towers, N. (2024). Evolution and trends in retailing: insights from International Journal of Retail & Distribution Management. *International Journal of Retail & Distribution Management*, Vol. 52 No. 6, pp. 647-670.

Watson, G.F., Beck, J.T., Henderson, C.M., & Palmatier, R.W. (2015). Building, measuring, and profiting from customer loyalty. *Journal of the Academy of Marketing Science, 43*, 790-825.

Weale, B.W. (1961), Measuring the Customer's Image of a Department Store, *Journal of Retailing*, Vol.37, n.2, Summer, pp.40-48.

Wen, C., R. Prybutok, V., Blankson, C., & Fang, J. (2014). The role of E-quality within the consumer decision making process. *International Journal of Operations & Production Management, 34*(12), 1506-1536.

Wilson, D.T. (1995), An Integrated Model of Buyer-Seller Relationships, *Journal of the Academy of Marketing Science*, 23 (4), pp. 335-345.

Wolfinbarger, M., & Gilly, M. C. (2003). eTailQ: dimensionalizing, measuring and predicting etail quality. *Journal of Retailing, 79*(3), 183-198.

Wolter, J. S., Bock, D. E., Hopkins, C. D., & Giebelhausen, M. (2022). Not the relationship type? Loyalty propensity as a reason to maintain marketing relationships. *Journal of the Academy of Marketing Science, 50*(5), 1052-1070.

Xue, M., Hitt, L. M., & Chen, P. Y. (2011). Determinants and outcomes of internet banking adoption. *Management Science, 57*(2), 291-307.

Yang, C., Guo, L., & Zhou, S. X. (2022). Customer satisfaction, advertising competition, and platform performance. *Production and Operations Management, 31*(4), 1576-1594.

Yin R.K. (2017). *Case Study Research and Applications: Design and Methods* (5th ed.). Sage, Thousand Oaks, CA.

Yoganarasimhan, H., Barzegary, E., & Pani, A. (2023). Design and evaluation of optimal free trials. *Management Science, 69*(6), 3220-3240.

Zeithaml, V. A., Berry, L. L., & Parasuraman, A. (1996). The behavioral consequences of service quality. *Journal of marketing, 60*(2), 31-46.

AUTHORS

Emanuele Acconciamessa is an Academic Fellow of the Department of Marketing at Bocconi University where he teaches Trade Marketing and Category Management in the Master of Science in Marketing Management. He is a member of the Channel & Retail Lab at SDA Bocconi.

Generoso Branca is a Post-Doc Researcher at the Department of Marketing, Bocconi University, and a Fellow in Marketing Management at SDA Bocconi. He received a Ph.D. from the University of Sannio, with an additional Doctor Europaeus Certificate. He is a member of the Channel & Retail Lab at SDA Bocconi.

Bruno Busacca is a Full Professor at the Department of Marketing and a member of the Bocconi University Board of Discipline. He was Dean of Development and Alumni Relations, Dean of SDA Bocconi School of Management, a member of the Rectors' Committee and the Academic Council of Bocconi University.

Sandro Castaldo is a Full Professor of the Marketing Department at Bocconi University. He is Editor in Chief of Economia & Management, and Scientific Director of the Channel & Retail Lab at Sda Bocconi. He is the President of the International Federation of Scholarly Associations of Management (IFSAM).

Andrea Ciacci is a Research Fellow of the Marketing Department at Bocconi University. He received a Ph.D. in Management from the University of Genoa, Department of Economics and Business Studies. He is a member of the Channel & Retail Lab at SDA Bocconi.

Alice Mantovani is a Ph.D. student in Management at the University of Genoa. She collaborated with SDA Bocconi and C.I.E.L.I. the Italian Center of Excellence on Logistics Transports and Infrastructures at the University of Genoa. She is a Research Fellow of the Channel & Retail Lab at SDA Bocconi.

Lara Penco, Ph.D., is a Full Professor of Management, Department of Economics and Business Studies, University of Genoa. She is the General Secretary of the Italian Society of Management (SIMA) and a member of C.I.E.L.I., the Italian Center of Excellence on Logistics Transports and Infrastructures.

Ginevra Testa is a Research Fellow at the University of Genoa, C.I.E.L.I. the Italian Center of Excellence on Logistics Transports and Infrastructures. She received a Ph.D. in Logistics and Transport at the University of Genoa. She is a Research Fellow of the Channel & Retail Lab at SDA Bocconi.

TCC is a retail performance company offering solutions that boost retail sales, improving marketing and loyalty performance, helping to enrich data and media networks. The company has successfully delivered more than 9000 loyalty promotion initiatives, across 70 countries.

Fabrizio Losa is Senior Commercial Director Italy, Iberia & Latam at TCC. He has over 20 years of experience in loyalty sector and he's responsible for developing and executing strategic initiatives to maximize revenue, expand market share, and strengthen TCC brand presence.

Chiara Landini is Head of Marketing Italy at TCC. She received a Ph.D. in Linguistic Sciences and Foreign Literatures from the Università Cattolica del Sacro Cuore of Milan. She coordinates the relations between TCC and the Channel & Retail Lab of SDA Bocconi within the Loyalty Monitor.

Damien Katris is Global Omnichannel, Data & Analytics Director at TCC. He is responsible for TCC's omnichannel solutions, data and analytics projects, and strategic initiatives, driving an integrated and data-driven approach to the design, analysis, and optimization of loyalty campaigns.

Yana Rubashkina is Head of Data Science at TCC. She is responsible for leveraging advanced analytics, predictive modelling, and data science tools to drive automation and deliver actionable insights into campaign performance and shopper behavior. She holds a Ph.D. in Economics from the Università Cattolica del Sacro Cuore of Milan. She supervises the contributions given by TCC to the Loyalty Monitor.